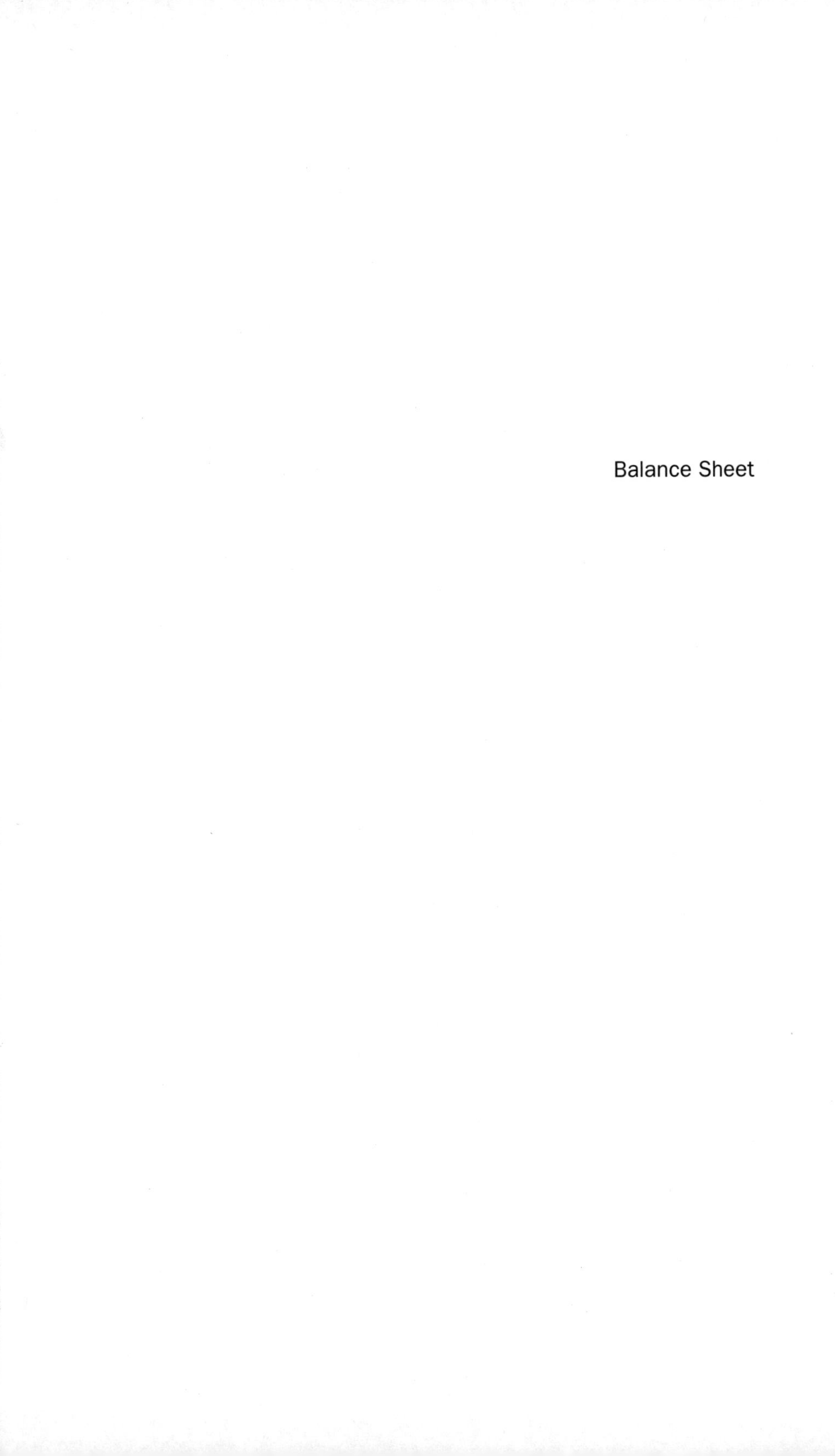

Balance Sheet

Balance Sheet

THE IRAQ WAR AND U.S. NATIONAL SECURITY

Edited by John S. Duffield and Peter J. Dombrowski

STANFORD SECURITY STUDIES
An imprint of Stanford University Press
Stanford, California

Stanford University Press
Stanford, California

Printed in the United States of America on acid-free, archival-quality paper.

Library of Congress Cataloging-in-Publication Data

Balance sheet : the Iraq War and U.S. national security / edited by John S. Duffield and Peter J. Dombrowski.
p. cm.
Includes bibliographical references and index.
ISBN 978-0-8047-6013-3 (cloth : alk. paper)
1. Iraq War, 2003--Influence. 2. National security--United States. 3. United States--Foreign relations--21st century. I. Duffield, John S. II. Dombrowski, Peter J., 1963-
DS79.76.B3517 2009
956.7044'32--dc22 2009012529

Typeset by Bruce Lundquist in 10/14 Minion

To Mom, Dad, Mary Ann, and Joe
J.S.D.

To Ann and JoJo
P.J.D

CONTENTS

CONTRIBUTORS

John S. Duffield is professor of political science at Georgia State University in Atlanta. He is the author of *Over a Barrel: The Costs of U.S. Foreign Oil Dependence* (Stanford University Press, 2008); *World Power Forsaken: Political Culture, International Institutions, and German Security Policy After Unification* (Stanford University Press, 1998); and *Power Rules: The Evolution of NATO's Conventional Force Posture* (Stanford University Press, 1995), as well as numerous other publications on international politics, institutions, and security. His current research focuses on the politics of energy security in the United States and other industrialized countries.

Peter J. Dombrowski is chairperson of the Strategic Research Department at the Naval War College in Newport, Rhode Island. He is the author of nearly forty articles, monographs, book chapters, and government reports. His most recent book, coauthored with Eugene Gholz, is *Buying Military Transformation: Technological Innovation and the Defense Industry* (Columbia University Press, 2006). Other publications include *Guns and Butter: The Political Economy of the New International Security Environment* (Lynne Rienner, 2005); *Naval Power in the Twenty-first Century: A Naval War College Review Reader* (Naval War College Press, 2005); *Policy Responses to the Globalization of American Banking* (University of Pittsburgh Press, 1996); and with Andrew Ross and Eugene Gholz, *Military Transformation and the Defense Industry After Next* (Naval War College Press, 2002).

Joseph Cirincione is the president of the Ploughshares Fund. He is the author of *Bomb Scare: The History and Future of Nuclear Weapons* (Columbia University Press, 2007). Previously, he served as senior vice president for national security and international policy at the Center for American Progress and as director for nonproliferation at the Carnegie Endowment for International Peace for eight years. He worked for nine years in the U.S. House of Representatives as a professional staff member of the Committee on Armed Services and the Committee on Government Operations and served as staff director of the bipartisan Military Reform Caucus. He teaches at the Georgetown University Graduate School of Foreign Service and is a member of the Council on Foreign Relations.

F. Gregory Gause III is professor of political science at the University of Vermont and served as director of the university's Middle East Studies Program from 1998 to 2008. He was previously on the faculty of Columbia University (1987–95) and served as fellow for Arab and Islamic studies at the Council on Foreign Relations (1993–94). He is the author of *Oil Monarchies* (Council on Foreign Relations Press, 1994) and is currently completing a book on the international politics of the Persian Gulf region since 1971.

Michael E. O'Hanlon is Senior Fellow in Foreign Policy and The Sydney Stein, Jr. Chair at the Brookings Institution. He specializes in U.S. national security policy and is senior author of the Iraq Index. A former defense budget analyst who advised members of Congress on military spending, he specializes in Iraq, North Korea, homeland security, the use of military force, and other defense issues. He was also director of Opportunity 08.

Clay Ramsay, director of research at the Program on International Policy Attitudes (PIPA) and a fellow at the Center for International and Security Studies at Maryland, cofounded PIPA in 1992. He regularly appears in the U.S. and international media providing analysis of public opinion. With a background in history and psychology, he has focused on the study of ideology and mass psychology. He received his PhD in history from Stanford University, has taught at Oberlin College, and is the author of *The Ideology of the Great Fear* (Johns Hopkins University Press, 1991). He is a faculty member of the School of Public Policy at the University of Maryland.

Steven Simon is Hasib J. Sabbagh Senior Fellow for Middle Eastern Studies at the Council on Foreign Relations. He previously served as a senior analyst at the Rand Corporation (2003–6), deputy director and Carol Dean Senior Fellow in U.S. Security Studies at the International Institute for Strategic Studies (1999–2003), and director for global issues and senior director for transnational threats on the National Security Council (1994–99). He is the coauthor of *The Age of Sacred Terror* (Random House, 2002) and *The Next Attack* (Times Books, 2005). His current work examines the consequences of the American intervention in Iraq, Muslim/non-Muslim relations, and the role of religion in U.S. foreign policy.

Thomas G. Weiss is Presidential Professor of Political Science at The CUNY Graduate Center and Director of the Ralph Bunche Institute for International Studies, where he is codirector of the United Nations Intellectual History Project. He is president of the International Studies Association (2009–10) and chairperson of the Academic Council on the UN System (2006–9). He was editor of *Global Governance*, research director of the International Commission on Intervention and State Sovereignty, research professor at Brown University's Watson Institute for International Studies, executive director of the Academic Council on the UN System and of the International Peace Academy, a member of the UN secretariat, and a consultant to several public and private agencies. He has written or edited some thirty-five books and one hundred fifty articles and book chapters about multilateral approaches to international peace and security, humanitarian action, and sustainable development. His latest book is *What's Wrong with the United Nations and How to Fix It* (Polity Press, 2009).

PREFACE

Some projects take a long time to come to fruition, and this one is no exception. Its origins date to the summer of 2003. That is when we first thought of conducting a comprehensive assessment of the impact of the Iraq War on U.S. national security, to be published around the first anniversary of the invasion. In retrospect, the notion of such a quick assessment so soon after the war began seems naive in the extreme. Nevertheless, that perhaps unrealistic initial inspiration laid much of the groundwork for the book you are now reading.

Although John Duffield came up with the initial idea and elaborated a clear vision for the volume, he immediately reached out to Peter Dombrowski, whom he knew could bring a wealth of relevant knowledge and experience to the project. Together, we developed a chapter outline that is very similar to the one contained in this book and began to contact potential contributors, several of whom are represented in these pages. For perhaps obvious reasons, however, it proved difficult to recruit a full complement of authors who would be willing and able to write chapters under such fluid circumstances and on such a short deadline. So we thanked those who had agreed to participate and moved on.

Then the idea returned at an opportune moment in the summer of 2007. John was able to take advantage of a meeting already scheduled with a representative of Stanford University Press to float the concept. This led to an exchange with Dr. Geoffrey R. H. Burn, the director and acquisitions editor of the press, who immediately took an interest in the project. The timing could not have been better. Despite his heavy responsibilities as chair of the Strategic Research Department at the Naval War College, Peter was once again available and willing to serve as coeditor. The press quickly reviewed a proposal and extended a generous advance contract. With the backing of the press, we were quickly able to assemble a world-class set of contributors.

Although many of those to whom we are indebted are apparent in the preceding paragraphs, we would nevertheless like to extend explicit thanks:

To the chapter authors, a veritable "who's who" of U.S. national security experts. That we were able to secure the participation of such an accomplished and knowledgeable group is testament to the importance of the topic.

To Dr. Geoffrey Burn, for making available the full resources of his dynamic university press. It is impossible to imagine a more helpful or supportive sponsor.

To Jessica Walsh, Mariana Raykov, Alexandria Giardino, and others at the press, who helped smooth the path from proposal to production.

In addition, John would like to express his gratitude to Peter, without whose partnership he would not have moved forward on this project; to Raluca Miller and Alla Manukyan, my graduate research assistants at Georgia State University (he is especially grateful to Alla for promptly and effectively handling what must have seemed like an unending series of "mini-projects" related to the book); and to his wife, Cheryl Eschbach, for encouraging him every step of the way. John dedicates his share of the book to his parents, Richard and Mary Rose Duffield, his mother-in-law, Mary Ann Eschbach, and his father-in-law, Joseph Eschbach, who passed away in September 2007 just as the project was getting underway. Joe was unstinting in his love and always took an interest in my work. I miss him greatly.

Peter would like to thank his wife Ann Martino who has patiently stood beside him through this project like all the others, and his daughter Johanna who someday will write a book or two of her own.

J.S.D.
Decatur, Georgia
P.J.D.
Newport, Rhode Island

Balance Sheet

1 TOWARD A BALANCE SHEET

What, Why, and How

John S. Duffield and Peter J. Dombrowski

I think that is where we must begin, by considering the overall security of this nation. . . . Iraq is an important piece of that overall equation, but it is only a piece.

Rep. Ike Skelton, Chairman of the House Armed Services Committee, September 10, 2007[1]

It is an iron law of warfare that the unintended consequences, for good and bad, are as important—if not more so—than the intended. Because these consequences take time to work themselves through, the long-term reputations of wars rarely reflect the first reviews.

Sir Lawrence Freedman, Professor of War Studies, King's College, London[2]

PURPOSE

In mid-March 2003, the Bush administration took the United States to war with Iraq. Members of the administration believed, or at least claimed, that the war would yield substantial benefits for U.S. national security at little cost. By deposing Saddam Hussein, the United States would eliminate a major threat to its vital interests. Among other things, the invasion would remove a regime that was hostile to the United States and its regional allies, including Israel, and that possessed, or would soon possess, nuclear weapons. Simultaneously, it would end the need to maintain the politically unpopular and increasingly expensive policy of containment using a porous sanctions regime and complex no-fly zones. In addition, attacking Iraq would open another front in the Global War on Terror (GWOT), albeit an increasingly controversial one that many would later judge unnecessary. In the place of Saddam's despotic regime, moreover, a democracy would be erected that could serve as a model for the rest of the region. Regional security for the United States, its allies, and friends would be further improved because a democratic Iraq would lead to a virtuous and reinforcing cycle. Not least important, a relatively small amount of American combat forces operating for a limited period in-country would win a swift victory, and the costs of rebuilding Iraq would be paid for largely out of the country's oil revenues.

Initially, events seemed to support the administration's arguments. U.S. and other coalition forces quickly overcame organized resistance. Within weeks, they had defeated the Iraqi army, captured Baghdad, and driven Saddam Hussein into hiding. At the beginning of May, President Bush declared the end of major combat operations.

Even this opening phase of the war was not without costs, however. The administration's insistence on using force strained relations with a number of major allies, and the invasion caused much anger throughout the Arab and Muslim worlds. Within Iraq itself, thousands of innocent civilians died, and much of the country was plunged into chaos.

As the quick initial victory turned into a prolonged occupation in the face of a fierce insurgency, both U.S. casualties and financial outlays steadily mounted.[3] Success proved to be much more elusive and expensive than the Bush administration had foreseen, or had been willing to admit. Nearly six years after the war began, the United States continued to maintain fifteen combat brigades and approximately 140,000 military personnel in Iraq. As of late 2008, the war's ultimate outcome remained uncertain.

Has the Iraq War been worthwhile? Has it made the United States safer? This book provides a comprehensive assessment of the consequences of the Iraq War for the national security of the United States. It is aimed in particular at those who have not already made up their minds about the ultimate merits of the Iraq War or wish to ground their opinions in a clearer understanding of what effects the war has actually had. What in fact have been the overall costs and benefits of the Iraq War to U.S. national security? Answering this question is a necessary first step in the process of drawing conclusions about the wisdom of the war as well as devising new policies toward Iraq and beyond.

JUSTIFICATIONS

Why is it important to prepare such a balance sheet, and why now? We recognize that a number of people may regard such an assessment as either unnecessary or irrelevant. Some made up their minds about the wisdom of the war long ago, although they may fundamentally disagree on whether it has been worthwhile. For members of the Bush administration and its supporters, the war, despite the many difficulties and challenges, has been a success, at least in terms of national security objectives.[4] Whatever the costs, they have been greatly outweighed by the benefits, such as the deposing of Saddam Hussein and the establishment of democratic institutions in the heart of the Middle East. As Vice President Richard Cheney declared in Baghdad on the fifth anniversary of the start of the war, it has been a "successful endeavor" and "well worth the effort."[5]

For many critics of the Bush administration's policy toward Iraq, the war has been an unmitigated disaster. As the *Atlanta Journal-Constitution* editorialized, "It seems fair to conclude that after five years of war, the sacrifice of almost 4,000 American lives and the expenditure of an estimated $1 trillion and counting, we have accomplished absolutely nothing in Iraq."[6] Whatever the ultimate outcome, it could never justify the human toll (in Iraqi as well as American lives) and the vast sums of money, perhaps as much as several trillion dollars or more, that will have been spent in the end.[7]

For die-hard proponents and opponents of the war alike, there is little point in conducting any further analysis. Still others may no longer be interested in thinking about the war, or they would simply rather avoid addressing the question of whether it has improved U.S. national security. Such strategic considerations often seem insensitive in the face of personal costs and private responses to the events of the war. Do I know anyone who has served in Iraq? Do I know anyone who has been killed or seriously wounded? How do the economic costs of the war affect my personal finances today or in the future? Do I feel that that the treatment of prisoners at Abu Ghraib was moral and ethical? How can I support the Iraq War when news accounts suggest that the reasons given for undertaking the war were exaggerated or even false?

In many respects, moreover, the Iraq War is a distant event growing evermore remote as the awe-inspiring fireworks of the initial invasion recede into memory. There has been no mass mobilization, no tax increases, and no rationing of consumer goods as in many other major conflicts. Political rallies against the war, while prominent before the invasion and sporadically thereafter, have received less and less national attention. News coverage of the war itself has faded, especially given the Bush administration's policy of minimizing access to stories that might inflame public opinion—no pictures of bodies returning to Dover, Delaware, and few means of covering the front lines short of being officially embedded with American military units.[8] By mid-2008 CBS no longer maintained a single full-time correspondent in Iraq. Nor were the other major TV news outlets much more engaged, with several employing a single correspondent to cover multiple countries in the Middle East. The result is that the "big three" news networks spent only 181 minutes of prime time covering Iraq in the first six months of 2008.[9] Yet, the Iraq War, including the decision to go to war, the prosecution of the war, and its wider effects, will shape national security policy for many years to come.

The Importance of Conducting an Assessment

We strongly believe, and we think most people would agree, that there is considerable value in this book's enterprise. Our justification begins with a simple proposition: the independent evaluation of public policies is vital to the health of representative democracies such as the United States. One of the hallmarks of representative democracy is the accountability of political leaders. The people in whom sovereignty ultimately resides must be able to hold their elected officials accountable for their actions—or inaction. And in order to hold their leaders accountable, the people must be able to evaluate the performance of those leaders, even in the face of possible efforts by leaders to hide or distort the truth in order to advance their personal and partisan agendas. This in turn requires that the people have access to reliable and adequate, if incomplete, information and analysis about the alternatives available to their leaders, the choices made by leaders among those alternatives, and the consequences of those actions. Where the meaning of the available information is not readily apparent, independent experts can play a valuable role in helping to provide reasonable interpretations.

This proposition is relevant to all public policies. But it should be particularly germane to policies that are especially costly or consequential. The Bush administration's decision to invade Iraq falls squarely in this category. Few would deny that it was one of most significant U.S. foreign policy decisions since World War Two, if not the entire history of the United States. It is comparable in importance, if not more so, to the U.S. intervention in the Korean War, the escalation in (and subsequent withdrawal from) Vietnam, and U.S. participation in the 1990–91 Gulf War. The Iraq War will clearly have far-reaching and what are likely to be long-lasting repercussions for the United States.

Not only that, but the Iraq War was in many respects a war of choice. Notwithstanding the alarming scenarios painted by members of the Bush administration, they had considerable leeway as to whether, when, and how to invade Iraq. The United States was not forced by circumstances beyond its control to act the way it did, when it did. In addition, a large number of Americans believed that a war was not necessary to address the threat posed by Iraq, or that war was at least premature.[10] Given the discretionary nature of the decision, it is all the more important to evaluate its consequences.

Why Now?

A secondary question concerns the timing of this appraisal. Some may agree in principle with the need to evaluate the consequences of the war, but they might ask whether this is the appropriate time.

In particular, some may feel that it is still too soon to render any useful judgment. Certainly, the situation within Iraq itself remains in flux. It is too early to tell what the ultimate political outcome will be.[11] Will the recently created political institutions remain in place and grow steadily in strength and legitimacy? Or will they be replaced by others, for example, a less centralized federal structure? Or could the whole country yet descend into all-out civil war?

In addition, some of the broader consequences of the war are still playing out. For example, what overall impact will the war have on the greater Middle East? Will it ultimately help to advance the cause of democracy and peace in the region? Or could it foment conflict and instability? And what will be the longer-term consequences for world energy markets?

Admittedly, it may never be possible to provide a definitive assessment of the costs and benefits of the Iraq War. Indeed, history is likely to render multiple, conflicting judgments. But that does not mean that there is no point in attempting to address this issue now. To the contrary, we would suggest several reasons for doing so.

First, more than half a decade after the war began, we are in fact beginning to be able to discern the broader impact. To be sure, many questions remain, but a number of the consequences can already be identified and measured, even if they have not fully worked themselves out. Thus regardless of the ultimate outcome within Iraq itself, it may not be too soon to begin to render an overall assessment. Certainly, it would be damning if, even assuming a favorable political result in Iraq, the costs were already judged to outweigh the potential benefits. Moreover, there are analytical risks associated with waiting longer. It is already difficult enough to isolate the effects of the Iraq War on some aspects of the security environment, such as U.S. alliance relations, Iran's nuclear policy, or world energy markets. As time passes, an increasing number of other developments are likely to intervene and impinge, complicating such an assessment.

A third reason follows from the peculiarities of the U.S. political system, specifically the presidential election cycle. Because of the American political calendar, this is a particularly useful time to evaluate the overall impact of the war. The arrival of a new administration in Washington, DC, in January 2009 represents the first opportunity since the war began for a complete rethinking of American strategy in Iraq as well as U.S. national security policy more generally. An important component of that review should be consideration of the full range of consequences of alternative courses of action. Not only will the new policymakers want to know what effects the various options are likely to have on the situation within Iraq, but they will also want to be aware of the wider potential implications of different choices.

What Others Have Written

The broad assessment of the consequences of the Iraq War envisioned by this book might not be worth conducting if a similar analysis had already been carried out. But, surprisingly, given the importance of the topic, no single comprehensive study exists.

To be sure, there has been a huge outpouring of books on various aspects of the Iraq War, including a number of outstanding analyses.[12] Among the most common topics are the causes of and reasons for the war, the conduct of the war's military operations, the management (and mismanagement) of the occupation, and the resulting developments within Iraq.[13] With regard to the broader consequences of the war, there have been a number of detailed analyses of the economic costs and of the impact on the U.S. military. The former in particular have provoked considerable debate, with estimates ranging as high as three trillion dollars or more in the long term.[14]

So far, however, relatively little has been written on the overall impact of the war in the way we intend. At this writing, only a few published works come close to fitting the bill. One is an edited volume by Rick Fawn and Raymond Hinnebusch on the causes and consequences of the Iraq War.[15] Yet even the section it devotes to the consequences is limited to a handful of short chapters running a mere seventy pages. Another is a chapter by Steven Miller in an edited book that is primarily concerned with globalization, national self-determination, and terrorism.[16] Although Miller does an excellent job of identifying many of the relevant consequences, his analysis is necessarily limited by his work's short length and the time at which he wrote, just three years after the war began. A third is a recent book by Peter Galbraith, who draws on his experience as a diplomat to address the consequences of Iraq for U.S. national security and the Middle East.[17] He does not, however, consider the implications of the war for the instruments of American power, such as the U.S. military or the fiscal health of the nation, or for other U.S. policies, such as for dealing with terrorism. Thus still missing—and needed—is a comprehensive, up-to-date assessment of the costs and benefits of the war, especially those that extend beyond the situation in Iraq itself. This book seeks to fill this significant hole in the literature on the war.

OUR APPROACH

Assuming the value of a broad assessment at this time, how should such an undertaking be conducted? We begin by addressing the issue of scope and then turn to the question of method.

What Is—and Is Not—Covered

Ideally, any comprehensive evaluation of the Iraq War would lay out all the relevant costs and benefits to the U.S. government and its people. It might even look more closely at the distribution of costs and benefits within the various governmental departments and agencies as well as among the American people, from the families of military personnel to the ordinary taxpayer. Often, however, discussions about the war have been framed primarily, if not exclusively, in terms of developments within Iraq and the direct costs of the war to the United States. How much has the war reduced the threat posed by Iraq to the United States and its vital interests? What have been the human and economic costs? What steps should the United States take there next in order to produce the best possible outcome, and what additional burdens should it be willing to bear?

While answering these questions is vital to a comprehensive assessment of the conflict, that approach is insufficient. We must also examine the broader, often overlooked, consequences of the war. To examine the war in isolation from the wide sweep of American public policies would be a serious error. Although what happens in Iraq is crucial, it is also essential to consider the full range of effects, especially those that have a bearing on U.S. national security.

We offer three further reasons for this position. First, it should be obvious by now that the war has had repercussions that extend far beyond the borders of Iraq. This is especially true of U.S. national security, few aspects of which would seem to be untouched. Arguably, the Afghan war, U.S. alliance relations, the stability of the Middle East, the health of the American military, and the war on terror have all been greatly affected by the war. In other areas, such as energy security and U.S. efforts to promote democracy, the effects may not yet be so apparent or easy to identify, but they could well be significant. One can at least say at this stage, however, that the Bush administration's rhetorical support for democracy has not been matched with resources, in part because of the costs associated with Iraq.[18] Thus whatever the ultimate outcome within Iraq itself, the consequences for U.S. national security are sure to be far reaching and long lasting.

A second reason for a comprehensive assessment concerns the rationales for the war that were offered by members of the Bush administration and its supporters. A number of these revolved around the particular threats posed by Iraq, including Saddam Hussein's alleged ties to global terrorist groups like al Qaeda, his efforts to acquire weapons of mass destruction, and his willingness to threaten or use force against his neighbors in the oil-rich Persian Gulf. But the war has often been justified in terms of the broader contributions it would make to U.S. national security. For example, U.S. policy in Iraq has often been linked with the war on terror. As President Bush himself noted while announcing the end of major combat operations: "The battle of Iraq is one victory in a war on terror that began on September the 11, 2001—and still goes on. . . . The liberation of Iraq is a crucial advance in the campaign against terror. We've removed an ally of al Qaeda, and cut off a source of terrorist funding. And this much is certain: No terrorist network will gain weapons of mass destruction from the Iraqi regime, because the regime is no more."[19]

Similarly, the war has been linked to U.S. efforts to promote democracy in the Middle East and beyond. Again, in the words of President Bush, "Iraqi democracy will succeed—and that success will send forth the news, from Damascus to Tehran—that freedom can be the future of every nation. The establishment of a free Iraq at the heart of the Middle East will be a watershed event in the global democratic revolution."[20]

Insofar as the war has been justified in terms of broader goals, it seems only fair to ask whether the achievement of these goals has in fact been furthered. More generally, insofar as the war was intended to make the United States more secure, the Iraq War should be evaluated in terms of the overall costs and benefits to U.S. national security including how they intersect with the broader objectives of American foreign policy. If removing Saddam Hussein from power was not key to democratization in the Middle East or winning the war on terror, then policymakers and the public need to know and understand why in order to craft a more effective approach in the years ahead.

Third, Iraq, by accident more than by design, became the focus of national security policymaking during the presidency of George W. Bush. Most of the key "doctrines" and themes identified with the Bush administration had their origins, or fullest expression, in the nation's approach to Iraq. Preemption, unilateralism, regime change, and democratization, among many other touchstones of the Bush administration's approach to the world, all played themselves out for better or worse in the context of the Iraq War in its various phases. Reinforcing, modifying, or rejecting elements of the Bush administration's policy may occupy the next several presidents, whether they like it or not. If nothing else, other countries around the world, both allies and adversaries, will not forget how the United States used—or did not use—the UN Security Council in the run up to the war, the treatment of coalition members over the course of the war, or the ways in which Iraq complicated dealings with Iran and its quest to obtain nuclear weapons. At home, as with the Ford, Carter, and Reagan administrations' efforts to put to rest the ghost of Vietnam, it will take some time for the military, Congress, and the American people to assimilate the lessons of Iraq and to understand their implications for U.S. national security now and in the future.

In sum, the success and failure of the war will have to be judged in terms of its overall contribution to U.S. national security. Such an assessment cannot be limited to what happens in Iraq. This reasoning may be especially true if the outcome within Iraq itself is ultimately deemed a favorable one. Even if that is the case, and we should all hope for such a result, it may be that success was purchased at too dear a cost. In other words, it may be possible to "win" in Iraq while ending up worse off. To paraphrase the Greek general Pyrrhus, who lost much of his force in dealing a defeat to the Romans, "another such victory and we are undone."

While we call for looking beyond the immediate situation in Iraq, this assessment of the impact of the war is bounded in two important respects, both of which are reflected in the subtitle of this book. Consideration is limited to consequences of direct relevance to the *national security of the United States*. This means, in the first place, that we will not address other types of actual or alleged consequences. Some have argued that the war has had significant implications for international law and world order, the United Nations, and even international relations theory.[21] But, important as they may be, such matters will not be taken up here. Likewise, we will not address the national security consequences for other countries, including Iraq, except where they have a direct bearing on the security of the United States itself. We justify this restricted focus on the twin grounds that the war would not have occurred but for decisions taken within the United States and that it was justified principally in terms of how it would enhance U.S. national security. Thus given constraints of time and space, and in order to maximize the coherence of the project, we find it useful to limit the scope of the volume in these ways.

The next question that must be addressed is how to structure the possible national security consequences of the war for the United States. We argue that these can usefully be conceptualized as falling into two broad categories. One category concerns the impact on the overall security environment, or the ends of U.S. national security policy. The other category concerns the impact of the war on the resources available to address threats and challenges, or the means of U.S. national security policy.

As noted above, the war was largely justified on the ground that it would increase the security of the United States. To what degree has the war in fact reduced the principal threats and challenges to the United States and its interests? One way of assessing the impact of the war on the security environment is to examine how it has contributed to or detracted from the achievement of the various goals of U.S. national security policy. Much will depend, of course, on the eventual outcome in Iraq. But the decision to go to war in and of itself as well as how the war has been prosecuted have arguably affected the conduct and outcomes of other important policies pursued by Washington, regardless of how Iraq turns out. Thus it is also relevant to look at the war's impact on these related efforts to address the threats faced by the United States.

Perhaps of most immediate concern have been U.S. efforts to combat terrorist groups that might strike against the United States and its allies and to slow or prevent the proliferation of weapons of mass destruction. Not to be overlooked, however, are longer-term U.S. efforts to promote democracy, stability in the Middle East, and energy security. How has the war furthered or hampered the achievement of these important goals?

Not only may the war have affected the broader security environment, but it may also have implications for the ability of the United States to achieve the goals of national security policy both now and in the future. Thus we must

also assess U.S. policy toward Iraq in terms of its overall impact on the tools and resources available for addressing the principal threats and challenges to the United States and its interests.

Of most immediate concern are the effects on the U.S. military, diplomatic corps, and intelligence assets. In view of the costs of the war for U.S. military personnel and the material resources they need to fight and win future conflicts, for example, it remains an open question as to whether Iraq has seriously damaged one of the primary instruments for ensuring the safety and security of the nation. Also of near-term importance is the overall standing of the United States in the eyes of others who may be critical to the success of U.S. efforts. How much support (or opposition) is there abroad for the United States and its policies? In the longer term, how and how successfully the United States is able to address its security concerns will depend on its fiscal and economic health. While the state of the economy and the federal budget have much broader implications, they are certainly relevant to the conduct of national security policy. After all, for example, in the face of federal budget deficits and reduced discretionary spending on domestic programs, will the American people be willing to bear the expense of recapitalizing and modernizing all the forces worn down by years in the Iraqi desert? The ability or inability to do so will in many ways determine the U.S. security posture in other areas of the globe, including Asia where the rise of China concerns strategists in the United States and abroad. Not to be overlooked are also public attitudes within the United States itself. Are the American people still willing to support the use of force and other potentially costly foreign engagements when these are deemed necessary by policymakers? The reservoir of trust and the willingness of the public to rally around the flag in times of crisis are important, but often taken for granted, resources for presidents and policymakers charged with responding to challenges by enemies and potential adversaries.

How We Plan to Cover It

Having addressed the issue of scope, we now turn to the question of method, although the two are closely interrelated. Despite our decision to limit the scope of this project to the consequences of the war for U.S. national security, the subject is still so broad and covers so many topics as to pose a considerable, if not insuperable, challenge to any one or two individuals. We immediately concluded that it would be advisable, if not absolutely necessary, to divide up the task, especially if this book were to be completed in time to contribute to policy debates in the early months of the Obama administration. Rather than write the book all by ourselves, therefore, we have enlisted noted subject-matter experts to prepare focused analyses. These experts represent a range of viewpoints and come from a variety of backgrounds, including academia and the policy community. One common denominator is that none represents the Bush administration, which we believe has had ample opportunity to present its case.

The principal disadvantage of this approach in our view was the risk that the coherence of the project would suffer. Such is the fate of many edited volumes. But we believed that this risk could be managed and reduced to acceptable levels. Our primary strategy for doing so was to request that each contributor try to address to the extent possible a parallel set of questions:

(1) What was the situation before the war? What were the goals of U.S. policy, and how was the United States pursuing them?
(2) What has been the impact of the war? In what ways and to what degree has it promoted, retarded, or altered U.S. policy efforts in the area?
(3) How might the situation have evolved if the United States had not invaded Iraq, or had not gone to war in the way that it did?
(4) What are the likely implications of different future policy choices in Iraq? Which steps would do the most to advance U.S. national security in the area of concern? What measures could or should be taken to remedy any setbacks or obstacles caused by the war in Iraq?

THE ORGANIZATION OF THE VOLUME

Paralleling the above categorization of the possible effects of the Iraq War, the volume is divided into two sections. Chapters 2, 3, and 4 consider the impact of the war on the achievement of U.S. goals in three closely related areas of national security policy. In Chapter 2, Steven Simon of the Council on Foreign Relations examines the impact of the war on the war on terror. Rightly or wrongly, the Iraq War has been justified and often described as an integral component of the war on terror. Initially, the Bush administration argued that Saddam Hussein had ties to international terrorist groups bent on attacking the United States and might someday provide them with weapons of mass destruction. More recently, it described Iraq as the central front in the war on terror. Critics contend that the war itself turned Iraq into a potential terrorist haven and that it has starved other fronts, especially Afghanistan, of the resources required to defeat al Qaeda and its patrons. What overall impact has the war in fact had on the prosecution of the war on terror? In what ways and to what degree has it made the situation better or worse?

Next, Joseph Cirincione, formerly of the Carnegie Endowment for International Peace and now president of the Ploughshares Fund, looks at the impact of the war on U.S. efforts to prevent the proliferation of nuclear weapons. A closely related rationale for going to war against Iraq was that country's continuing efforts to develop weapons of mass destruction. In his 2002 State of the Union Address, President Bush identified Iraq as one of three countries—the so-called axis of evil—seeking to acquire weapons of mass destruction (WMD) that could be used, directly or indirectly, to attack or threaten the United States and its allies. Iraq had come close to acquiring a nuclear capability before the 1991 Gulf War, and it was viewed by the Bush administration as determined to achieve that goal—and capable of doing so—despite international sanctions. Some hoped that bold action against Iraq would not only eliminate the threat posed by that country but also deter other potential proliferators from moving forward. Critics have charged that the state of Iraq's WMD programs was exaggerated and that the invasion has only convinced other countries that they must have nuclear weapons in order to deter U.S. aggression against them. While subsequent developments have borne out the charge that the threat from Iraq was greatly overstated, what overall impact has the war in fact had on U.S. efforts to prevent proliferation?

In Chapter 4, F. Gregory Gause III of the University of Vermont discusses the impact of the war on U.S. national security interests in the Middle East. The well-being of the United States and its economic and security partners is closely bound up with the reliable flow of oil from the Persian Gulf. Arguably, Iraq under Saddam Hussein posed an even greater potential threat to the stability of that region than it did to the United States itself. After all, the Iraqi leader had already launched two wars that had, at least temporarily, disrupted a substantial share of the world's oil supply. By removing Saddam Hussein from power, then, a principal source of regional instability might thereby be eliminated as well. Critics argue that the war, by fostering sectarian violence within Iraq between Sunnis, Shiites, and Kurds, has heightened the risk of a regional conflagration. What in fact has been the net overall effect of the war in the region?

Chapters 5, 6, and 7 address the consequences of the war for different resources and instruments of U.S. national security policy. In Chapter 5, Michael

O'Hanlon of the Brookings Institution examines the impact on the U.S. military. The Bush administration believed that the Iraq War could be won quickly with a relatively small force. Indeed, the U.S. military rapidly overcame the Iraqi army, but it soon became bogged down in an extended counterinsurgency and civil war. To be sure, the U.S. armed forces have gained valuable lessons and experience in postconflict operations and nation-building, but this has come at great cost in terms of lives lost, equipment damaged, and military readiness. What impact has the war had on the ability of the U.S. armed forces to deal with contingencies not only in but also outside Iraq? How quickly can any damage be repaired, and at what cost?

In Chapter 6, Thomas Weiss of the City University of New York considers the impact of the war on the international standing of the United States. A state's prestige, moral authority, and overall standing in the world can be valuable resources in the pursuit of national security. They can affect, among other things, whether it receives support or resistance from others for its policies. Some proponents of the Iraq War hoped that a quick and decisive victory there would enhance the influence of the United States, increasing its ability to persuade or coerce others to do its bidding. Subsequent polls, however, have suggested that the United States has lost favor in much of the world. What has been the impact of the war on the international standing of the United States? Has it in fact fallen? If so, can the damage be repaired, and what will it take to do so?

Finally, Clay Ramsay of the Program on International Policy Attitudes explores the impact of the war on U.S. public opinion. Ultimately, the ways in which the United States can pursue its national security interests depend on the backing of the American public. It is widely believed that the Vietnam War resulted in sharp public constraints on the ability of the U.S. government to engage in certain types of external policies, especially those involving the use of force, for many years thereafter. More recently, the debacle in Somalia inhibited American leaders from responding to genocide in Rwanda. Some have argued that the tremendous cost of the Iraq War and the loss of so many American lives for uncertain benefits will have a similar effect. What impact has the war in fact had on public attitudes toward foreign involvements and the use of force? How much are such attitudes likely to constrain U.S. policy, and how long might they last?

Our concluding chapter has several objectives. We first review initial expectations of the broader consequences of the war for U.S. national security. We then offer our own overall assessment of the national security benefits and costs of the war. On balance, we find that the costs will almost certainly outweigh the benefits by a significant degree, even assuming a favorable political outcome in Iraq. We complement this assessment with a counterfactual analysis of the likely consequences of other courses of action that the Bush administration might plausibly have pursued and argue that all of the alternatives would most likely have resulted in a more favorable balance of costs and benefits. We end the chapter with a discussion of the lessons of the war for future U.S. policy in Iraq and beyond.

2 THE IRAQ WAR AND THE WAR ON TERROR

The Global Jihad After Iraq

Steven Simon

The immediate effects of the war in Iraq on global terrorism have included a worldwide spike in terrorist attacks, a sharp decline in favorable perceptions of the United States that, in turn, has increased the appeal of Islamic militancy, the intensification of violence in insurgencies in Afghanistan and North Africa, and the diversion of military and intelligence counterterrorism resources to Iraq. The long-run effects of the war may not be known for a decade or more. The Afghan generation did not mature as terrorists until well after the Taliban put an end to the civil strife that followed the expulsion of the Soviets from Afghanistan. It is likely that a corresponding lag will follow the end of al Qaeda's activities in Iraq. There are already indications, however, of blowback of some sort, as scattered jihadist attacks outside of Iraq would suggest. The societies that will bear the brunt of the blowback are as yet unknown, although those from which the jihadists emerged will be clearly at risk. At present, the largest question mark concerns whether the setbacks suffered by al Qaeda in Iraq (AQI) between the fall of 2007 and mid-2008 will discredit the group's reputation and reduce its appeal to recruits worldwide. What is known, however, is that the invasion of Iraq revived a jihadist movement that was all but dead in the wake of the 2001 defeat of the Taliban by U.S. forces in Afghanistan.

AL QAEDA'S VISION: THE LONG WAR

Al Qaeda had high hopes for Iraq. Following losses suffered in Afghanistan in 2002, al Qaeda began to look toward Iraq as a replacement beachhead. The group had long believed that in order to spread the true faith and retake the

Muslim world, it must first control a state. In time, with the haven in Afghanistan under attack, Iraq would become just such a beachhead.

Thus, on the eve of the American invasion, Osama bin Laden announced to the world that al Qaeda was "following with great interest and extreme concern the crusaders' preparations for war to occupy a former capital of Islam, loot Muslims' wealth, and install an agent government, which would be a satellite for its masters in Washington and Tel Aviv."[1] Jihadists argued that Iraq would be the disaster for America that Afghanistan was for the Soviet Union. "We believe these infidels have lost their minds," one correspondent wrote on a Pakistani militant Web site called Jamaat ud-Daawa. "They do not know what they are doing. They keep on repeating the same mistake."[2] Al Qaeda leader Ayman al-Zawahiri assessed that the United States was caught between two fires, namely, the humiliation of withdrawal and the losses that would result from continued commitment. In his view, the American intervention constituted a comprehensive strategic failure that jihadists would exploit ruthlessly.

Al Qaeda's main objective in Iraq was to establish an Islamic state that would form the basis of a renewed caliphate. Zawahiri expressed this objective in a question-and-answer session with journalists in early 2008: "The Islamic State [of Iraq] is a step towards the establishment of the caliphate, and is superior to the other armed jihadi movements [in Iraq]."[3] In a statement commemorating the fifth anniversary of the invasion, Zawahiri spoke of the importance of the Iraqi front in the wider jihad: "Soon, Iraq will become a fortress of Islam from whence the squadrons and regiments tasked with liberating the Al-Aqsa mosque [in Jerusalem] will burst forth, with the help of Allah."[4] The strong territorial impulse of the jihad comes across clearly in these statements, as it does in contemporary jihadist strategic thinking along the lines of Abu Bakr al-Naji's treatise *Management of Savagery*.[5]

In al Qaeda's worldview, Iraq is a battleground, though not the only one, in which the decisive confrontation with the West will unfold. Thus, from 2003 until late 2007, the country dominated the group's attention. From bin Laden's perspective, as he explained in a January 2006 audio recording aired on al Jazeera, while the war against the U.S. crusaders "was not just restricted to Iraq as he [President Bush] claims," Iraq had nonetheless become "a gravitational point and a recruiting ground for qualified [mujahidin]."[6] In a December 2007 message, bin Laden referred to Iraq as the "first line of defense for the Islamic nation."[7] Deploying the same talking points, Zawahiri characterized Iraq in

2008 as "the most important frontline for the participation of our Islamic nation against the forces of the crusader Zionist invasion."[8]

Despite these widely disseminated declarations, the flow of fighters to Iraq did not rise to bin Laden's expectations. Bin Laden drew attention to the shortfall of Muslims willing to travel to Iraq for jihad in an October 2007 audio message: "Where are the soldiers of the Levant and the reinforcements from Yemen?" he pleaded, "Where are the knights of Egypt and the lions of Hejaz? Come to the aid of your brothers in Iraq!"[9]

Bin Laden's disappointment notwithstanding, damage to U.S. interests had already been done. The Iraq jihad, as the declassified key judgments of a National Intelligence Estimate (NIE) on "Trends in Global Terrorism" acknowledged in April 2006, has done irrevocable harm to U.S. efforts in the global war on terrorism. This assessment judged that "the Iraq jihad is shaping a new generation of terrorist leaders and operatives" and that the Iraq conflict had become "the cause célèbre for jihadists, breeding a deep resentment of U.S. involvement in the Muslim world and cultivating supporters for the global jihadist movement."[10]

Successive polls during this period corroborated this intelligence assessment. Support for the United States in Jordan, an important regional security partner for the United States, dropped from 25 percent in 2002 to 1 percent in 2003. In Lebanon, U.S. approval ratings fell from 30 to 15 percent during the same period. Majorities in Jordan, Turkey, Egypt, Indonesia, and Pakistan said the U.S. effort to remove Saddam Hussein made the world more, not less, dangerous. The decline in U.S. approval ratings coincided with falling support for the U.S.-led war on terror. In Jordan, support fell from 13 percent in 2002 to 2 percent in 2003.[11]

Although the great majority of insurgents was made up of Ba'thist "deadenders" and Moktada al-Sadr's Mahdi Army, there is ample evidence that foreign fighters under the influence of al Qaeda played a significant role in Iraq's accelerating spiral of violence early on. Jihadists under the command of Abu Musab al-Zarqawi, who affiliated himself with al Qaeda, were responsible for the most gruesome attacks in Iraq during the early months of the insurgency. Attacks on the Jordanian embassy as well as the UN and International Red Cross headquarters in Baghdad were deliberate attempts by al Qaeda to foster chaos, force the withdrawal of the international community from Iraq, and trigger sectarian violence; these attacks ultimately tipped Iraq into civil war. This was a deliberate strategy on the part of al Qaeda in Iraq.

BLOWBACK FROM THE IRAQ WAR

In 2005, Peter Bergen and Alex Reynolds argued that the Iraqi insurgency could result in a "ferocious blowback of its own," one longer and more powerful than that which resulted from the Soviet invasion of Afghanistan in the 1980s. The insurgents in Iraq today, warned the authors, could become tomorrow's terrorists.[12] In 2007, Bergen (together with Paul Cruickshank) wrote that the rate of terrorist attacks around the world by jihadist groups and the rate of fatalities in those attacks increased dramatically after the invasion of Iraq. Specifically, they argued that the Iraq War has generated a sevenfold increase in the yearly rate of fatal jihadist attacks. Still, the authors noted that a large part of this rise occurred in Iraq, which accounted for half of the global total of jihadist terrorist attacks during that period. Outside of Iraq and Afghanistan, the study found an increase of 35 percent in the number of jihadist terrorist attacks.[13]

To be sure, al Qaeda in Iraq has, to date, been operationally linked to only one attack outside of the Middle East: the failed 2007 Glasgow International Airport and London club bombings. Nevertheless, this meager record masks a serious jihadist effort to internationalize the conflict in Iraq. This effort predates the official start of the Iraq War. In October 2002, Abu Musab al-Zarqawi (Ahmad Fadeel al-Nazal al-Khalayleh), a proponent of expanding the war, engineered the murder of an American diplomat, Laurence Foley, in Jordan. In 2005, he orchestrated the bombing of three American-owned hotels in Amman. All three successful bombers were Iraqi. (A fourth, the wife of another bomber, fled after her vest failed to detonate.) Zarqawi's group also explored the possibility of attacks against Saudi Arabia and at least one other Gulf Cooperation Council (GCC) state.

Zarqawi set his sights on Europe early on. According to U.S. and European intelligence officials, the creation of the AQI leader's European network predated the Iraq War. In April 2002, Shahdi Abdellah, a former Zarqawi associate, told German interrogators that the Jordanian terrorist "needed people outside of Afghanistan . . . and particularly in Europe" and that he was "very interested in accomplishing something in Europe."[14] Based in part on Abdellah's testimony, European authorities rounded up 116 suspected terrorists linked to Zarqawi the following February. Former director of Central Intelligence George Tenet characterized the disruption of Zarqawi's European-based network during late 2002 and early 2003 as "one of the great successes of the post-9/11 war on terrorism." Acting together with two dozen other intelligence services, the United States disrupted plots in the UK, France, Spain, and Italy during this period.[15]

Zarqawi and other Iraqi insurgents were linked to Younis Tsouli, a twenty-two-year-old West Londoner of Moroccan origin using the Internet handle "Irhabi 007."[16] Tsouli, whose on-line presence was first noticed by authorities in 2004, was the top jihadi Internet expert until his capture by Scotland Yard in fall 2005. In the spring of 2004, keenly aware of the power of the Internet, Zarqawi's group began to distribute communiqués on extremist Arabic-language message forums. One of the first to take note was Tsouli, who made contact with al Qaeda in Iraq's chief spokesman, Abu Maysara al-Iraqi. Irhabi 007's services, which included hacking into servers owned by the Arkansas State Highway and Transportation Department as well as the George Washington University to post videos of insurgents attacking U.S. forces in Iraq, were critical to AQI's propaganda operation. So useful were Tsouli's services that even al-Sahab, al Qaeda's media organization, relied on him to disseminate its propaganda.[17]

The European network played a role in providing funds and recruits for Zarqawi. Among those who made their way to Iraq was Muriel Degauque, a thirty-five-year-old Belgian Muslim convert who blew herself up in an attack on an American convoy south of Baghdad in 2005.[18] Around the same time, European counterterrorism officials began to worry aloud that Zarqawi could be planning to use his base in Iraq to attack Europe. Earlier that year, the U.S. National Counterterrorism Center had reported that Zarqawi's operatives were linked with twenty-four extremist organizations and at work in forty countries.[19] Plots in Britain, Germany, Bosnia, Denmark, France, and Spain linked to the insurgent leader were uncovered. Although the tempo of activity is strikingly clear, the record of the ensuing prosecutions has not demonstrated a clear operational link between Zarqawi and the conspirators. As of 2008, however, the Iraq War appears to have inspired these plots rather than to have served as a source of command and control.

The bungled terrorist attacks in London and Glasgow of 2007, therefore, remain the sole known evidence of an operational nexus between the Iraqi and European theaters, a connection confirmed by the discovery of Iraqi al Qaeda telephone numbers on the European plotters' cell handsets. One of the plotters, Bilal Abdullah, was of Iraqi descent. The use of vehicle-borne explosive devices (VBEDs) aimed at multiple targets also pointed to al Qaeda in Iraq. British intelligence officials told foreign diplomats they believed the attacks were the first sign of blowback from Britain's involvement in the Iraq War, but they stopped short of saying that the plot originated or was directed by the group.[20]

Whether Zarqawi's death at the hands of U.S. forces in 2006 has diminished the threat of jihadist terror in Europe, especially given the role of Pakistan-based militants in fostering attacks there, is currently unclear. Although the Iraq War certainly contributed to radicalization among European Muslims, social and economic exclusion combined with political alienation would seem to have been an equally compelling explanation for extremism. These explanations, however, are not mutually exclusive. The individual experiences of European youths are said to align with their observations about the condition of Muslims in the Middle East in a way that reinforces resentment against non-Muslims and Western governments more generally.[21] At a 2007 London conference of leading experts on the sociology of Muslims in Europe, one French participant explained that European Muslims view the war in Iraq "as European Muslims, not just Muslims"; that is, through the prism of European historical and cultural contexts. For them, the war is "just an add-on," one of a list of grievances European Muslims have but by no means the most significant.[22] The picture is nonetheless complicated, as shown by the case of the 19th Arrondissement cell, a French jihadist recruitment ring made up of mostly North Africans, who traveled to Iraq to fight alongside Zarqawi. During their trial in 2008, French prosecutors presented no evidence that any of the men intended to carry out terrorist attacks against France. Farid Benyettou, a twenty-six-year-old janitor-turned-jihadist and the group's leader, insisted in his testimony that he preached against committing jihad in France. "We are in France, we are in France," Benyettou told the court repeatedly, "We enjoy a certain number of liberties" and the laws should be obeyed.[23]

On balance, the paucity of cases of European Muslims going to fight in Iraq—fewer than one hundred cases exist—warrants a degree of skepticism about the likelihood of massive near-term bleed out from Iraq to Europe.[24] Logistical difficulties entailed in travel to Iraq, aggressive policing by European security services, the unpopularity of European volunteers within Iraq, and the confusing nature of a war that pits Muslim against Muslim all contribute to the low rate of flow. The fact that many volunteers who have made the journey have been employed in suicide missions also obviates the problem of blowback.

The origins of most of the foreign fighters in Iraq suggest that blowback in the shape of returning veterans will likely be felt most powerfully in the Muslim world rather than in Europe. The most recent figures were gleaned from documents and computer files found in 2007 during a U.S. military raid of an AQI camp in the desert close to Sinjar, located by the Syrian border. According to the *New York Times*, the cell was "responsible for smuggling the vast majority of foreign fighters in Iraq."[25] More than seven hundred profiles of fighters entering Iraq since August 2006 were recovered, including details such as the militant's hometowns, occupations, and roles once inside Iraq. The records provide a rare snapshot into the operation of bringing foreign fighters into Iraq.

The Sinjar records, as outlined by the Combating Terrorism Center (CTC) study, indicate that Saudis, at 41 percent, made up an overwhelming majority of fighters traveling to Iraq. Libya provided the second largest contingent at 19 percent, followed by Syria (8 percent), Yemen (8 percent), and Algeria (7 percent).[26] The CTC study also indicates that on a per capita basis, Libya contributed the majority of foreign fighters, followed by Saudi Arabia, Tunisia, Syria, and Yemen.[27] The authors note that it is the apparent prominence of Libyan fighters that sets their study apart from previous ones, pointing out that as recently as 2007, a U.S. Army source was quoted as stating that only 10 percent of foreign militants in Iraq come from North Africa.

Local governments are aware of the danger. The Saudis in particular have taken measures to deal with the threat of bleed out from Iraq. In 2004, following a wave of extremist violence, the government launched a new prisoner reeducation and rehabilitation program aimed at de-radicalizing militants and curbing terrorism. The program, which is run by the Ministry of Interior and pairs prisoners with state-sanctioned religious leaders and counselors, is designed to de-radicalize extremist sympathizers. Participants in the program include not only jihadist sympathizers but also a number of Saudis who have fought in Iraq and were later repatriated.

An estimated two thousand prisoners are reported to have participated in the program to date. Of these, the Saudi government reports that seven hundred prisoners have renounced their former beliefs and been released while one thousand remain incarcerated. Another fourteen hundred prisoners have refused to participate in the program altogether. Officials maintain the program has an 80 to 90 percent success rate and point out that only ten individuals have been rearrested to date since leaving the program, suggesting a relatively low rate of recidivism.[28] General Petraeus has praised the Saudi initiative, saying it may have contributed to the decline in the number of foreign fighters in Iraq.[29] Other regional countries, including Yemen and Egypt, have also begun to experiment with de-radicalization programs.[30]

SHIFTING SANDS: THE IRAQIFICATION OF GLOBAL JIHAD

By 2008, the Iraqi insurgency had come full circle. Prior to 2001, al Qaeda trained its fighters at camps in Afghanistan and exported them to wage war in Chechnya and Kashmir, or to carry out attacks against U.S. targets in Africa and elsewhere. The U.S. invasion of Afghanistan after the attacks of September 11, 2001, caught al Qaeda off guard. The group's leaders were forced into hiding, the conveyor belt of radicals from South Asia stalled, and the movement as a whole seemed to have come to a dead end. The invasion of Iraq by the coalition in 2003 effectively reversed this outcome.[31] Abu Musab al-Zarqawi exploited this new lease on life to create serious difficulties for the U.S. occupation of Iraq and indeed for attempts to unify the Iraqi state. Since then, the flow of jihadist traffic has reversed, with tactics and fighters from Iraq making their way back to Afghanistan and beyond. So significant did the relationship between fighters in Afghanistan and insurgents in Iraq become that before his death in 2007 senior Taliban commander Mullah Dadullah boasted to al Jazeera, "We have [a] 'give and take' with the mujahedin in Iraq."[32]

The earliest evidence that the jihadists in Iraq were collaborating with those in Afghanistan and elsewhere came to light two years after the start of Operation Iraqi Freedom (OIF), in the fall of 2005. Although Vice President Dick Cheney had declared the Iraq insurgency to be in its "last throes" the previous spring, fighting claimed seventy-seven American lives in October 2005 alone, making it the third deadliest month for U.S. forces in Iraq at the time.[33] In comparison, the death toll for that entire year in Afghanistan was sixty-six. Yet that figure represented a more than twofold increase over casualties from 2004 and, at that point, the deadliest year since the invasion. The increase in U.S. military fatalities coincided with the arrival of Iraqi-style improvised explosive devices (IEDs) in Afghanistan. Other tactics honed in Iraq would follow, leading to what one former senior Bush administration official dubbed the "Iraqification of Afghanistan."[34]

The radical Islamists' prominence in the Iraqi insurgency may owe in part to their early start. Before the U.S. invasion, Abu Musab al-Zarqawi was of concern to Washington. Secretary of State Colin Powell and other administration officials pointed to Zarqawi as evidence of cooperation between al Qaeda and the regime of Saddam Hussein. But the truth was that Zarqawi and bin Laden were more rivals than anything else prior to the 2003 invasion.[35]

Although Zarqawi attended the Sada training camp run by bin Laden's military chief Mohammed Atef in the early 1990s, he neither pledged fealty to bin Laden nor joined al Qaeda during this period. Instead, he returned to Jordan, where he was apprehended and sentenced to fifteen years in prison. Released in 1999 as part of a general amnesty, Zarqawi traveled to Pakistan to reconnect with other like-minded jihadists. He carried a letter of introduction from Abu Kutaiba al-Urduni, a prominent Jordanian jihadist who had once served as recruiter for Sheikh Abdullah Azzam in Afghanistan. The letter was addressed to Osama bin Laden.[36]

The two men are alleged to have met for the first time in late 1999 or early 2000. According to a former Israeli intelligence official, "It was loathing at first sight."[37] In addition to suspecting that members of Jordan's intelligence services had infiltrated Zarqawi's cell, bin Laden was put off by Zarqawi's un-Islamic tattoos and his conviction that all Shiites "should be executed." (Bin Laden's mother is an Alawite.) Nevertheless, the al Qaeda leader provided Zarqawi with funds to set up a training camp near the Afghan-Iranian border for his group, Jund al-Sham, or Soldiers of the Levant. Although he had declined to swear *bayat*—an oath of allegiance—to bin Laden, Zarqawi joined forces with al Qaeda's fighters after the U.S. invasion of Afghanistan in October 2001. Two months later, he fled Afghanistan for Iran. During the next year and a half, Zarqawi crisscrossed the region to recruit and form an insurgent force in the Sunni Triangle in Iraq in anticipation of U.S. intervention.

In mid-2002, Zarqawi relocated to northern Iraq. According to George Tenet, the then director of Central Intelligence (DCI), Zarqawi set up base in the northern Iraqi town of Khurmal, where he ran a chemical and poisons laboratory and training facility and began to forge ties to Algerians, Moroccans, Pakistanis, Libyans, and other Arab extremists located throughout Europe. The U.S. intelligence community estimated that Zarqawi had connections to terrorist cells in more than thirty countries during this period.[38] Although the camp at Khurmal was established by Ansar al-Islam (AI) as a safe haven in northeastern Iraq in the event that Afghan sanctuary was ever lost, it was supervised by Zarqawi. As Afghanistan came under siege in the fall of 2001, al Qaeda fighters began relocating to the AI camps in ever-larger numbers.[39]

In 2003, with the U.S. invasion underway, Zarqawi—by then strategically positioned near Baghdad—was contacted by bin Laden and asked to join al Qaeda. Meanwhile, bin Laden is alleged to have opened an underground railroad to and from jihadist training camps in the Sunni Triangle through which Taliban leaders, branded by U.S. officials as a "spent force," traveled to Iraq to get training.[40] This informal collaboration between insurgents in Iraq and the Taliban would impart new life to an Afghan insurgency knocked back on its heels by the U.S. assault. Starting in 2005, Afghan officials began to warn of "strong indications" that the group had brought in instructors from Iraq to teach Taliban fighters the latest insurgent techniques. Arab manuals depicting insurgent combat techniques also began turning up in Afghanistan.[41]

While the total number of Taliban who graduated from training courses in Iraq is estimated to be as high as five hundred, the actual figure may never be known.[42] Nonetheless, information about the relationship between jihadists in Iraq and abroad has become available through interviews given to *Newsweek* in 2005 by former insurgents, such as Mohammed Daud, a thirty-eight-year-old graduate of the program, and Hamza Sangari, a Taliban commander from Khost Province.[43]

According to these accounts, the then-thirty-four-year-old Sangari received an invitation in late 2004 from Abdul Hadi al-Iraqi, bin Laden's chief envoy to the Iraqi insurgency. Along with fellow Afghan jihadists, Sangari traveled to the Sunni Triangle where he received advanced combat training, including ambush tactics and urban warfare techniques. Graduates of the program returned to Afghanistan with enhanced skills and greater commitment to the jihadist code. Daud, who commanded the largest Taliban force in Ghazni Province upon his return from Iraq, attributed his operational effectiveness as a commander and the "new momentum and spirit" of his trainees to his experience in Iraq.

Esprit d'corps was not the sole training objective. In at least one camp, Ashaq al Hoor, Afghans received demolition training and were taught to fabricate armor-penetrating munitions. Iraqi insurgents also trained the Afghans to build the remotely detonated shaped charges that were responsible for the majority of American deaths in Iraq.[44]

Within a few years, Iraqi-style IEDs began making their appearance in Afghanistan. Prior to 2006, large roadside bombs, the hallmark of the Iraqi insurgency, were rare events in Afghanistan. Increasingly, however, roadside bombs have become the weapon of choice for Afghan insurgents. From fewer than two dozen improvised explosive devices in 2002, the number grew to 83 in 2003 and by 2006 had ballooned to 1,730.[45]

Since then, the trend has shown no sign of abating. The first half of 2007 saw one thousand IED attacks alone.[46] The 2007 annual report of the Joint IED Defeat Organization (JIEDDO), created by the U.S. military to eliminate the threat posed by this new weapon, noted that the "number of IEDs employed against U.S. forces in FY07 reached an all-time high, more than doubling over the last half of the fiscal year."[47] British forces in Helmand Province alone reported encountering one hundred fifty IEDs between April and June 2008.[48]

The increase in the number and sophistication of IED attacks is largely attributable to advances made by insurgents in Iraq, although this trend could also be the result of natural progress made by Afghan jihadists learning from mistakes, as did the IRA in the 1970s. The truth may lie somewhere in-between. Whatever the case, official U.S. analyses lean toward the view that Afghan jihadists are watching and learning from Iraqi insurgents. A 2007 report by the Congressional Research Service observed, "Taliban forces in Afghanistan appear to have learned some IED techniques from the Iraqi insurgents."[49] In February 2008, the director of the JIEDDO, U.S. Army Lieutenant General Thomas Metz, referred to the tactical shift underway in the Taliban, saying, "They have decided through the networks and learned from Iraq that IEDs are the way to go. So they are out here with a larger [IED] capacity."[50] Throughout the early months of 2008, NATO forces in Afghanistan continued to report a sharp shift in Taliban tactics away from frontal attacks toward roadside bombings and ambushes.

One such technique adopted by Afghan fighters was the use of near-simultaneous IED attacks. In 2006, authorities began to notice the appearance of multiple IEDs linked together used to target moving vehicles, a common tactic in Iraq.[51] Still, the attacks, with only two or three IEDs connected together, were less advanced than the more sophisticated and deadly "daisy chains"—strings of multiple IEDs wired together—widely used then in Iraq. This was to change, however, by 2008, as daisy-chain ambushes became a reality on the Afghan scene.[52]

Taliban fighters who traveled to Iraq brought back other deadly skills as well, including the use of suicide bombers against both noncombatant and combatant targets. While insurgents in Iraq embraced martyrdom operations as their tactic of choice from 2003 onward, the practice was considered taboo in the Afghan context. No suicide attacks were reported to have taken place during the entirety of the Soviet jihad, although insurgents were observed to demonstrate reckless regard for their lives in combat. Nor were suicide bombings a feature of the Afghan civil war that followed.[53]

The first recorded suicide attack in Afghanistan occurred on June 9, 2003, and is believed to have been carried out by Arab Afghans. Similarly, a December 2003 suicide attack in Kabul was described as the work of "either Arabs or Pakistanis." The first such attack attributed to an Afghan took place in January 2004, when Hafez Abdallah, a Taliban fighter from Khost, threw himself on a coalition jeep and detonated explosives strapped to his body.[54]

Between 2002 and 2004 there were fewer than half a dozen suicide bombings in Afghanistan. (Two failed suicide bombings in Kabul in 2002 were carried out by foreigners linked to al Qaeda, not the Taliban.[55]) Thereafter, the number of such attacks grew steadily, as Afghans and Pakistanis began to replace Arabs in suicide missions. In 2005, the figure climbed to seventeen. In contrast, there were an estimated five hundred and fourteen suicide attacks in Iraq between March 22, 2003, and August 18, 2006. Together, these attacks killed hundreds and wounded thousands more.[56] By 2006, however, the annual number of suicide attacks in Afghanistan had increased by more than sevenfold to one hundred and twenty-three. An additional seventy-seven attacks were carried out in the first six months of 2007 alone.[57] This trend continues to accelerate.

A 2007 UN report commissioned to investigate the background to the spiraling rate of suicide attacks in Afghanistan concluded that "suicide attackers . . . may have been inspired by such attacks in Iraq and neighboring Pakistan."[58] Still, differences have been noted, most notably in the targeting patterns of the bombers. Whereas Iraqi insurgents often attacked soft targets, such as crowded markets and mosques, with the goal of high casualties and deepening ethnic hatreds, suicide bombers in Afghanistan have favored hard targets such as government or military installations.[59]

There are disturbing signs that these deadly tactics may be migrating to other battlegrounds in the war on terror as well. Makeshift bomb attacks by insurgents are on the rise around the world, suggesting that the tactic perfected in Iraq, where an estimated six hundred IED explosions were occurring each month in early 2008, and Afghanistan, with sixty-four bombings recorded for the month of February 2008, is fast becoming the weapon of choice for terrorist groups. According to the British consulting firm HMS, which advises JIEDDO, there are an additional two to three hundred attacks using IEDs every month outside of Iraq and Afghanistan. After Iraq and Afghanistan, Pakistan, India, Sri Lanka, Thailand, Russia, and Nepal report the highest rates of IED activity.[60]

IEDs have also made an appearance in the Maghreb. In Algeria, intelligence suggests that the Salafist Group for Preaching and Combat (GSPC), which merged with al Qaeda in 2006 to become al Qaeda in the Maghreb (AQIM), is abandoning its traditional guerrilla tactics and attempting to develop sophisticated IED capabilities of its own.

The GSPC, which fought a ten-year war from 1991 until 2002 against the Algerian government that left more than one hundred thousand dead, revived the conflict in 1998. Although the Bush administration designated the group as a terrorist organization after 9/11, the GSPC has blurred the line between terrorist organization and full-fledged insurgency.[61]

The merger with al Qaeda was a response to GSPC's plight in March 2004, when a trilateral counterterrorism initiative staged by the United States, Chad, and Algeria led to the capture of the group's head and the scattering of the remaining leadership. The group's new leader, Abdelmalek Droukdal, appealed to Zarqawi in Iraq to kidnap French citizens who might then be traded for the release of his imprisoned predecessor. Zarqawi had more in mind, however, and proposed a merger between the GSPC and al Qaeda. In a retrospective interview with the *New York Times*, Droukdal said Zarqawi played a "pivotal role" in the subsequent merger of the two groups, arranging for the transfer of badly needed weapons and funds to the Algerian group.[62]

The union with al Qaeda brought with it the organization's institutional skills in tactics and weaponeering. By January 2005, Zarqawi was singling out the GSPC for praise in his statements. In 2006, the arrangement was formalized, with the GSPC adopting the label of "al Qaeda in the Maghreb." Shortly thereafter, Algerian authorities reported that IEDs began to surface in Algeria.[63] In 2006, Algerian security forces began reporting that the group has begun to experiment with mobile detonators, "a more sophisticated method than time or manual detonation," and one perfected by insurgents in Iraq.[64]

The GSPC-AQI merger resulted not only in the transfer of capabilities but also the transformation of the Algerian movement from a nationalist insurgency to a component of the global jihad. In addition to sophisticated bomb-making techniques, members of GSPC/AQIM absorbed other tactics from their jihadi brethren in Iraq, most notably in the area of targeting. Although insurgents in Iraq would later turn their wrath on Iraqi civilians, the movement initially targeted international assets such as foreign embassies and the UN headquarters. In late 2004, GSPC/AQIM followed suit, carrying out an attack on Westerners. This was a genuine departure. According to the 2007 annual State Department Country Report on Terrorism, the group had previously avoided targeting foreign entities in favor of government targets.[65] A December 2006 attack on a bus carrying foreign oil workers outside Algiers confirmed the group's commitment to wage jihad against Westerners.[66]

Algerian authorities have also noted an increase in suicide attacks since the merger.[67] In December 2007 twin suicide car bombs detonated outside UN headquarters in Algiers, killing seventeen UN staff members and more than a dozen others. AQIM immediately claimed responsibility. The attack was the deadliest against the international organization since the bombing of the UN headquarters in Iraq in August 2003, which claimed the lives of twenty-two UN employees.[68] The group's bombing of the prime minister's office and a police building in Algiers the previous April was also the work of three suicide truck bombers.[69]

Having recast the regional jihad and widened its targets to include foreign nationals and assets, GSPC/AQIM began to place greater emphasis on recruiting and carrying out attacks in neighboring states. Intelligence services have disrupted several AQIM plots in recent years, including one in late 2007 that targeted the U.S. and UK embassies in Tunisia. Additional plots have been disrupted in Morocco and Egypt.[70]

Finally, the Iraq War has also provided terrorist groups with opportunities to expand their international networks. The GSPC/AQIM is known to have facilitated the flow of Algerian and other foreign fighters from Northern Africa to the Iraqi theater. At the height of the insurgency, the U.S. military estimated that up to 20 percent of the suicide bombings in Iraq were carried out by Algerians.[71] (The Sinjar papers, however, found that Algerians constituted just 7 percent of the foreign contingent.[72]) Though the true size of the Algerian contingent may never be revealed, graduates of the Iraq insurgency have been exposed to sophisticated bomb-making techniques and related capabilities that, as noted above, have appeared in North Africa. In the longer term, the relationships formed by the network of foreign fighters traveling to Iraq may prove the most dangerous of Iraq's implications for the evolution of global terrorism.

IRAQ'S PROPAGANDA VALUE

Aside from "hard" tactical changes like the spread of IED technology, the targeting of Westerners, and an increase in suicide and other assault tactics intended to kill large numbers, the Iraq War has also contributed to the way the global jihad is packaged and marketed. Indeed, the jihadist's propaganda victories may be one of the most lasting legacies of the Iraq War.

Although al Qaeda was no stranger to the power of the media before 2003, the Iraq War has transformed the way the group spreads its message to the world. Experts cite the emergence of post-2003 Iraqi videos depicting beheadings, IED attacks, and suicide bombings against coalition forces as providing inspiration for jihadists around the world.[73] No single person has been more responsible for this development than Abu Musab al-Zarqawi.

Before his death in June 2006, Zarqawi, who viewed the camera as a weapon of war, ordered his fighters to record every insurgent operation. Former insurgents say each cell had "a little office where someone did film operations."[74] The footage, showing IED and other attacks against U.S. forces, was then set to music and uploaded to jihadist Web sites, often finding its way onto YouTube and other popular outlets on the World Wide Web. Initially produced in Arabic, subtitles were later added in order to give the videos a wider audience.

So gripping were the Iraqi jihadi videos that the Taliban quickly set out to imitate them. Graduates of the Iraq insurgency returned to Afghanistan fresh with the equipment and know-how needed to produce and disseminate videos on the Internet. By 2004, videos of Taliban attacks were showing up in bazaars along the Pakistani border.[75] Gruesome videos showing the beheading of a "Crusader Spy," eerily similar to Zarqawi's infamous videotaped beheadings from Iraq, began to appear on Taliban Internet sites around this same time.

In addition to inspiring sympathizers around the world and helping with fund-raising and recruiting efforts, the videos serve another, equally sinister purpose: allowing insurgents to spread their dangerous skills to jihadists in far-off lands. Zarqawi reportedly had his bomb classes taped so that his expertise would not be lost if he were killed.[76]

Insurgent propaganda also helped redirect the traffic flow of foreign fighters. In the summer of 2005, the SITE Institute reported an "unbelievable increase of publications coming from Afghanistan," many of which said, "Stop going to Iraq, start going to Afghanistan. We need you here."[77]

The result has been profound. Analysts believe the Iraq War has had a documented radicalizing effect on more than a dozen known plots to date from Europe to the United States and beyond. In each case, the conspirators drew on al Qaeda for inspiration. The Madrid bombers, for example, are known to have watched videos of Spaniards fighting and dying in Iraq before they carried out their March 11, 2004, attack. Moreover, the goal of the bombers, to compel the Spanish government to withdraw Spanish forces from Iraq, was linked to their pre-attack obsession with the Iraq War.[78]

Muhammad Bouyeri, the murderer of Theo van Gogh and ringleader of the Hofstad group in Amsterdam, was similarly motivated by events in Iraq, among a host of other fixations. He was outraged by the Dutch deployment of troops in support of the invasion. In an open letter written in the summer of 2004, he raged about the torture inflicted by the United States on Iraqis.[79]

The London bombers proclaimed their July 7, 2005, subway attack an act of revenge for British "massacres" in Afghanistan and Iraq. In a video aired by al Jazeera two months after the attacks, one of the four suicide bombers, Mohammed Siddique Khan, told viewers, "Your democratically elected governments continually perpetrate atrocities against my people all over the world. Your support makes you directly responsible. We are at war and I am a soldier. Now you too will taste the reality of this situation."[80] Khan's associates have confirmed that the occupation of Iraq was, in his view, one such atrocity. On the eve of the one-year anniversary of the attacks, al Jazeera aired a video in which a second bomber, Shehzad Tanweer, declared, "What you have witnessed now is only the beginning of a string of attacks that will continue and become stronger until you pull your forces out of Afghanistan and Iraq."[81]

The four men responsible for the failed copycat bombings two weeks later were likewise inspired by what they saw in Iraq. One of the men, Hussein Osman, told police he watched videos with fellow suspects. According to the *Observer*, upon arrest Osman said, "More than praying we discussed work, politics, the war in Iraq. . . . We always had new films of the war in Iraq. . . . More than anything else those in which you could see Iraqi women and children who had been killed by U.S. and UK soldiers."[82]

In the United States, the six men who plotted to attack Fort Dix in New Jersey in 2007 were also radicalized by the war. In addition to watching videos "depicting armed attacks on and the killing of U.S. military personnel [in Iraq]," investigators say the war affected the choice of the target, a military base that served as a transit point for soldiers departing for Iraq.

AL QAEDA OVERREACH?

In the immediate aftermath of the Iraqi invasion, the global jihad ideology was ascendant. The Iraq War validated the bin Laden narrative for many in the Muslim world. Media coverage outside the United States of collateral damage resulting from U.S. operations as well as revelations of abuses at Abu Ghraib and Haditha legitimated the insurgency in the opinion of many Muslims.

Beginning in 2006, however, the trend began to shift as Muslims began to pull away from the group in response to Zarqawi's brutal tactics against fellow Muslims. The November 9, 2005, Amman hotel bombings triggered a backlash. In the wake of these horrific attacks, Jordanians took to the streets in droves to denounce terrorism and fellow-Jordanian Zarqawi.[83] Members of Zarqawi's own family disowned him. Elsewhere in the region, Muslims were also beginning to turn away from Zarqawi's brutal attacks next door in Iraq, many of which targeted civilians.

The attacks prompted criticism within al Qaeda's ranks as well. In April 2006, the son of bin Laden's mentor Abdullah Azzam announced to the world that Zarqawi had been stripped of his political duties due to concerns that his actions were hurting the Iraqi insurgency's support in the Arab world.[84] The previous summer, U.S. intelligence intercepted a letter from Zawahiri in which the Egyptian jihadist leader issued a mild reprimand to Zarqawi for his repeated targeting of Iraqi Shi'a, saying, "Many of your Muslim admirers amongst the common folk are wondering about your attacks on the Shi'a. The sharpness of this questioning increases when the attacks are on one of their mosques." Zawahiri went on to question the "correctness of this conflict" and wondered if the operations could not be put off "until the force of the mujahed movement in Iraq gets stronger?"[85] He turned next to the matter of Zarqawi's brutal tactics, including the beheadings of hostages: "Among the things which the feelings of the Muslim populace who love and support you will never find palatable . . . are the scenes of slaughtering the hostages. You shouldn't be deceived by the praise of some of the zealous young men and their description of you as the shaykh of the slaughterers," Zawahiri cautioned. In addition, the letter demonstrated that al Qaeda was keenly aware that "more than half of this battle is taking place in the battlefield of the media. And that we are in a media battle in a race for the hearts and minds of our Umma."[86]

Polling by the Pew Global Opinion Trends survey indicated that Zawahiri was right to be concerned. A 2007 survey found that support for suicide bombings against civilians fell sharply across the Muslim world in the five years between 2002 and 2007, declining by half or more in Lebanon, Bangladesh, Jordan, Pakistan, and Indonesia. The largest recorded change was in Lebanon, where 34 percent of Muslim respondents in 2007 said suicide bombings were "often/sometimes justified" compared with 74 percent five years earlier.[87] Alongside declining support for suicide bombings, the Pew study noted declining Muslim confidence in Osama bin Laden, buttressing the argument that a broader rejection of extremist tactics among the Muslim world is underway. In Jordan, those expressing "a lot/some confidence" in bin Laden fell from 56 percent in 2003 to 20 percent in 2007, while in Lebanon the numbers declined from 20 to just 1 percent.[88] A separate Pew study showed that among Muslims, bin Laden is widely mistrusted in all but a handful of countries. In only two countries—Nigeria and the Palestinian Territories—do the majority of Muslim respondents say they have at least some confidence in bin Laden.[89]

Alongside this backlash from the Muslim world, al Qaeda has been hurt by the emergence of critics from within the movement itself. In the past few years, several formerly staunch supporters of jihad have repudiated al Qaeda and the tactics the group employs. Among these ideological defectors are Sheikh Abu Muhammad al-Maqdisi, an influential jihadi theorist, Sayyid Imam Al Sharif also known as "Dr. Fadl," who is widely regarded as an "ideological godfather" of al Qaeda, and Noman Benotman, a former leader of the Libyan Islamic Fighting Group and al Qaeda ally.[90] In 2007, Fadl, Zawahiri's mentor, published "Rationalization of Jihad," in which he argued that al Qaeda's bombings in Egypt, Saudi Arabia, and elsewhere are illegitimate and the killing of civilians wrong. "What good is it," wrote Fadl, "if you destroy one of your enemy's buildings, and he destroys one of your countries? What good is it if you kill one of his people, and he kills a thousand of yours? . . . That, in short, is my evaluation of 9/11."[91] As he told al-Hayat, Zawahiri and bin Laden were simply immoral.

The cumulative effect of the repudiation of al Qaeda's leaders by its former religious scholars, argue Peter Bergen and Paul Cruickshank, could "help hasten the implosion of the jihadist terrorist movement."[92] Others are less sanguine. Bruce Hoffman contends that the reality is more complex and that while the defections of many leading jihadi ideologues are admittedly a major blow to al Qaeda, neither recent public opinion polling in the Muslim world nor the defections "constitutes a knock-out punch." Even with these developments, Hoffman concludes, al Qaeda could soldier on for decades.[93] To the extent there is a serious schism, it should more properly be located in the argument between proponents of the bottom-up approach to jihad championed by Abu Musab al-Suri and the vanguard strategy of old-guard militants like Ayman al-Zawahari. Counterjihadist sheikhs, in any case, tend to stick to utilitarian objections to the jihad, rather than question the underlying grievances that mobilize militants. Moreover, these clerics do not command the organizational structures and disciplined cadres that enabled the Gama'at al Islamiyya leadership, for example, to make its 1997 cease-fire stick.[94] Given these factors, the Iraq War will likely continue to motivate jihadists both in Europe and the Middle East for some time.

THE "UNDERRESOURCED" WAR

Finally, the decision to go to war in Iraq had serious consequences for the fight against al Qaeda in Afghanistan. A handful of experts have long warned that the war in Iraq was hurting the U.S. mission there by distracting from and undermining the central front in the war on terrorism.[95]

Former military and intelligence officials report having to consistently divert resources and high-level attention from Afghanistan to Iraq. By early 2002, equipment and personnel were being transferred from Afghanistan for operations in and around Iraq. U.S. intelligence officials admit that the Iraq War drained most of the CIA officers with field experience in the Muslim world. After noting that there were only so many experienced officers, one former senior intelligence official continued, "Those people all went to Iraq. We were all hurting because of Iraq."[96] The CIA also postponed an $80 million plan to set up a new Afghanistan intelligence service and moved the Islamabad station chief to Washington to work on the Iraq portfolio. As the *Washington Post's* Barton Gellman reported, "By the time war came in Iraq nearly 150 case officers filled the task force. . . . The Baghdad station became the largest since the Vietnam War, with more than 300."[97] According to one senior intelligence official, this was a "huge diversion of resources in terms of intelligence assets. The requirements of the two areas of operation meant that when you consider the area and language expertise [available] in the ops world, there was a huge overlap," and Afghanistan lost. Of the more than one thousand people who worked on the Iraq Survey Group, which conducted the postwar hunt for weapons of mass destruction, scores or more might have been working on counterterrorism instead—including some of the nine hundred people translating documents for the effort. But when terrorist activity near the Pakistani border flared up, requests from Kabul for additional personnel were turned down.[98]

The commando team that was charged with hunting for Osama bin Laden and other al Qaeda leaders reportedly shrank as its equivalent unit in Iraq expanded in the first half of 2003 to more than two hundred troops to cope with a spreading insurgency, pursue the hunt for Saddam Hussein, and help in the search for weapons of mass destruction. When replacements were sent to Afghanistan, they were often reservists whose skills were not as fresh as those of the top "operators" who had departed. "The SOF [Special Operations] guys sent the A team to Iraq," says one individual who was deeply involved in the hunt for bin Laden. "They kept a capability but it wasn't the A team."[99] In at least one instance, officials were told no Predator Unmanned Aerial Vehicles (UAVs) were available for use in Afghanistan because they had all been allocated to Iraq.[100]

Senior military and administration officials only began to speak publicly about these concerns in 2008. In January 2008, the chairman of the Joint Chiefs of Staff Admiral Michael Mullen acknowledged the tendency for the Bush administration to prioritize Iraq over Afghanistan, telling Congress, "In Afghanistan, we do what we can. In Iraq, we do what we must."[101] (Defense Secretary Robert Gates had admitted as much the previous October in a closed-door session with Democratic lawmakers.[102]) Lt. Gen. John Sattler, the director for strategic plans and policy at the Department of Defense, told the Senate Armed Services Committee, "The priority now for resources is going towards Iraq at this time. . . . There are some things we could do and, as Admiral Mullen said, we may like to do, we would like to do, but we can't take those on now until the resource balance shifts."[103] Before leaving his post as senior commander in Afghanistan in June 2008, General Dan McNeil referred to the conflict there as an "underresourced war," saying the mission required "more maneuver units, it needs more flying machines, it needs more intelligence, surveillance and reconnaissance units."[104] The relative lack of resources needed to prosecute the war in Afghanistan has taken on greater salience as the epicenter of the jihad shifted from Iraq to other, more promising, theaters of operation.

REVERSE FLOW

"Should jihadists leaving Iraq perceive themselves and be perceived, to have failed," concluded the 2006 NIE, "fewer fighters will be inspired to carry on the fight."[105] The resurgence underway in the Maghreb and Afghanistan casts doubt on this assertion.

Recent reporting discloses the diversion of fighters from Iraq to Afghanistan and elsewhere, a response to deteriorating conditions for insurgents in the wake of the Anbar Awakening and the U.S. troop "surge" of 2007. U.S. and Iraqi officials began to refer publicly to the new trend for the first time in the spring and summer of 2008. In July 2008, General Petraeus told the Associated Press that senior leaders of al Qaeda were redeploying fighters from the front in Iraq to the Pakistan-Afghanistan border region, implicitly indicating that Iraq was no longer their highest priority. Referring to "unsubstantiated rumors and reflections," Petraeus said the U.S. military believed the group was redirecting some foreign fighters originally intended for Iraq to the Federally Administered Tribal Areas of Pakistan (FATA) instead.[106] While emphasizing that al Qaeda was not going to abandon Iraq, Petraeus noted that the evidence suggested the group was reassessing its chances of success in Iraq. "They're not going to write [Iraq] off. None of that," Petraeus said. "But what they certainly may do is start to provide some of those resources that would have gone to Iraq to Pakistan, possibly Afghanistan."[107]

The following week the Iraqi ambassador to the United States, Samir Sumaida'ie, confirmed the trend, telling the *New York Times* that his government had heard reports that many of the foreign fighters in Iraq had left, either returning to their homeland or "going to fight in Afghanistan." According to Sumaida'ie, al Qaeda has found it "increasingly difficult to operate in Iraq" since 2006 and 2007. Foreign fighters in Iraq, he said, were coming around to the conclusion that Afghanistan was seemingly "more suitable" for jihad.[108]

Senior U.S. counterterrorism officials have since staked out a more cautious view, suggesting foreign fighters already in Iraq are generally not leaving for Afghanistan. Rather, al Qaeda is channeling new recruits, who previously would have been directed to Iraq, toward Afghanistan and Pakistan. U.S. military analysts believe this trend explains, in part, the decline in the foreign-fighter flow to Iraq from as many as eighty to one hundred per month in 2004–5 to as few as twenty in 2008.[109] In a further sign that al Qaeda in Iraq may be undergoing a transformation, Iraqi intelligence reported that several top lieutenants, including Abu Ayyub al-Masri—al Qaeda in Iraq's leader since 2006—left Iraq for Afghanistan in early June 2008.[110] Brigadier General Brian Keller, the senior intelligence officer to General Petraeus, concluded that al Qaeda "will never give up entirely on Iraq, but they may in the future see Afghanistan or some other location yet to be determined as a place where their resources may be more effectively employed."[111]

WILL WITHDRAWAL FROM IRAQ AFFECT OUTCOMES?

Intelligence services are split as to whether the radicalism precipitated by the invasion of Iraq will diminish in the coming years as the coalition presence in Iraq recedes. Some analysts fear that the Iraq War has set in motion a self-sustaining momentum. In this scenario, what the United States or the UK does or does not do with respect to Iraq becomes irrelevant to the future of radicalism among Muslims in Europe.[112]

Indeed, it is Pakistan, rather than Iraq, that poses the greatest danger of bleed out. Bruce Hoffman and Seth Jones stress that "virtually every major al-Qaeda attack or plot of the past four years has emanated from the [South Asia] region."[113] The lawless Afghanistan-Pakistan border is home to more than fourteen different terrorist groups. In several instances, conspirators attended training camps in Pakistan. The London Tube bombers Mohammed Siddique Khan and Shahzad Tanweer both attended an al Qaeda facility in Malakand; Zawahiri later claimed credit for the London attack in an audiotape produced by al Sahab, al Qaeda's communications department. Senior al Qaeda commanders—including Abu Faraj al-Libi, Abu Hamza Rabia, and Abu Ubaidah al-Masri—have been linked to the failed August 2006 Heathrow transatlantic plot.[114] Al Qaeda has been an effective force multiplier by aligning with many of these groups.

At this juncture, it is fair to conclude that the Pakistan/Afghanistan region is likely to eclipse Iraq as a direct radiator of global terrorism. The enduring significance of the Iraq War, in this respect, will be the way in which it transformed the South Asian jihad into a much more lethal phenomenon.

CULT OF THE INSURGENT

In 1968, an Israeli raid on a PLO encampment at Karameh in Jordan led to a minor, but bloody skirmish. No strategic advantage accrued to either side through this engagement. Although the IDF formation took casualties and lost a handful of tanks and other vehicles, Jordanian and Palestinian casualties were far higher. Yet, neither the military insignificance of the encounter nor the disproportionate beating taken by the Arab side seemed to matter once the PLO propagandists succeeded in a media characterization of the event as a colossal, David versus Goliath victory for the *fedayeen*. Returning to this episode, Bruce Hoffman has argued that a "cult of the insurgent" has arisen as a result of the "aura of success" surrounding the Iraqi insurgency and Hizballah's victory against Israel in the 2006 war.[115] The cult of the insurgent creates an environment "where guile and a flair for publicity count more than firepower," argues Hoffman. This development could be the most critical factor in inspiring, motivating, and animating the next generation of terrorists worldwide.

CONCLUSION

A definitive assessment of the effects of the Iraq War on global terrorism, even as most analysts expect a large U.S. military force to remain in Iraq until 2010, or even beyond, is impossible. Certain conclusions, however, can be ventured. First, the intensive nature of U.S. combat operations in Iraq deprived the Afghan theater of critical military and intelligence assets when they would have been most useful. Insurgencies left unsuppressed when they first form become extremely difficult to defeat once they have matured. Second, Iraq served as a training ground and test bed for weapons and tactics that have revitalized insurgencies in Afghanistan, Pakistan, and the Maghreb. (Yemen might be next.) Third, global perceptions of U.S. operations in Iraq have fueled anti-American and anti-Western sentiment that intelligence and security services believe has radicalized Muslim populations. There is no turnstile at the doorway to the jihad, however, so the precise effect of this on recruitment can only be guessed. It is indisputable, though, that the Iraq War has inspired violent attacks outside of Iraq, both in Europe and the Middle East. Lastly, the war in Iraq reaffirmed bin Laden's narrative, just when the horror of 9/11 had begun to elicit sympathy for the United States and the defeat of the Taliban threw al Qaeda into profound disarray. It is indisputable that many Muslims have recoiled from the excesses of al Qaeda in Iraq. Their disgust with *takfiri* violence against Muslims, however, should not be confused with approbation for the invasion and occupation of Iraq, which many still see as a gross injustice.

3 THE IRAQ WAR AND THE FAILURE OF U.S. COUNTERPROLIFERATION STRATEGY

Joseph Cirincione

The central rationale for war with Iraq was the threat posed by Saddam Hussein's alleged stockpiles of chemical, biological, and nuclear weapons. Bush administration officials argued that the threat that Hussein would use these weapons or give them to al Qaeda was so great that war was the only reasonable response. The plan was not only to eliminate the immediate danger but also to demonstrate the utility of a new strategy—the Bush Doctrine—for the direct use of U.S. military action to prevent the spread of these weapons and to respond, should prevention fail. Iraq was only one part of an "axis of evil." Other states would either learn the lesson of the war and abandon similar efforts, or they would suffer the consequences.

The new strategy was a failure. The war promoted as quick, easy, cheap, and essential proved long, difficult, expensive, and unnecessary. Saddam Hussein did not have any chemical, biological, or nuclear weapons, or programs or plans to restart such programs. Nor did Iraq have any operational ties to those who attacked the United States on 9/11.

Globally, the strategy backfired: almost every proliferation problem grew worse after the war. The other members of the axis of evil were more dangerous to the United States in 2008 than in 2001. Both Iran and North Korea accelerated their nuclear programs, each making more progress in the five years after the war than they had in the ten years before. The risk of nuclear terrorism grew as the terrorist threat increased, and programs that would eliminate the ability of terrorists to obtain nuclear weapons or materials languished from lack of attention and funding. Al Qaeda fully reconstituted itself in secure havens in Pakistan, an unstable, nuclear-armed nation. Osama bin Laden was closer to getting a nuclear weapon in 2008 than he was in 2001. Many nations, observing these trends, began to contemplate their own nuclear programs.

Nevertheless, these dangerous trends can be reversed. There is nothing inevitable about the spread of nuclear weapons. A new strategy must, however, be grounded in an understanding of the failures of the Iraq War to provide a new counterproliferation model and an appreciation for the strengths and weaknesses of previous approaches.

BEFORE THE WAR

From the dawn of the nuclear age in 1945 until the start of the Iraq War, efforts by the United States and most other nations to prevent the use and spread of nuclear, biological, and chemical weapons rested on a combination of international agreements, alliance systems, and security commitments. Treaties prohibiting or limiting these weapons were coupled with export controls to limit key technologies, positive security assurances to defend nations that did not acquire these weapons, and threats to retaliate against those that would dare use them. In the jargon of international relations theorists, this means that for most of the past six decades policies and programs have been based on a "liberal internationalist" view of the world, coupled with a realist understanding of national interests and the importance of military force. President Woodrow Wilson is perhaps the first modern example, but, with the exception of Herbert Hoover and George W. Bush, presidents since, including Franklin Roosevelt, Dwight Eisenhower, Richard Nixon, Ronald Reagan, and Bill Clinton, have favored a more integrated liberal international system, whatever their domestic agendas. From Wilson's idea of a League of Nations, FDR's United Nations and Bretton Woods, Truman's NATO alliance, to Clinton's idea of free trade and economic liberalization, U.S. presidents since World War Two have used elements of liberal internationalism in their foreign policy to project U.S. power.

Within the United States, this approach enjoyed broad bipartisan support. After amassing arsenals far in excess of any rational security need, American presidents focused on eliminating the enormous stockpiles through treaty constraints. The weapons themselves began to be seen as the problem: so long as they existed, they would be used. "The weapons of war must be abolished before they abolish us," President John F. Kennedy declared before the United Nations in September 1961. "The mere existence of modern weapons . . . is a source of horror and discord and distrust."[1] This belief led Kennedy to start, Lyndon Johnson to complete, and Richard Nixon to sign the nuclear Nonproliferation Treaty (NPT). The treaty bound the nuclear powers to eventual disarmament while nonnuclear signatories agreed to forgo the development of nuclear weapons.

Bipartisan efforts to eliminate chemical and biological weapons progressed as well, with a continuity of effort spanning several administrations. President Richard Nixon unilaterally ended the U.S. biological weapons program in 1969 and negotiated the Biological Weapons Convention that bans these deadly arsenals. President George H. W. Bush negotiated and in January 1993 signed the Chemical Weapons Convention that similarly bans chemical weapons, and President Bill Clinton won its ratification in 1997. In all, 162 nations have ratified the Biological Weapons Convention and 184 have ratified the Chemical Weapons Convention. While some nations, notably Israel, Egypt, and Syria, remain outside the treaty regime, and a few, including Iran or China, are suspected of pursuing some research on these weapons, neither biological nor chemical weapons are considered a major state threat. Nations that once insisted on their value now regard them as taboo. Now, rather than a source of pride, they are considered evil weapons that no civilized nation would use. No nation admits to their possession.

The bipartisan approach of seven presidents worked. Though proliferation was not prevented altogether, it was greatly slowed. Rather than the twenty or twenty-five nations that Kennedy in 1960 feared could soon obtain nuclear weapons, by 2003 there were only eight nuclear-armed states. In order of when they acquired a nuclear bomb, they were: the United States, Russia, the United Kingdom, France, China, Israel (undeclared), India, and Pakistan.

The number of nuclear weapons in the world had also been cut by more than half, from a cold-war high of sixty-five thousand in 1986 to about twenty-five thousand in 2008. The reductions resulted from bilateral agreements between the United States and the Soviet Union negotiated under Presidents Ronald Reagan, George H. W. Bush, and George W. Bush and were seen by other nations as the partial fulfillment of these two nations' commitment under Article VI of the NPT "to pursue negotiations in good faith on effective measures relating to cessation of the nuclear arms race at an early date and to nuclear disarmament." The agreements had the dual effect of reducing the risk of nuclear war and encouraging other states to honor their commitments to refrain from developing nuclear weapons. The treaty regime was working. President Reagan began to envision "arms control measures to eliminate the [nuclear] weapons themselves."

The facts gave reason for this ambitious hope. Far fewer countries possessed nuclear weapons or weapons programs at the beginning of the twenty-first century than at any point during in the 1960s, 1970s, or 1980s. In the 1960s, twenty-three countries had weapons, were conducting weapons-related research, or were discussing the pursuit of weapons, including Australia, Canada, China, Egypt, India, Japan, Norway, Sweden, Switzerland, and West Germany. In 2003, the only countries of serious proliferation concern apart from the known nuclear-armed states were North Korea, which had suspended its program under the 1994 Agreed Framework, Iraq (suspected of still holding chemical or biological weapons), Iran, and Libya (the last two are suspected of importing nuclear weapon technology).

The cornerstone of the global nonproliferation regime, the NPT, is widely considered one of the most successful security pacts in history, with every nation of the world a member except for Israel, India, Pakistan, and North Korea. Most of the 183 nation-states that do not have nuclear weapons believe what the treaty says: we should eliminate nuclear weapons. Most of the American public agrees. An Associated Press poll of March 2005 showed that 66 percent of Americans believe that no country should be allowed to have nuclear weapons, including the United States.[2]

THE ORIGINS OF REGIME CHANGE

Despite the overall success of more than fifty years of U.S. nonproliferation strategy, its failures were heavily criticized in the years preceding the 2000 election. For these critics, the fact that 183 countries lacked nuclear weapons was outweighed by the efforts of a few nations to acquire them.

For example, John Bolton, then at the American Enterprise Institute, said in 1999 that the Clinton administration suffered from a "fascination with arms control agreements as a substitute for real nonproliferation of weapons of mass destruction."[3] Gary Schmitt, an analyst at the neoconservative Project for the New American Century, said more directly, "Conservatives don't like arms control agreements for the simple reason that they rarely, if ever, increase U.S. security. . . . The real issue here, and the underlying question, is whether the decades-long effort to control the proliferation of weapons of mass destruction and the means to deliver them through arms control treaties has in fact worked." He contended that it was no longer "plausible to argue that our overall security was best served by a web of parchment accords, and not our own military capabilities."[4]

Such voices argued for new, more aggressive policies directed against a few selected states. This radical new approach maintained that the foundations that presidents from both parties had built for more than half a century were hopelessly weak and had to be torn up and replaced with a brand-new structure.

This was not "new thinking" as much as a continuation of the philosophy generally known as neoconservatism that developed during the 1960s and 1970s. Neoconservatives had long toiled, often with great success, to force the government to adopt a more militant approach to America's adversaries. Through campaigns, institutes, and organizations such the Committee on the Present Danger, they had popularized an exaggerated view of the Soviet military threat, promoted increased defense budgets, and opposed arms control agreements. They now brought their cold-war ideology to bear on Iraq.

In 1998, a group of experts wrote to President Bill Clinton, urging him to take direct measures to remove Iraqi dictator Saddam Hussein from power. Their main argument was that the threat of nuclear, biological, and chemical weapons posed an unacceptable risk to the United States that could only be addressed through military action. The authors of this letter included Paul Wolfowitz, Donald Rumsfeld, John Bolton, Richard Perle, Elliott Abrams, and William Kristol. They described what they saw as the failure of traditional international approaches:

> The policy of "containment" of Saddam Hussein has been steadily eroding over the past several months. . . . We can no longer depend on our partners in the Gulf War coalition to continue to uphold the sanctions or to punish Saddam when he blocks or evades UN inspections. Our ability to ensure that Saddam Hussein is not producing weapons of mass destruction, therefore, has substantially diminished. Even if full inspections were eventually to resume, which now seems highly unlikely, experience has shown that it is difficult if not impossible to monitor Iraq's chemical and biological weapons production. The lengthy period during which the inspectors will have been unable to enter many Iraqi facilities has made it even less likely that they will be able to uncover all of Saddam's secrets. As a result, in the not-too-distant future we will be unable to determine with any reasonable level of confidence whether Iraq does or does not possess such weapons.[5]

Most of these thinkers were neoconservatives who combined different elements of realism, liberal internationalism, and idealism to develop a new direction for U.S. foreign policy. They believe in the "democratic peace" espoused by liberal internationalists, but substantially mistrust international institutions. In pursuit of freedom and security, they favor a more assertive use of military force than traditional realists. Rather than simply manage the world, they favor using the U.S. military as a tool to transform it. Thus, the experts argued in their letter to Clinton: "The only acceptable strategy is one that eliminates the possibility that Iraq will be able to use or threaten to use weapons of mass destruction. In the near term, this means a willingness to undertake military action as diplomacy is clearly failing. In the long term, it means removing Saddam Hussein and his regime from power."[6]

Although many of these thinkers assumed high-level government positions after the elections of 2000,[7] it was not until the attacks of September 11, 2001, that they were able to profoundly change the course of American antiproliferation policy. In the wake of the attacks, the Bush administration reassessed proliferation threats to U.S. security. In early 2002, then assistant secretary of state for nonproliferation John Wolf noted, "The President has said that halting proliferation is not one of many objectives of U.S. foreign policy; it is a central framing element."[8]

ELIMINATING REGIMES, NOT ARSENALS

Many officials in the Bush administration believed that the entire process of negotiating and implementing nonproliferation treaties was both unnecessary and harmful to U.S. national security interests. They argued that some of the treaties, such as the Comprehensive Test Ban Treaty, the Anti-Ballistic Missile Treaty, and the Landmine Treaty, restrict necessary armaments, thus weakening the principal nation that safeguards global peace and security. Other treaties, such as the Chemical Weapons Convention and the Biological Weapons Convention, promote a false sense of security as some nations sign, and then cheat, on the agreements. Multilateral meetings were often seen as opportunities for the global Lilliputians to gang up on the American Gulliver.

The perceived failures of the treaty regime led the Bush team to demand more flexibility in its options to combat proliferation. Although the administration remained committed to export controls and strengthening some international agencies, the core strategy relied on direct military means to eliminate threats they believed were obvious. This view held that preventive war, even waged unilaterally, must be considered a valid and necessary response to certain threats. The strategy became known as the Bush Doctrine, with three interrelated parts.

First, the administration pivoted from terrorist groups to nation-states, linking the attackers of 9/11 directly to regimes officials believed hostile to U.S. interests. President Bush reiterated the point in numerous statements, dramatically declaring, "America will not permit terrorists and dangerous regimes to threaten us with the world's most deadly weapons."[9] Deputy Secretary of Defense Paul Wolfowitz proclaimed, "It's going to be a broad campaign; it's not going to end quickly. One of those objectives is the al Qaeda network. The second objective is state support for terrorism, and a third is this larger connection between states that support terrorism and states that develop weapons of mass destruction."[10]

Second, the United States would favor direct military action over diplomacy and containment. In a speech delivered at West Point in June 2002 President Bush explained why:

> New threats also require new thinking. Deterrence—the promise of massive retaliation against nations—means nothing against shadowy terrorist networks with no nation or citizens to defend. Containment is not possible when unbalanced dictators with weapons of mass destruction can deliver those weapons on missiles or secretly provide them to terrorist allies.
>
> We cannot defend America and our friends by hoping for the best. We cannot put our faith in the word of tyrants, who solemnly sign non-proliferation treaties, and then systemically break them.[11]

Third, the United States would take these military actions preemptively to prevent serious threats from developing. Bush argued, "Some have said we must not act until the threat is imminent. Since when have terrorists and tyrants announced their intentions, politely putting us on notice before they strike? If this threat is permitted to fully and suddenly emerge, all actions, all words, and all recriminations would come too late."[12]

Together, these three postulates strongly supported the case for war with Iraq.

There was no secret to this strategy. The new, action-oriented approach was detailed in two key documents—*The National Security Strategy of the United States of America* (September 2002) and *National Strategy to Combat Weapons of Mass Destruction* (December 2002)—and reinforced in several speeches, particularly Bush's West Point address.[13] The latter document, detailing the new plan, called it "a fundamental change from the past."[14] The *National Security Strategy* emphasized the direct application of U.S. military, economic, and political power: "The United States possesses unprecedented—and unequaled—strength and influence in the world. . . . The great strength of this nation must be used to promote a balance of power that favors freedom." As Thomas Donnelly, an analyst at the conservative American Enterprise Institute, explained, "The task for the United States is nothing less than the preservation and expansion of today's Pax Americana, the extension of the 'unipolar moment' for as long as possible."[15]

Proliferation was seen as part of this larger, global struggle, not as an end in itself. The primary challenge to continued American supremacy, they argued, was the proliferation of nuclear, biological, and chemical weapons to states hostile to the United States.

In this view, there was bad proliferation and good proliferation. Whereas previous presidents treated the spread of these weapons as the core problem and sought their elimination through treaties, the Bush administration saw the threat as existing in a small number of states, particularly the nexus of these states, weapons, and terrorists. Meanwhile, nuclear weapons in the hands of responsible states, that is, the United States and its allies, were seen as necessary instruments for preserving peace and security. Whereas previous presidents would cite, as President Bill Clinton did, the grave threat to the nation "from the *proliferation of nuclear, biological and chemical weapons*,"[16] President Bush said in his 2003 State of the Union address, "The gravest danger facing America and the world is *outlaw regimes that seek and possess nuclear, chemical, and biological weapons*" (emphasis added). President Bush, in effect, changed the focus from "what" to "who." The new strategy sought the elimination of regimes rather than weapons, believing the United States could determine which countries were responsible enough to have nuclear weapons and which were not. American power, not multilateral treaties, would enforce this judgment.

Strategy documents and speeches often obscured the true strategy, assuaging some critics who could note the balance of force and diplomacy, for example, in the official National Security Strategy. Administration officials would detail their "three pillars" of antiproliferation policy: traditional nonproliferation agreements, counterproliferation (including antimissile systems and military action), and consequence management (responding to the use of nuclear, biological, or chemical weapons).[17] Yet most of the effort and funding flowed to the second pillar. In 2001, counterproliferation efforts received approximately $9 billion (mostly for antimissile weapons), compared to $1.5 billion each for nonproliferation and consequence management efforts. By the end of 2005, programs to try to intercept ballistic missiles were funded at $9 to 10 billion annually, and the war in Iraq, launched in an effort to disarm Saddam Hussein, had cost almost $300 billion. Funding for traditional nonproliferation efforts, including all diplomatic activity and cooperative threat-reduction programs, remained at $1.5 billion. By mid-2008, the diplomatic pillar was a toothpick compared to the accumulated $700 billion of the war in Iraq and the nearly $60 billion spent on antimissile systems since 2001.

SELLING THE THREAT

Standing before the joint session of Congress, President Bush outlined the new strategy in the 2002 State of the Union address. He warned, "Some governments will be timid in the face of terror. And make no mistake about it: If they do not act, America will."[18] He would not let existing international institutions or treaties hinder U.S. freedom of action. The new focus of U.S. nonproliferation efforts would be ad hoc coalitions of countries and American military might. Regimes that could not be persuaded would be eliminated, with the idea that other recalcitrant governments would take notice and fall in line with U.S. demands.

President Bush then spelled out the first targets of the new U.S. strategy clearly. North Korea, Iran, and Iraq were "an axis of evil, arming to threaten the peace of the world. By seeking weapons of mass destruction, these regimes pose a grave and growing danger. They could provide these arms to terrorists, giving them the means to match their hatred. They could attack our allies or attempt to blackmail the United States. In any of these cases, the price of indifference would be catastrophic."[19]

For the Bush administration, the danger from Iraq was too great to risk further delay. Days before the war began, Vice President Richard Cheney warned that Iraqi President Saddam Hussein "has, in fact, reconstituted nuclear weapons."[20] U.S. officials warned that Iraq had imported key elements for new nuclear weapons, improved its facilities to produce thousands of chemical weapons, and expanded its biological weapons program to pre-1991 levels. President Bush himself claimed that Iraq had hundreds of tons of chemical weapons and thousands of liters of biological weapons that could kill millions and a hidden fleet of missiles and unmanned aerial vehicles to deliver them. Worse, Saddam's "long-standing, direct, and continuing ties to terrorist networks," the president said, meant that "trusting in the sanity and restraint of Saddam Hussein is not a strategy, and it is not an option."[21]

This was the principal rational offered at the onset of the war. As President George Bush told the world on March 17, 2003, "Intelligence gathered by this and other governments leaves no doubt that the Iraq regime continues to possess and conceal some of the most lethal weapons ever devised. . . . The danger is clear: Using chemical, biological or, one day, nuclear weapons obtained with the help of Iraq, the terrorists could fulfill their stated ambitions and kill thousands or hundreds of thousands of innocent people."[22]

There were, in fact, no credible connections between Baghdad and al Qaeda, but in the president's mind the two were one in the same; thus, he promised the nation that "the terrorist threat to America and the world will be diminished the moment that Saddam Hussein is disarmed."[23]

THREAT INFLATION

As the result of several official studies, including the work of the Iraq Survey Group and the Senate Intelligence Committee's 2004 and 2008 reports on prewar intelligence, we now know with a high degree of certainty that many of the claims made by the administration before the war were false.

Specifically:

a. Iraq did not have militarily significant quantities of chemical or biological weapons.
b. Iraq was not producing chemical, biological, or nuclear weapons.
c. Iraq did not have ongoing chemical, biological, or nuclear weapons programs.
d. Iraq did not pose an immediate threat to the United States, Europe, or the region.
e. None of the key findings in the 2002 U.S. National Intelligence Estimate (NIE) on Iraq were accurate, with the exception of the finding that Saddam was highly unlikely to transfer any weapons to terrorist groups.
f. U.S. and UK officials went far beyond the intelligence findings in their public statements.

The Senate Intelligence Committee report of July 2004 is still the most authoritative account of what is one of the worst intelligence failures in U.S. history. But because it and other official reviews (until the same committee's report of June 2008) limited their examination only to the process inside the intelligence community and did not consider the role of the White House or of the Department of Defense, the assessment remains incomplete.

We now know that intelligence assessment done prior to the Bush presidency showed that Saddam was growing weaker, not stronger. The April 1999 NIE, from before this inflationary period, provides a more sober and more accurate estimate than that asserted by Bush administration officials before the war—and to this day—that Saddam was "a growing threat" and that "we would have to confront him sooner or later." On the contrary, the intelligence community concluded:

> Iraq's military capabilities have deteriorated significantly as a result of UN sanctions and damage inflicted by Coalition and US military operations. Its military forces are even less well prepared for major combat operations than we judged in the National intelligence Estimate . . . of July 1994 and in an Update Memorandum published in January 1995. . . . They remain more capable than those of regional Arab states, but could not gain a decisive military advantage over Iran's forces. . . . Iraq's military capabilities will continue a slow and steady decline as long as both economic sanctions and the arms embargo are maintained. Smuggling and other efforts to circumvent the embargo will be inadequate to halt the trend. . . . Saddam probably realizes that a reinvasion of Kuwait is now more likely to provoke a Coalition military response that could destroy his regime.[24]

In January 2003, when officials were ratcheting up their warnings of a growing threat and immediate danger, the intelligence community issued its final appraisal: "Saddam probably will not initiate hostilities for fear of providing Washington with justification to invade Iraq. Nevertheless, he might deal the first blow, especially if he perceives that an attack intended to end his regime is imminent."[25]

WE WERE NOT ALL WRONG

Supporters of the U.S. and UK administrations assert that everyone—including the United Nations—got it wrong. This claim is also repeated by many experts and journalists who, when using it, often mean that they, too, got it wrong. It is offered as an explanation and an excuse, as if their conclusion that war was necessary was the only reasonable judgment possible at the time given the available evidence.

But not everyone got it wrong. The United Nations inspectors in particular turned out to be more accurate and more precise than the intelligence agencies of the United States, the United Kingdom, and Israel, all of which asserted that

Saddam had large stockpiles of ready to use weapons. The UN inspectors, by contrast, never said that Iraq *had* nuclear, biological, or chemical weapons—only that Iraq *might have* some components or materials for such weapons. As Hans Blix told the Security Council one month before the war, "One must not jump to the conclusion that they exist."[26]

The administration and many experts ignored the new intelligence coming in from the UN inspectors during the three months they were permitted to operate. The official report on the UK process (conducted by Lord Butler of Brockwell and released July 14, 2004) notes the failure of the British government to "re-evaluate" its intelligence estimates in light of the inspectors' findings in 2003.[27] The same could be said of the U.S. intelligence agencies. In the months before the war, the inspectors reported back that there was no evidence of the large-scale, ongoing production programs the United States and UK claimed. The inspectors have said they would have needed only a few more months to give definitive answers.[28] Dr. Hans Blix, former executive director of the United Nations Monitoring, Verification and Inspection Commission (UNMOVIC), said after the war:

> Saddam Hussein did not have any weapons of mass destruction in March 2003, and the evidence invoked of the existence of such weapons had begun to fall apart even before the invasion started. Saddam Hussein was not a valid object for counterproliferation. He was not an imminent or even a remote threat to the United States or to Iraq's neighbors. The ousting of his bloody regime could have been urged on the basis that it was a horror to the Iraqi people, but this was not argued at the time. A continuation of the inspections, as desired by the majority of members of the Security Council, would have allowed visits to all sites suspected by national intelligence agencies and would have yielded no weapons of mass destruction because there were none.

Dr. Mohammed ElBaradei, director general of the International Atomic Energy Agency (IAEA), concluded in 2004:

> The Iraq experience demonstrated that inspections—while requiring time and patience—can be effective even when the country under inspection was providing less than active cooperation. All evidence to date indicates that Iraq's nuclear weapons program had been effectively dismantled in the 1990s through IAEA inspection—as we were nearly ready to conclude before the war. Inspections in Iran over the past year have also been key in uncovering a

nuclear program that had remained hidden since the 1980s—and in enabling the international community to have a far more comprehensive picture of Iran's nuclear program than at any time before.

Many experts, including several at the Carnegie Endowment for International Peace, urged the president to continue inspections and containment. We now know that these measures were working; that Saddam was growing weaker, not stronger; that his army was deteriorating and his rule shaky. As David Kay later testified before Congress, Saddam's regime "was in a death spiral."[29]

One of the central lessons drawn from the Iraq War must be the value of inspections. United Nations inspection agencies worked well when supported by a unified Security Council. We now know that from 1991–98 the United Nations Special Commission (UNSCOM) and the IAEA were ultimately able to discover and eliminate most of Iraq's unconventional weapons and production facilities (including nuclear) and to destroy or monitor the destruction of most of its chemical and biological weapons agents. This was accomplished despite unrelenting opposition and obstruction by the Iraqi regime. UNMOVIC, working in conjunction with the IAEA from October 2002 to March 2003, operated, with only a few exceptions, freely and without significant obstruction. The team visited more than six hundred sites, discovered and destroyed several items that were prohibited by UN resolutions, and was close to verifying the absence of any significant programs or weapons.[30]

U.S. officials at the time mocked the inspectors. Vice President Dick Cheney said before they even entered Iraq that "a return of inspectors would provide no assurance whatsoever of his compliance with UN resolutions,"[31] while Secretary of Defense Rumsfeld said the return of inspectors to Iraq would be a "sham."[32]

Independent monitoring and verification organizations like London-based VERTIC confirmed that the UN-supported inspection process in Iraq worked.

> The first strategic lesson to be drawn from the cases of UNSCOM and UNMOVIC, and the experiences of their partner in the nuclear field, the IAEA, is that international verification can work effectively even under the most disadvantageous of conditions. Despite Iraq's noncooperation and deliberate attempts at sabotage all three bodies broadly succeeded in their verification mission. All demonstrated that an international inspection regime can perform creditably: they were able to prepare themselves well, deploy quickly,

> use technology skillfully, organize efficiently, maintain their impartiality and produce sober, balanced reports of a high technical standard. They were also able to follow intelligence leads successfully and reach quick and decisive, albeit suitably caveated, conclusions.[33]

Further, not all national intelligence agencies "got it wrong." Many, including the French, German, and Russian governments, suspected that Saddam could have some chemical or biological weapons and were concerned that some nuclear weapon activity might be underway. But they did not believe these weapons, if they existed, posed an immediate danger. The French certainly got it right. And they were not alone. The majority of nations on the UN Security Council appeared to agree with French Foreign Minister Dominique de Villepin, who elaborated the French position before the United Nations Security Council in March 2003:

> It is clear to all that in Iraq, we are resolutely moving towards the complete elimination of weapons of mass destruction programmes. The method that we have chosen works. The information supplied by Baghdad had been verified by the inspectors and is leading to the elimination of banned ballistic equipment.
>
> We must proceed the same way with all the other programmes—with information, verification, destruction. . . . With regard to nuclear weapons, Mr. ElBaradei's statements confirm that we are approaching the time when the International Atomic Energy Agency (IAEA) will be able to certify the dismantlement of the Iraq programme.
>
> What conclusions can we draw? That Iraq, according to the very terms used by the inspectors, represents less of a danger to the world than it did in 1991, and that we can achieve the objective of effectively disarming that country. . . . There is nothing today to indicate a link between the Iraqi regime and al Qaeda. Will the world be a safer place after a military intervention in Iraq? Let me state my country's conviction: it will not.

Whatever one may think about French motives, it is now clear that, on the merits, France was largely right about the threat of Iraq's weapons and how to address it prior to the war.[34]

Politics and pressure pushed CIA leaders to take concerns and fragments of information and turn them into definitive findings and a casus belli. A Senate Intelligence Committee report of June 2008 confirms this finding. As the *New*

York Times editorialized, "The report shows that there was no intelligence to support the two most frightening claims Mr. Bush and his vice president used to sell the war: that Iraq was actively developing nuclear weapons and had long-standing ties to terrorist groups. It seems clear that the president and his team knew that that was not true, or should have known it—if they had not ignored dissenting views and telegraphed what answers they were looking for."[35]

Senator Jay Rockefeller (D-WV), chairman of the committee, summed up the majority view:

> In making the case for war, the Administration repeatedly presented intelligence as fact when in reality it was unsubstantiated, contradicted, or even non-existent. As a result, the American people were led to believe that the threat from Iraq was much greater than actually existed. . . . It is my belief that the Bush Administration was fixated on Iraq, and used the 9/11 attacks by al Qa'ida as justification for overthrowing Saddam Hussein. To accomplish this, top Administration officials made repeated statements that falsely linked Iraq and al Qa'ida as a single threat and insinuated that Iraq played a role in 9/11. Sadly, the Bush Administration led the nation into war under false pretenses.[36]

THE BUSH DOCTRINE GAINS STEAM

One problem with evaluating the effectiveness of the Iraq War as a counterproliferation model is that the war was never primarily about weapons. The war was the start of a plan for serial regime change in the Middle East. "There is tremendous potential to transform the region," said Richard Perle at the time. "If a tyrant like Saddam (Hussein) can be brought down, others are going to begin to think and act to bring down the tyrants that are afflicting them."[37] Joshua Muravchik, a prominent neoconservative thinker with the American Enterprise Institute, argued that "democratic regimes in Tehran and Baghdad would unleash a tsunami across the Islamic world."[38] Mark Danner of the *New Yorker* wrote that the neoconservatives in the Bush administration "take a somewhat ideological and almost evangelical view of the world." They believe that American power "should be used to change the world, not simply to manage it."[39] When then undersecretary of state John Bolton was asked what lesson Iran and North Korea should draw from the Iraq War, he replied, "Take a number."[40]

Thus, weapons elimination was a subset of regime elimination, but became the leading public justification and the principal justification for rejecting negotiations. Vice President Cheney crystallized the Bush administration's approach, reportedly commenting, "I have been charged by the president with making sure that none of the tyrannies in the world are negotiated with," and concluding, "We don't negotiate with evil; we defeat it."[41]

In short, the ideals and attitudes that led to the invasion of Iraq would be applied to the other members of the "axis of evil" Iran and North Korea. The attempt of neoconservatives to mirror the Iraq strategy as closely as possible with Iran and North Korea, however, would prove to be disastrous to nuclear nonproliferation with both countries.

THE BUSH DOCTRINE AND IRAN

As American troops secured Baghdad, a remarkable proposal came from another member of the "axis of evil," Iran. As one observer summarized it, "The proposal . . . offered a dramatic set of specific policy concessions Tehran was prepared to make in the framework of an overall bargain on its nuclear program, its policy toward Israel, and al Qaeda. It also proposed the establishment of three parallel working groups to negotiate 'road maps' on the three main areas of contention—weapons of mass destruction, terrorism and regional security, and economic cooperation."[42]

Neoconservatives within the administration scuttled the opportunity, however. Regime change, not diplomacy, was the best way to handle Iran, they argued. In reaction, Iran accelerated its then covert nuclear program. Dr. Trita Parsi, who conducted numerous interviews with top Iranian leaders in 2004, believes that "if the United States had engaged Iran in 2003 . . . Iran would not be enriching now."[43]

Then, on October 21, 2003, after public disclosure of its then-secret program, Iran announced that it would suspend its efforts to enrich uranium and allow expanded inspections by the IAEA, letting inspectors perform spot checks of any suspicious sites. Iran's decision came after two days of intense negotiations between top Iranian officials and the British, French, and German foreign ministers. The European diplomats reportedly offered technological assistance and an assured supply of nuclear fuel in exchange for full Iranian cooperation. As a European Union official said at the time, "It's a real success for our engagement policy instead of the American confrontation policy."[44]

After European Union ministers won a freeze in Iran's nuclear uranium enrichment activities, U.S. officials had an opportunity to exploit this breakthrough and negotiate an end to a potentially hostile program. The right combination of force and diplomacy might have worked to allow Tehran to build nuclear reactors, but not the nuclear fuel-fabrication processes that keep Iran's nuclear bomb-making capabilities alive. Administration hard-liners prevailed, however, and the United States pursued a more confrontational approach.

Iran froze its enrichment program for almost two years. Negotiations with the EU offered Iran substantial economic and trade incentives, but without direct U.S. participation, Iran could not get the security assurances its leaders believed were a necessary part of any final deal. As the stalemate with Iran continued, a push for a renewal of the Bush Doctrine began in neoconservative circles. In early 2006, *Weekly Standard* editor William Kristol argued that Iran's "nuclear program could well be getting close to the point of no return."[45] *Washington Post* columnist Charles Krauthammer wrote, "Instead of being years away from the point of no return for an Iranian bomb . . . Iran is probably just months away."[46]

In reality, Iran was still five years away from the ability to enrich uranium for fuel or bombs. Even that estimate, shared by the Defense Intelligence Agency and experts at International Institute for Strategic Studies, the Institute for Science and International Security, and the University of Maryland, assumes that Iran would go full-speed ahead and would not encounter any of the technical problems that typically plague such programs.[47]

In December 2007, a new NIE was released. The NIE presented a far more nuanced picture of both the nuclear program and the Iranian government's intentions than previous estimates, directly contradicting the one-dimensional portrait painted by some neoconservatives, including many in the White House. The new report allowed U.S. policymakers and the American public to engage in realistic debate over Iran's uranium-enrichment program, which without a doubt poses a significant challenge to U.S. interests in the Middle East and beyond.

The Iran NIE strongly countered the caricature of mad mullahs bent on hastening Armageddon. "Tehran's decisions," according to the NIE, "are guided by a cost-benefit approach rather than a rush to a weapon irrespective of the political, economic, and military costs."[48] This, perhaps, is the most significant finding and squares with what independent experts have been saying for years.

The NIE finding pointed the way for a new U.S. policy toward Iran. Specifically, "some combination of threats of intensified international scrutiny and pressures, along with opportunities for Iran to achieve its security, prestige, and goals for regional influence in other ways, might—if perceived by Iran's leaders as credible—prompt Tehran to extend the current halt to its nuclear weapons program."[49] Put differently, if Iran is backed into a corner and then offered a constructive, mutually beneficial way out, it might be possible to get Iran to halt its nuclear program. At least within the intelligence agencies there seemed to be an acknowledgment of the failure of the Iraq War and the need for an alternative approach.

FAILURE WITH NORTH KOREA

The Bush Doctrine also failed with respect to North Korea. In October 2002, a U.S. official confronted North Korea with evidence of a covert uranium-enrichment program, a clear violation of the 1994 Agreed Framework. After angry denunciations, North Korea relented, admitting to violating the Agreed Framework and offering to negotiate a new agreement to give up its program. U.S. officials wanted unilateral concessions before talks could begin (similar to the tactic being used against Iran). North Korea offered to put everything on the negotiating table, not just its enrichment program, but Bush administration officials remained unbending in their demands. The talks collapsed.

While the United States had effectively blocked diplomacy with both Iran and North Korea, it was unable to mount any credible alternative policy. U.S. forces were bogged down in an increasingly violent insurgency, sapping the main tool of the Bush Doctrine, U.S. military might. After confronting North Korea in 2002, the administration's policy floundered. The United States stood aside as North Korea abandoned the Agreed Framework and kicked out international inspectors.

On September 19, 2005, the United States, China, Russia, South Korea, Japan, and North Korea negotiated a pact to end North Korea's nuclear program. The chief U.S. negotiator at the talks, Assistant Secretary of State Christopher Hill, praised the agreement as a "win-win situation." Indeed, all successful negotiations have to be so. The parties must be able to leave the table declaring victory and returning to their countries and peoples with tangible achievements.

But the Bush administration was still internally divided, with some, led by Vice President Dick Cheney, favoring the counterproliferation policy of the Iraq War, and others, now led by Secretary of State Condoleezza Rice, favoring a more pragmatic policy of forceful diplomacy. The opponents of negotiations moved in the days after the September accord to effectively freeze North Korean assets in the Macau-based bank, Banco Delta Asia. The squeeze move infuriated the North Koreans, who broke off the talks again and proceeded step by step to a nuclear test in October 2006. The lessons of the Iraq War had still not been learned; U.S. officials could not decide whether their main objective was to end the North Korean regime or to end the nuclear program.

REVERSING COURSE

The North Korean nuclear test helped break this policy deadlock, demonstrating to many that the regime-change policy not only had failed in Iraq, but would not succeed with North Korea (or Iran). Pragmatic realists threw their weight behind diplomacy, working with the North's neighbors to force it back to the negotiating table. Secretary of State Rice and Assistant Secretary Hill forged an international united front to isolate North Korea and then followed up with the direct talks with North Korea organized by China. Beijing increased its pressure, too, restricting oil supplies and talking tough with the Kim regime in the days prior to direct talks between Hill and his North Korean counterpart, Vice Foreign Minister Kim Gye-gwan.

Finally, in February 2007, an agreement was reached with North Korea to abandon its nuclear program, verifiably dismantle key installations, and provide the United States with information on all its past proliferation activities. In return, the North Koreans would receive security guarantees from the United States, aid, and the possibility of normalizing relations between the two countries if North Korea complied with the agreement.

The policy that defused this crisis was the opposite of the policy prescription of the original Bush Doctrine. North Korea was not invaded and Kim Jong Il was not deposed. Carrots and sticks were used to press the North Koreans into granting major concessions, allowing unprecedented international access to their nuclear program. The shift was part of an overall swing in the administration toward a centrist pragmatism. The *Washington Post* concluded that "the fist-shaking that characterized much of the first six years of the Bush administration's North Korea policy has been replaced by a dogged insistence on negotiations and by offers of aid and other concessions—contingent on verified moves to get rid of nuclear facilities."[50]

Neoconservatives never quit, however, and attempted to kill the agreement, with John Bolton leading the charge against the "bad deal" of the six-party agreement.[51] The *National Review* editors questioned whether any compromise could be reached with Kim Jong Il, while Elliott Abrams, a deputy national security adviser, sent angry comments to fellow officials in Washington, questioning the deal.[52] However, the arrangement, while obviously not perfect, helped reverse the damage done by years of U.S. disengagement with North Korea.

A closer look at the various elements contributing to this apparent nonproliferation success with North Korea provides a clearer understanding of both the policy reversal and the broader policy trends.

The first element was the situation of North Korea itself. A poor, isolated country that produces little save fear and tyranny, it was in a weak strategic position. The multilateral sanctions and economic incentives clearly played a part in the decision of the North Korean leadership to compromise.

Second was the unanimity of the other five nations in the six-party talks. All five wanted to stop a nuclear-armed North Korea from emerging. Their tactics differed, but they were united in their efforts to stop Pyongyang from trying to perfect the flawed nuclear device it tested in October 2006. That unity extended to the unanimous declaration of the Security Council condemning North Korea and imposing sanctions on the regime after its nuclear test.

The third element contributing to the shift was the more assertive role played by China. The October 9 test surprised and angered China, upsetting its greater strategic plans. China does not want North Korea destabilizing its borders or provoking Japan, and that is just what happened after the test. Japan started a public debate over whether it should possess its own nuclear weapons—the last thing China wants. State Counselor Tang Jiaxuan, China's third-highest-ranking official, quickly visited Pyongyang to deliver a message asserting China's displeasure directly to North Korean leaders. China cannot dictate North Korea's actions, but the pressure brought a halt to North Korean nuclear tests and an agreement to return to negotiations. China also convinced the United States to come to the table, choreographing talks in Beijing that produced the first of several breakthrough bilateral sessions.

Fourth was the power shift in Congress as a result of the November 2006 elections. The Democratic control of Congress flipped the pressures on the Bush administration, with immediate effect. Shortly after the elections, at a November House International Relations Committee hearing still under Republican rule, members led by Rep. Tom Lantos (D-CA) hammered Undersecretary of State Nicholas Burns over the failed administration policy, cajoling him into engaging in direct talks with North Korea.

Fifth was the change in Defense Department leadership. Donald Rumsfeld, an ardent opponent of direct negotiations with North Korea, resigned as defense secretary, and he was replaced by pragmatist Robert Gates, who is more inclined to engage in the direct negotiations previously seen as appeasement. Vice President Dick Cheney alone among the senior ranks remained opposed to dealing with Pyongyang, but his influence waned in the closing years of the administration.

Sixth, the political fortunes of the president of the United States had deteriorated. In the end, it was the president's call: deal or no deal. Formerly, President Bush lined up with Cheney, Rumsfeld, and UN Ambassador Bolton, but with two of these officials gone and badly in need of some success for his beleaguered administration, the president tilted toward pragmatism. North Korea was one of the few possibilities for a foreign policy victory during the remainder of his term.

The deal faltered again when hardliners convince the president not to take North Korea off the list of state sponsors of terrorism after Pyongyang had begun the promised dismantlement of its plutonium-production reactor. North Korea, predictably, began to restart some of the halted programs. By the end of 2008, pragmatists in the administration had reestablished control, the deal was back on, and North Korea was steadily taking apart its facilities for nuclear weapons.

SUCCESS WITH LIBYA

The North Korea agreement shares key similarities with the deal struck between the United States and Libya and offers similar lessons for future policy. In a stunning transatlantic announcement on December 19, 2003, British Prime Minister Tony Blair and President Bush said Libya had agreed, after nine months of secret talks, to publicly disclose and dismantle all nuclear, chemical, and biological weapons programs; to limit its missiles to a range of less than three hundred kilometers; and to open the country immediately to comprehensive inspections to verify its compliance. Even more importantly, Libya agreed to provide information on its dealings with the nuclear black market.[53]

Why did this deal occur, and to what degree can it be attributed to the Bush Doctrine? In March 2003, shortly before the Iraq War began, Musa Kussa, President Qaddafi's chief of intelligence, approached British M16 officials seeking to finalize ongoing negotiations for the end of its unconventional-weapons programs in exchange for normalization of ties. Some officials and experts link Libya's decision to President Bush's national security strategy and the invasion of Iraq. The presence of 250,000 U.S. forces in the region undoubtedly had an impact, but it does not seem that President Qaddafi feared a U.S. invasion of Tripoli.

More likely, Qaddafi had concluded that he needed Western contracts and markets more than he needed chemical or nuclear weapons. In fact, efforts to end Libya's weapon programs spanned four presidential administrations. The UN had imposed sanctions in 1992 in response to the downing of an airliner over Lockerbie in Scotland in 1988. Some U.S. sanctions were already in place by then, having been imposed in 1986 by President Ronald Reagan after Libya was linked to an act of terrorism in Germany. More U.S. sanctions followed in 1992 and 1996. In the late 1990s Libya approached the second Clinton administration with hopes of ending its international isolation. The Clinton administration made Libyan cooperation in the Lockerbie bombing case a prerequisite to normalizing U.S.-Libya relations. Qaddafi's acceptance of responsibility for the destruction of Pan Am Flight 103 led to the suspension of UN sanctions in 1999. However, U.S. sanctions remained in place. U.S. officials made clear that Libya would have to address concerns over its weapons programs before U.S. sanctions would be lifted. These discussions continued in the Bush administration.

Whether by design or by chance, the United States and the UK in 2003 struck the right combination of force and diplomacy. Prime Minister Tony Blair seems to have been a decisive influence on President Bush, overcoming opposition from the U.S. Department of Defense to any "deals with dictators." Former State Department official Flynt Leverett, who was involved in these negotiations, notes, "The lesson is incontrovertible: to persuade a rogue regime to get out of the terrorism business and give up its weapons of mass destruction, we must not only apply pressure but also make clear the potential benefits of cooperation."[54]

With the agreement, British, U.S., and IAEA officials visited ten previously secret facilities and removed twenty-seven and one-half tons of documents and components for Libya's nuclear and missile programs, including uranium hexaflouride, centrifuge parts, and guidance devices for long-range missiles. The United States also removed Scud-C missiles and their launchers, as well as more than fifteen kilograms of highly enriched uranium. Libya destroyed three thousand chemical munitions, consolidated and secured its stocks of chemical weapons agents and precursors for destruction, and joined the Chemical Weapons Convention. IAEA and U.S. officials have verified that Libya's disarmament was transparent and almost complete.

The world now has two very different models for how to eliminate a threatening nation's nuclear and missile capabilities. The Iraq model of regime change has been enormously costly, chaotic, and uncertain. The Libyan model of changing regime behavior has been efficient, effective, and almost cost-free.

NET ASSESSMENT OF THE SUCCESSES AND FAILURES OF THE IRAQ WAR COUNTERPROLIFERATION STRATEGY

Supporters of the Iraq War model point to several significant successes as indicators of its viability. They believe that the war led directly to Libya's capitulation and cite the key role of information provided by Libyan officials (and later Iranian admissions to IAEA inspectors) in the public exposure of the A. Q. Khan network.[55] They believe that the demonstration of U.S. strength in the war helped the United States convince the United Nations Security Council in 2004 to adopt UN Resolution 1540, committing all nations to adopt laws to strengthen their export-control regimes and to criminalize illegal trade in biological, chemical, and nuclear weapon-related technologies. U.S. and Russian nuclear arsenals continued to decrease with good prospects for accelerating the dismantlement of nuclear weapons.

Unrelated to the war but also cited as a nonproliferation success is the 2002 Strategic Offensive Reduction Treaty to draw down U.S.- and Russian-deployed, strategic nuclear arsenals to between 1,700 and 2,200 warheads by the end of 2012. Progress has also been made on efficient implementation of nuclear security and nonproliferation programs in the former Soviet Union, even if those programs could still use more attention and funding.[56] In 2004, the U.S. Department of Energy established the Global Threat Reduction Initiative (GTRI), an umbrella program to unite ongoing efforts to secure and remove highly enriched uranium from research reactors and other civilian nuclear facilities around the world.

Part of the Bush alternative strategy was the effort to get the cooperation of key nations in the Proliferation Security Initiative (PSI) to interdict illegal trade in weapons components. According to Secretary of State Rice, by 2005 PSI was already responsible for at least eleven interdictions of goods related to nuclear and ballistic missile programs.[57] In November 2005, Undersecretary of State for Arms Control and International Security Robert Joseph stressed the importance of PSI, telling a Washington conference, "PSI has transformed how nations act together against proliferation. . . . It is not a treaty-based approach involving long, ponderous negotiations that yield results only slowly, if at all. Instead it is a true partnership."[58]

The failures of the Bush administration's counterproliferation strategy, however, outweigh the gains. In 2005, former national security advisor Zbigniew Brzezinski summarized the ripple effect many saw from the Iraq invasion and the selective approach to nonproliferation: "America's ability to cope with nuclear nonproliferation has also suffered. The contrast between the attack on the militarily weak Iraq and America's forbearance of the nuclear-armed North Korea has strengthened the conviction of the Iranians that their security can only be enhanced by nuclear weapons."[59]

Speaking in 2007, Brzezinski noted, "American leadership, in all of its dimensions, has been damaged. American legitimacy has been undermined by unilateral decisions. [Iraq] is a failed occupation as a consequence of a decision-making process that compounds errors, that involves a very narrow group of true believers, and that evades responsibility and accountability for errors and even crimes."[60]

More specifically, the war in Iraq contributed to three key failures of the new proliferation policy:

- The danger of nuclear terrorism increased. When the United States turned its attention away from Afghanistan and toward Iraq, it allowed al Qaeda and the Taliban to regroup in nuclear-armed Pakistan. After the Iraq invasion terrorist attacks rose globally and al Qaeda grew in influence and adherents.[61] Further, U.S. intelligence officials concluded in February 2005 Senate testimony that American policy in the Middle East has fueled anti-U.S. sentiment and that the Iraq War has provided jihadists with new recruits who "will leave Iraq experienced in and focused on acts of urban terrorism."[62] At the same time, nuclear sites around the world remain susceptible to theft, diversion, or terrorist attack, while weapons and materials are being secured more slowly than expected. The amount of nuclear material secured in the two years after 9/11 was at best equal to the amount secured in the two years before 9/11.[63] CIA Director Porter Goss said in his February 2005 Senate testimony that he could not assure the American people that some of the material missing from Russian nuclear sites had not found its way into terrorist hands.[64]

- Iran accelerated its nuclear efforts—whether peaceful or not—by moving from nuclear research and experimentation to industrial-scale uranium enrichment. A large part of Iran's nuclear infrastructure was developed after 2000, including the operation of uranium-gas production plants, a vast facility that houses more than fifty thousand centrifuges vital to uranium enrichment and, by the end of 2008, almost four thousand working centrifuges that had produced more than one thousand kilograms of low-enriched uranium. Iran was far closer to a nuclear weapon in 2008 than it was in 2000, while the Bush administration lacked a coherent plan for stopping the program. Bush administration officials blocked attempts by European allies to negotiate an end to the program and any real effort to engage Iran directly. Former undersecretary of state Nicholas Burns said, "I served as the Bush administration's point person on Iran for three years, but was never permitted to meet an Iranian."[65] Senator Chuck Hagel (R-NE) warned that ignoring Iran will not solve the problem. "America's refusal to recognize Iran's status as a legitimate power does not decrease Iran's influence, but rather increases it."[66] Five former secretaries of state and two former national security advisors also encouraged direct negotiations with Iran at senior levels, but their advice fell on deaf ears in the Bush administration.[67]

- North Korea also dramatically accelerated its program, increasing fivefold its amount of bomb material, withdrawing from the NPT, detonating a nuclear device, and declaring itself a nuclear-armed state. Absent serious negotiations with the United States, the U.S. invasion of Iraq seemed to convince officials in Pyongyang that a nuclear deterrent was essential for protection. Further, while the United States was bogged down in Iraq, it also failed to deter North Korea's forays into nuclear and missile technology sales, including possible assistance to Syria's construction of a nuclear reactor.

More generally, the administration failed to recognize that its strategy was producing the opposite of the results intended. The Iraq quagmire was part of the overall strategic collapse of the Bush Doctrine. As the administration clung to its failing policies, it neglected other, more traditional levers of U.S. power including multilateral diplomacy and bilateral negotiated nuclear reduction and security arrangements. This led, indirectly, to other key proliferation failures:

- Though the A. Q. Khan nuclear black market was disrupted in 2004, failure to do so earlier allowed Iran, Libya, and possibly North Korea to acquire key components for nuclear weapons production. The failure to get more cooperation from the government of Pakistan (which used the network for its own nuclear imports) made it difficult to determine if the network had been shut down completely or simply gone further underground. European intelligence reports indicate that Pakistani-based illicit nuclear sales may still thrive.[68]

- More nations declared their intentions to develop the ability to enrich uranium for nuclear reactor fuel—the same technologies that can be used to enrich uranium for nuclear bombs.[69] U.S. proposals to curtail these technologies failed to win any significant support.
- The United States and Russia ended the process of negotiating reductions in their nuclear arsenals, and the reductions themselves proceeded at a slower pace than previous administrations planned.[70] The U.S. desire to bring Ukraine and Georgia into NATO and plans to deploy antimissile military bases in Poland and the Czech Republic aggravated Russian concerns over U.S. intentions. By late 2008, the Russian-Georgian conflict brought U.S.-Russian relations to their worst point since before the collapse of the Soviet Union.
- Administration proposals to develop new nuclear weapons (coupled with new doctrines for nuclear weapons use against even nonnuclear targets) encouraged other nations, such as Russia, to develop similar plans and encouraged the view that nuclear weapons should be an essential component of a nation's security program.
- Concern grew that the entire nonproliferation regime was in danger of a catastrophic collapse. The NPT Review Conference of May 2005 ended acrimoniously, failing to act on the consensus of the majority of states for stronger nonproliferation and disarmament efforts or to adopt any of the dozens of useful suggestions proposed by many of the nations present.
- President Bush's July 2005 decision to reverse U.S. policy toward India and begin selling sensitive nuclear technology seemed to reward India's nuclear proliferation. The action seemed to be a de facto recognition of India as a nuclear-armed state, with all the rights and privileges reserved for those states that have joined the NPT, raising concerns that other states, such as Pakistan and Israel, might demand the same status.
- A core part of the counterproliferation strategy realized little progress. From 2000 to 2007, the United States spent almost $60 billion

on antimissile systems without realizing any substantial increase in military capability. The antimissile system under construction in Alaska is widely regarded as ineffective.[71] If current plans are implemented, spending from fiscal years 2009 to 2013 will amount to an additional $62.3 billion.

By the beginning of 2006, a broad, bipartisan consensus had developed that the failures of the new approach outweighed the benefits. Former director of policy planning in the Bush State Department Richard Haass criticized the reliance on regime change: "The uncertainties surrounding regime change make it an unreliable approach for dealing with specific problems such as a nuclear weapons program in an unfriendly state. . . . Regime change cannot be counted on to come quickly enough to remove the nuclear threat now posed by [North Korea and Iran]."[72]

For some, the greatest failure of the new approach was its belief that it could indefinitely maintain a global double standard. This, they felt, tainted American credibility. Representative John Spratt (D-SC), a leader on defense issues in the Congress, said, "My greatest concern is that some in the administration and in Congress seem to think that the United States can move the world in one direction while Washington moves in another; that we can continue to prevail on other countries not to develop nuclear weapons while we develop new tactical applications for such weapons and possibly resume nuclear testing."[73]

Similarly, former assistant secretary John Wolf, after leaving the State Department, said that while he supported many administration policies, he was worried by the current U.S. approach to nonproliferation: "The [nonproliferation] treaty fails if it differentiates or if members try to differentiate between good states who can be trusted with nuclear weapons and all others. We have never been further from the treaty's goals and we are moving in the wrong direction. . . . It's been fashionable recently to talk a lot about counterproliferation, but that's really a defensive concept. Nonproliferation done right is bigger. . . . In the end, I think you get a better result."[74] Wolf shared Spratt's concerns about programs for new nuclear weapons and new nuclear missions: "One set of concerns relates to the Department of Energy's program to research a new penetrator warhead," he said. "Far more worrisome though is the proposed change in weapons doctrine that envisions using nuclear weapons for WMD pre-emption." Pointing to the risks of preemptive attack illustrated by the Iraq War, he noted that many officials believed Iraq had chemical and biological weapons: "Suppose instead some had argued to use nuclear weapons preemptively, and suppose we had. What would have been the implications of doing so and being wrong? Whoops is not a good enough response."[75]

IAEA Director General Mohammed ElBaradei believes that the American emphasis on nuclear superiority and military force may, in fact, increase insecurity: "In the wake of the Cold War, many of us were hopeful for a new global security regime, a regime that would be inclusive, effective, and no longer dependent on nuclear weapons. But regrettably, we have made little or no progress." ElBaradei argues that a main objective for international security in the twenty-first century should be to establish a system "that would make the use of force—including the use of nuclear weapons—less likely as a means of conflict resolution."[76]

CONCLUSION

Some believe that the counterproliferation strategy exemplified by the Iraq War, or some modified variation, could still prove its worth. However, a combination of approaches would seem to offer the best chance of success—a comprehensive strategy that combines the best elements of the U.S.-centric, force-based approach with the traditional multilateral, treaty-based approach. Any enforcement mechanisms should be in support of the treaty regime, not a replacement for it.

The Iraq War strategy—like the diplomatic strategy it replaced—has proven insufficient. Stopping the spread of nuclear weapons requires more international resolve than previous administrations could muster, but it also demands more genuine international teamwork than the Bush administration recognized. Nuclear weapons and fissile materials are problems wherever they are, not just in a handful of "evil" states. The threat cannot be eliminated by removing whichever foreign governments the United States finds most threatening at any given time. History has shown again and again that today's ally can become tomorrow's problem state. Moreover, terrorists will seek nuclear weapons and materials wherever they can be found, irrespective of a state's geopolitical orientation.

The United States cannot defeat the nuclear threat alone, or even with small coalitions of the willing. It needs sustained cooperation from dozens of diverse nations—including the leading states that have forsworn nuclear weapons, such as Argentina, Brazil, Germany, Japan, South Africa, and Sweden—in order to broaden, toughen, and stringently enforce nonproliferation rules. To get that cooperation, the nuclear-armed states must show that tougher nonproliferation rules not only benefit the powerful but constrain them as well.

There is a clear alternative to the Bush Doctrine. Modern American foreign policy boasts a set of diplomatic, economic, and military tools known collectively as the policy of containment that has stood the test of time. President Bush's ten predecessors in one fashion or another deployed these tools to end the Korean War, win the cold war, extricate our military forces from Vietnam, forge an international coalition to win the first Gulf War, and craft a lasting peace in the Balkans.

Success will depend on the United States's ability to marshal legitimate authority that motivates others to follow. As Francis Fukuyama notes, "Other people will follow the American lead if they believe it is legitimate; if they do not, they will resist, complain, obstruct, or actively oppose what we do."[77]

4 THE IRAQ WAR AND AMERICAN NATIONAL SECURITY INTERESTS IN THE MIDDLE EAST

F. Gregory Gause III

There is a persistent story that Chou En Lai, premier of the People's Republic of China from 1949 to his death in 1976, was once asked to assess the historical impact of the French Revolution. His pithy reply: "It is too soon to tell."[1] One could make the same remark about the effects of the Iraq War on American national security interests in the Middle East. Nevertheless, the end of the Bush administration is one convenient point from which to survey the consequences of the war for the position of the United States in the region. With the understanding that judgments can change as events develop, it is hard to argue from this vantage point that the Iraq War has advanced American national security interests in the Middle East. The few positive effects directly traceable to the war are vastly outweighed by the negative regional repercussions.

This chapter begins with an argument about American interests in the Middle East and how the Bush administration, in the wake of the September 11 attacks, altered what had been a relatively consistent definition of those interests over previous administrations. It then assesses the consequences of the Iraq War in six areas of American concern: proliferation of weapons of mass destruction, terrorism, democracy promotion, Arab-Israeli peace, oil, and the overall American strategic position in the region. It will not discuss the costs in blood and treasure paid by the United States in the war, a subject discussed elsewhere in this volume. It will also not discuss the important topic of the costs and benefits to Iraqis of this war—the hope of a more decent and representative politics weighed against the reality of the death, displacement, and chaos the war has brought to that country.[2] That is the topic for an entirely different assessment, made by Iraqis themselves.

AMERICAN INTERESTS IN THE MIDDLE EAST, 9/11, AND THE IRAQ WAR

The Iraq War marked an important shift in how the American political leadership defined its interests in the Middle East. In general, the United States supported the Middle Eastern status quo in the decades after World War Two because that status quo served American oil and strategic interests. There were, of course, exceptions. Washington actively opposed pro-Soviet regimes (or regimes believed to be pro-Soviet) during the cold war, including in the 1950s working to overthrow a number of sitting governments. In 1967 and 1982 American administrations gave Israel a nod and a wink approval to go to war. These exceptions aside, however, the mantra of Washington in the Middle East was "stability." Various administrations tried to advance the cause of Arab-Israeli peace in order to lessen the chances of regional war and remove a major tension in American relations with Arab states. The United States fought the Gulf War of 1990–91 to restore the Kuwaiti monarchy and preserve the geopolitical order in the Persian Gulf. Instability harmed American interests; witness the oil embargoes that accompanied the 1973 Arab-Israeli War and the Iranian Revolution of 1979. Stability in the Middle East, particularly after the cold war, when the United States was the unchallenged dominant outside power in the region, was good for America. Indeed, Washington put such a premium on regional stability that it did very little to try to reverse the Iranian Revolution, the single most damaging event for American interests in the Middle East, or to unseat Saddam Hussein after 1991.

The attacks of September 11, 2001, changed that perspective. The threat of terrorism of Middle East origin became much more salient for Americans, and the risks of such attacks with weapons of mass destruction became a major focus of the Bush administration. The Bush Doctrine linked the terrorist threat and the WMD threat, asserting that the United States would not allow hostile regimes with ties to terrorist groups to obtain such weapons.[3] This was the rationale put forward by the administration for the Iraq War. But the 9/11 attacks led to a more thorough-going reassessment of America's interests in the Middle East. The Bush administration, along with many in the American political class, diagnosed the cause of 9/11 as follows: Middle East terrorism is the product of authoritarian systems that do not allow open political competition. Opposition is thus forced underground, where it becomes violent and elements are attracted to terrorist methods. Middle Eastern regimes try to deflect popular opposition by encouraging anti-American sentiments, thus Middle Eastern terrorists direct their violence against the United States. The root causes of terrorism can therefore only be addressed through changes in the domestic political systems of Middle Eastern states. Arab (and Iranian) democracy is therefore the cure for anti-American terrorism.[4] If not Arab democracy, then at a minimum a profound change in the domestic political arrangements of Arab countries was required. The stability that American administrations in the past had prized in the Middle East rested, at least in part, upon those Arab authoritarians. So American interests had to change; stability gave way to an agenda of regime change and political reform in the region.[5]

One can question the logic of this argument.[6] It is, however, hard to question the sincerity with which it was held by the Bush administration, at least through 2006. This new agenda of "creative instability" in the region began with the invasion of Iraq in 2003, but it did not end there. The Iraq War was meant to catalyze broader changes in the Middle East. There were efforts to isolate and destabilize enemies of the United States, most notably Iran and Syria. But there was also pressure on friendly states to reform and democratize their political systems, an unprecedented step in American Middle East policy. Besides the elections in Iraq itself, Washington encouraged presidential and parliamentary elections in the Palestinian Authority, multicandidate presidential elections and parliamentary elections in Egypt, parliamentary elections in Lebanon, and municipal elections in Saudi Arabia. In the post-9/11 period, American policy aimed not just to change hostile regimes but also to alter the domestic political systems of friendly states. It is hard to imagine that the Bush administration would have engaged in all of these reform efforts in the region if the democracy rhetoric were just meant as a smokescreen to cover more traditional imperial goals in going to war in Iraq.[7]

This ambitious agenda of domestic political change ran into numerous problems, in Iraq itself and throughout the region. As the Bush administration came to a close, its emphasis on domestic political reform in allied states gave way to a more traditional emphasis on regional power issues, with Washington rallying its friends in the region to balance Iranian power. But that change was itself a recognition that the results of the "creative instability" push were largely negative for American interests in the Middle East. The remainder of this chapter analyzes the consequences of the Iraq War and the broader push for regional change in six areas. Three are "new" policy goals that were present in the American rhetoric on the Middle East before 9/11 but gained unprecedented salience in the aftermath of the attacks: stopping terrorism, preventing the proliferation of weapons of mass destruction (WMD), and promoting democracy. Three are traditional goals from the "stability" period of American policy in the region that were not abandoned in the post-9/11 period: encouraging Arab-Israeli peace, maintaining the free flow of oil at reasonable prices, and sustaining American strategic dominance.

THE NEW AGENDA: WMD, TERRORISM, AND DEMOCRACY

Nonproliferation, the containment and elimination of terrorism, and the spread of democracy are not entirely new goals of American foreign policy in the Middle East. They were part of the litany of American interests various administrations put forward to explain and justify American policy in the region. But after 9/11, they took on a new salience for the Bush administration. In terms of their prominence, they formed the new agenda for American interests in the Middle East. The Iraq War had some positive effects on each of these goals, but those effects were more limited than the administration had hoped. The war also had some unforeseen negative implications in each of these areas, which cancelled out whatever gains had been made.

Nonproliferation

The dominant public rationale given by the Bush administration for the Iraq War was to prevent a hostile state with ties to terrorist groups from obtaining weapons of mass destruction or distributing them to terrorists. On the WMD front, the Bush administration can claim one success. In December 2003 Libya declared that it would give up its nuclear, biological, and chemical weapons programs and its medium- and long-range missiles. It opened its facilities to international and American officials, who shipped considerable amounts of nuclear material and missile components out of the country.[8] The Bush administration was convinced that Libya had truly abandoned its WMD ambitions, and in May 2006 restored diplomatic relations with the country and took it off the list of countries supporting terrorism.[9] There are indications that Libya sought to improve relations with the United States before the Iraq War, offering to put its WMD programs on the table in exchange for a lifting of international sanctions.[10] Nevertheless, it was only after the Iraq War, and shortly after, that the Qaddafi regime gave up its programs. The timing seems something more than coincidence (Joseph Cirincione's discussion in Chapter 3 of this book presents a different interpretation of the Libyan case).

Against the putative Libya success, however, must be set a number of failures and setbacks on the WMD front in the Middle East since the Iraq War. The most notorious was the lack of weapons of mass destruction in Iraq itself. This was an intelligence failure more than a policy failure, and the mistaken belief that Iraq had WMD was a cause of the Iraq War, not a consequence.[11] Still, the absence of WMD in Iraq, after the United States had emphasized the presence of these programs in making its case for war, severely damaged American credibility on WMD issues.

The most high-profile regional case of nuclear proliferation in the wake of the Iraq War is Iran. The Iranian program was relatively well concealed during the 1990s, but in 2002, in the lead-up to the Iraq War, an Iranian opposition group revealed that Tehran was secretly developing two parallel nuclear programs: a uranium-enrichment program at its nuclear facility at Natanz and a plutonium program at its facility at Arak. In February 2003 Iranian President Khatami publicly acknowledged the accuracy of the charges. Iran defended the programs, stating (correctly) that it was allowed to develop its nuclear industry for civilian purposes under the Nuclear Nonproliferation Treaty (NPT). Its critics, including the International Atomic Energy Agency, the UN body that monitors the NPT, responded that Iran was obligated to report these programs to the IAEA under the terms of the NPT. The secrecy of the programs raised questions about Iran's intentions.[12]

In the wake of the Iraq War, it appeared that Iran was rethinking its nuclear plans. The remarkable success of American arms in deposing Saddam Hussein's regime might have given the Iranians pause, at least temporarily. The National Intelligence Estimate (NIE) released in December 2007 concluded that in early 2003 Iran suspended work on the development of nuclear weapons, though not on the nuclear program itself.[13] In October 2003, in negotiations with representatives of the European Union, Iran agreed to suspend uranium enrichment and accede to the Additional Protocol of the NPT, which allowed the IAEA to conduct more intrusive inspections of Iranian facilities. In November 2004, the EU and Iran reconfirmed their earlier deal, with Iran continuing its suspension on enrichment and the EU-3 (Great Britain, France, and Germany, the countries leading the EU negotiations with Iran) promising no UN sanctions against Iran.[14]

Rather than follow up on these indications of potential changes in Iranian policy after the fall of Saddam Hussein, including an offer of direct talks in 2003, the Bush administration refused to engage Iran.[15] The hints of Iranian flexibility on the nuclear issue disappeared with the election of Mahmoud Ahmadinejad as president of Iran in June 2005. With his subsequent bellicose statements about Israel and the United States, fears of Iranian intentions in Washington and in Europe, not to mention Jerusalem, increased. In February 2006, Iran resumed uranium enrichment.[16] Despite the findings of the 2007 NIE, the Bush administration has continued to emphasize that it believes that Iran is developing nuclear weapons. However, in a tacit admission that its policy of relying solely on isolation of and pressure against Iran was not working, the administration in its second term softened its opposition to multilateral diplomatic approaches toward Tehran and eventually even joined EU-led negotiations with the Iranians.[17] By the administration's own admission, Iran has been a nonproliferation failure.

Syria also was not dissuaded by the Iraq War from pursuing what appears to have been a nuclear program. In September 2007 Israeli planes bombed a military installation in Syria. The details about the target were shrouded in secrecy, as both the Syrians and the Israelis largely kept quiet about the operation and the Syrians bulldozed the site shortly after the attack. However, information subsequently leaked to the press indicated that the facility was most likely a North Korean-built nuclear reactor.[18] While definitive proof about what the Syrians were building is not available in the public sphere, it seems reasonable to conclude that the Iraq War did not serve as a deterrent to Syrian proliferation desires.

America's regional allies, in the wake of the Iraq War and Iran's continued progress on its nuclear program, have manifested a new interest in developing their own nuclear programs. Egypt, Turkey, Saudi Arabia, and some of the smaller Gulf states have all taken tangible steps either to revive or begin nuclear projects. King Abdallah of Jordan said, "The rules have changed. . . . Everybody's going for nuclear programs."[19] The Gulf Cooperation Council in its December 2006 summit ordered a study on the feasibility of a joint nuclear program.[20] The United States signed bilateral agreements with Saudi Arabia in May 2008 and Bahrain in March 2008 to assist them in developing civilian nuclear programs; France signed similar agreements with Saudi Arabia, the UAE, Qatar, and Egypt, among other countries, in late 2007 and early 2008.[21] In none of these cases is there any indication that the Middle Eastern countries are seeking to develop a nuclear-weapons program. Still, the rush in interest across the region in nuclear technology is clearly related to Iran's program. Since the Iraq War, the risk of nuclear proliferation in the Middle East seems to have increased, not decreased.[22]

The War on Terror

The Iraq War was also meant to decrease the terrorist threat emanating from the Middle East. It is beyond the scope of this chapter to discuss the issue of al Qaeda's reemergence in Pakistan and Afghanistan (see Steven Simon's discussion in Chapter 2 of this book). However, the director of national intelligence, Michael McConnell, publicly testified in February 2008 that al Qaeda is steadily improving its "ability to recruit, train and position operatives capable of carrying out attacks in the United States."[23] While there have been no terrorist attacks in the United States since the Iraq War, al Qaeda, its affiliates, and/or groups inspired by it have launched attacks across the globe, in Great Britain, Spain, Morocco, Tunisia, Turkey, Jordan, Saudi Arabia, Iraq, and Indonesia, along with Afghanistan and Pakistan. It is difficult to conclude with any certainty what role the Iraq War had in motivating new recruits to the radical Islamist cause. But it is clear that the American war and occupation has hardly reduced the appeal of Islamist radicalism globally.

In the Middle East itself, two countries saw a substantial increase in al Qaeda activity after the Iraq War. The first was Iraq itself. While Abu Musab al-Zarqawi, who would go on to become the leader of al Qaeda in Iraq, had found a haven in the border area between Kurdish Iraq, Iran, and Saddam-controlled Iraq in the months between the fall of the Taliban regime in Afghanistan and the Iraq War, there is no evidence that al Qaeda had a following or an organization in Iraq before the war. There is also no evidence that Saddam's regime had a relationship with al Qaeda, despite the frantic efforts of the Bush administration to make that case. But as the American occupation of Iraq continued, al Qaeda in Iraq (AQI) became a potent player in the insurgency and a spur to the brutal sectarian civil conflict that engulfed Iraq in 2006 and early 2007. AQI and its allies were even able to take control of some major cities in western Iraq during that period. The year 2007 seems to have been their high-water mark. Their brutal tactics, both against Iraqi Shi'a and against Iraqi Sunnis who did not toe their line, led to a reaction against them. Tribal and insurgent groups, which came to be called the Awakening Movements and the Sons of Iraq, turned against AQI. With the assistance of the United States, they were able to drive AQI out of much of western Iraq and Baghdad; campaigns continued as of the fall of 2008 in the north and northwest of Baghdad. AQI's fortunes were clearly on the decline in Iraq by then. But this decline was the result of dynamics within the Iraqi Sunni Arab community and better counterinsurgency tactics by American forces.[24] The Iraq War itself opened the country to al Qaeda influence.

The other Middle Eastern country that saw an increase in al Qaeda activity after the Iraq War was Saudi Arabia. In May 2003 al Qaeda in the Arabian Peninsula (AQAP) staged a large-scale attack on housing compounds in Riyadh. There were a number of attacks on foreign interests (including the American consulate in Jiddah), Saudi state agencies (including a car bombing of the Interior Ministry), and economic targets (including a foiled attack on the major Saudi oil-processing complex in Abqaiq) in the next four years. By 2005 the Saudi security forces had gained the upper hand in their struggle with AQAP. Whereas in 2003 and 2004, most incidents were initiated by the insurgents, from 2005 onward most of the armed encounters were initiated by the security forces. While AQAP is clearly on the defensive and was not able to mobilize the Saudi public against the regime, as of 2008 it remained capable of sporadic violent attacks.[25]

Al Qaeda has not been able to come to power in any Middle Eastern state, as it had in Afghanistan during the Taliban period, nor has it been able to find a stable safe haven where it can enjoy freedom of action, as it apparently has in Pakistan. But the Iraq War does not appear to have been the cause of al Qaeda's failures. On the contrary, the war seems to have encouraged a brief upsurge in al Qaeda's fortunes in both Iraq and Saudi Arabia. Moreover, the post-Iraq War successes of Hizballah and Hamas, both listed on the official American roster of terrorist organizations, also call into question the idea that the war helped U.S. interests in the Middle East on the terrorism front.

Promoting Democracy

The Iraq War had very mixed consequences for the new American interest in encouraging democracy in the Middle East. To be certain, it destroyed a particularly loathsome dictatorship and created a formally democratic political system in Iraq. It also encouraged an inspiring popular revolt in Lebanon against Syrian occupation, allowing free Lebanese elections for the first time in decades. However, these successes, and other moves toward free elections in the region, brought results that greatly surprised the Americans who encouraged and supported them. Islamists were the primary beneficiaries of the postwar democratic openings in the Arab world. Whether the democratic rise of Islamists in the region helps or hurts American interests in the long term is a matter of debate. It is also an open question whether the violence that accompanied the development of Iraqi democracy has done more to discredit democracy in general in the region than to encourage it. The jury remains out, but there are good reasons to question whether the gains outweigh the costs.

There is no denying the initial excitement in the Middle East after the fall of Saddam Hussein. Anecdotes about cab drivers in Damascus and Tehran asking American visitors when Washington was going to liberate their country and give them democracy abounded. The Iraqi elections of January and December 2005, held amid a deteriorating security situation, were well managed, saw high turnout levels (particularly in December 2005, after Sunni Arabs dropped their earlier boycott of elections), and produced affecting images of Iraqis voting in free elections for the first time in half a century. The new American emphasis on elections pushed friendly regimes like Egypt and Saudi Arabia to adopt political reforms. The most dramatic spill-over effect of the war for democratic advances was in Lebanon. The assassination in 2005 of former prime minister Rafiq al-Hariri led to massive demonstrations and the withdrawal of Syrian forces. Lebanese Druze leader Walid Jumblatt, no friend of the United States in the past, said, "It's strange for me to say it, but this process of change has started because of the American invasion of Iraq.

I was cynical about Iraq. But when I saw the Iraqi people voting three weeks ago, 8 million of them, it was the start of a new Arab world."[26] The Lebanese parliamentary elections of May-June 2005 produced a parliamentary majority for the anti-Syria, pro-American bloc of Sunni, Druze, and Christian movements headed by Jumblatt and Hariri's son Saad.

While this wave of elections in the Arab world fit the model the Bush administration had hoped to see as a result of the Iraq War, the results of the elections were a rude surprise. In Iraq, Islamist forces in both the Shi'a and the Sunni Arab communities did very well (the two main Kurdish nationalist parties formed a single list and dominated the Kurdish voting). The major cross-sectarian, multiethnic secular party, Prime Minister Iyad Allawi's Iraqi List, received only 15 percent of the seats in the January 2005 parliamentary elections (when he had the advantage of incumbency) and even less, around 9 percent, in the December 2005 elections. The elections were dominated by the United Iraqi Alliance, an amalgam of the Islamic Supreme Council of Iraq (formerly the Supreme Council for the Islamic Revolution in Iraq), the movement of Moktada al-Sadr, and the Da'wa Party of current prime minister, Nouri al-Maliki. All three components are sectarian Shi'a movements, close to Iran (the Sadrists were the least beholden to Iran of the three components in 2005, but Iran's influence among them has grown) and Islamist in orientation. The major force emerging from the Sunni Arab community in the December 2005 election was the Accordance (al-Tawaffuq) Front, comprising the Iraqi Islamic Party, which is the Iraqi branch of the Muslim Brotherhood, and other Sunni Islamist currents.[27] New elections in Iraq might alter the political map in the future, particularly on the Sunni side, but the immediate consequence of Iraqi elections was to harden sectarian and ethnic identities and to empower Islamists in both the Shi'a and the Sunni Arab communities. Iraq could develop into a stable democracy, but it could also degenerate into an even more calamitous civil conflict.

Islamist successes were not limited to Iraq. In Egypt's parliamentary election of November-December 2005, the Muslim Brotherhood, although technically an illegal organization, won 20 percent of the seats. More telling, Brotherhood candidates won about 60 percent of the seats they contested. In Lebanon's elections of May-June 2005, Hizballah, designated a terrorist organization by the United States, led an electoral coalition that swept the Shi'a seats and formed a powerful opposition bloc with dissident Maronite leader Michel Aoun. Perhaps the most surprising result to the Bush administration was in the Palestinian parliamentary elections of January 2006. Hamas, another officially designated terrorist organization in Washington's eyes, won an absolute majority of the seats and formed the Palestinian government. In terms of democracy promotion, the Iraq War and subsequent Bush administration diplomacy certainly advanced the cause, but the results of those democratic elections were hardly reassuring to Washington.[28]

The results of those elections led to a noticeable cooling of American enthusiasm for Arab electoral experiments in the final years of the Bush administration (though, incongruously, not to a change in President Bush's rhetorical support for freedom in the Muslim world). The Egyptian government quickly reverted to its authoritarian tendencies after the 2005 elections (to some extent, during those elections) with little reaction from the Bush administration. Saudi Arabia did nothing to follow up on the municipal elections of 2005, again without having to pay a price to Washington. As the Bush administration ended, the United States was in the uncomfortable position of continuing to preach democracy without pushing its allies to practice it.

THE OLD AGENDA: OIL, ARAB-ISRAELI PEACE, AND AMERICA'S STRATEGIC POSITION

While the 9/11 attacks introduced new elements into the agenda of American interests in the Middle East, they did not remove the important interests that had driven American involvement in the region for decades before: oil, the Arab-Israeli peace process, and America's overall strategic position in the region. The war's effects on these traditional American interests were almost completely negative.

Oil

The argument over the importance of oil in the war decision itself will undoubtedly continue for some time, but there is no argument about the fact that the Bush administration hoped that the war would bring Iraq back into the world oil market as a major player, producing more oil than it had under Saddam. That assumption was implicit in the administration's claim that Iraq would be able to pay for its own reconstruction after the war.[29] This has not happened. Iraqi production in 2002 averaged just over 2 million barrels per day (MBD). In the first three months of 2008, some five years after the war began, Iraqi production still averaged just 2.25 MBD.[30] In the meantime, oil prices skyrocketed. In 2003 a barrel of oil (West Texas Intermediate, the highest-priced marker crude) averaged $31.07; in 2007 the average price was $72.20.[31] In the summer of 2008 prices on occasion exceeded $140, an all-time high, though by the fall of 2008 prices had fallen below $90 per barrel in the wake of the global financial crisis. The Iraq War clearly did not increase the amount of oil on the market nor did it contribute to a stabilization of the world oil market. On the contrary, the war and occupation were accompanied by an unprecedented increase in the price of oil.

A persistent criticism of the Bush administration's Iraq policy is that it fought the war to exert "control" over Iraqi oil or to deny Iraqi oil-development contracts to Russian, French, and Chinese companies. On this criticism, even if the war did not stabilize oil prices, it would have been a success for American interests if it led to American "control" of Iraqi oil. I do not believe that "control" of Iraqi oil was a major goal of the Bush administration. Those who talk about foreign "control" over oil ignore the past forty years of history in the world oil market, where the overwhelming trend has been for the producer government—not a foreign company—to control oil-production decisions and the revenue from crude-oil production. But even if such chimerical "control" were a goal of the Bush administration, five years after the war the United States has no more "control" over Iraqi oil than it did before the war, which is to say, none. The essential first step for securing American commercial control of Iraqi oil resources would have been the privatization of the Iraqi oil industry. However, in the sweeping privatization regulations issued by the Coalition Provisional Authority in September 2003, the Iraqi National Oil Company (INOC) was pointedly exempted.[32] While the CPA ruled Iraq, it did not take Iraq out of OPEC. If the war was about American commercial control of Iraqi oil, the Bush administration did a remarkably poor job in consolidating that control while it had the chance.

It is true that in June 2008, the Iraqi Oil Ministry began to negotiate with a number of Western oil companies, including Exxon Mobil and Chevron from the United States, Shell and BP from Great Britain, and Total from France, on no-bid contracts to service existing Iraqi oil fields.[33] The prominence of American (and British) firms in this first move by Iraq to develop its oil industry excited the expected reactions among those who believed that the Iraq War was "really" about American control of Iraqi oil.[34] Perhaps in response to those reactions, the Iraqi government subsequently cancelled the no-bid contracts.[35] The Iraqi Oil Ministry at about the same time signed a $3 billion deal with the China National Petroleum Corporation to develop an oil field near the Iranian border. The spokesman for the Iraqi Oil Ministry commented that Iraqi officials hoped that this agreement would "refute all the rumors that say the American companies are the only ones benefiting from the American occupation."[36] In October 2008 the Iraqi oil ministry opened bidding to international oil companies to participate in the development of a number of Iraqi fields. While the details of the Iraqi offer were not made public, it appears that the terms on offer are a hybrid between service contracts, where the companies are paid a fee for technical assistance in restoring and developing fields, and participation agreements where the companies will obtain an equity stake in the fields. The legal framework for Iraqi oil development remains unclear, as the Iraqi parliament as of October 2008 had yet to adopt a new oil law and the Kurdish Regional Government continued to question the right of the central government to administer oil fields in its territory.[37]

It is hard to imagine that Iraq, starved of capital and oil technology since the international sanctions of 1990, could restore and develop its fields on its own. In announcing the October 2008 bidding round, Iraqi oil minister Hussein al-Shahristani told reporters that "current production is by no means meeting demand for the reconstruction of the country. International companies are needed to fast track development."[38] It seems a stretch to consider such moves as evidence of a successful American project to "control" Iraqi oil. It is also a stretch to imagine that the Iraqi government, which in 2008 successfully resisted pressure from the Bush administration to negotiate a Status of Forces Agreement governing the American military presence in Iraq that would give American forces in Iraq blanket immunity from Iraqi law and American commanders complete discretion in ordering military operations, would be putty in the hands of any American administration pushing it to give oil contracts to American companies.[39]

Of course, if American companies eventually monopolize the more important and potentially more lucrative contracts to develop (as opposed to simply service) new and existing fields, then there will be more cause to wonder about Washington's political influence in Iraqi oil decisions. But, until then, it is hard to argue that any American interests in the oil area have been served by the Iraq War.

Arab-Israeli Peace Process

The Bush administration came to office with the intent of de-emphasizing the Arab-Israeli peace process. It had seen how much time President Clinton had invested in the issue in the last year of his presidency and how little he had accomplished. However, in the lead-up to the Iraq War, the administration sought to rally Arab support by reengaging in Arab-Israeli diplomacy. Along with the EU, the UN, and Russia, Washington formed a new diplomatic group—dubbed the Quartet—and formulated a roadmap of steps for Israel, the Palestinian Authority, and the international parties to take on the road to a final settlement of the Israeli-Palestinian conflict. President Bush also stated publicly that the United States supported the establishment of a Palestinian state as the end result of that settlement. There were hopes that a successful war against Iraq would jump-start the peace process in much the same way as in 1991, when the Gulf War was followed by the Madrid Conference, the Oslo Accords, and the Jordanian-Israeli peace treaty.[40]

Unfortunately, this was not to be. The Israeli government of then prime minister Ariel Sharon focused immediately after the Iraq War on a unilateral withdrawal from the Gaza Strip, not on negotiations with the Palestinian Authority. The Gaza withdrawal in August 2005 was followed shortly by the January 2006 Palestinian elections, in which Hamas won a parliamentary majority. With Hamas forming the new Palestinian government, neither Israel nor the United States had an interest in pursuing negotiations. The summer of 2006 witnessed the border war between Hizballah and Israel, and the summer of 2007 saw civil conflict among the Palestinians, with Hamas consolidating its control of the Gaza Strip and Palestinian President Mahmoud Abbas's Fatah organization holding on to power in the West Bank. Violence between Hizballah and Israel and Hamas and Israel, combined with the political divisions and disarray among the Palestinians, made the prospects for peace seem more distant than ever. In 2007 Israeli prime minister Ehud Olmert, under fire domestically for a corruption scandal, pushed for progress in talks with Abbas and opened a channel through Turkey for indirect talks with Syria.[41] The Bush administration, while leery of the Syrian opening, strongly supported the Olmert-Abbas negotiations. It convened an international conference in Annapolis, Maryland, in November 2007 to try to push the process forward.[42] But with Hamas in control of Gaza and claiming majority support in the suspended Palestinian parliament, it is hard to see how any deal between Olmert and Abbas could be implemented. Moreover, it is hard to attribute Olmert's initiatives of 2007–8 to the American victory in Iraq years earlier. Unlike the Gulf War, the Iraq War did not lead to breakthroughs on the Arab-Israeli peace front.

America's Strategic Position

In terms of America's strategic position in the Middle East, the Iraq War produced a few benefits and one very significant problem. The major benefit was the removal of Saddam Hussein from power in Iraq. Although hardly the threat to American regional interests that he was in 1990, when he invaded Kuwait, Hussein was an irritant and a problem, and now he is no more. Iraq will not be able to threaten its neighbors anytime soon (except with the potential spill-over effect of its own internal violence). The Iraqi government is now much more amenable to cooperation with the United States, though how long that will last is an open question. During 2008 there were contentious and protracted negotiations between the Bush administration and the Maliki government on a Status of Forces Agreement (SOFA) to govern the American military role in Iraq. With the United Nations mandate authorizing the American military role in the country set to expire at the end of 2008 (it could be extended, but that would require Security Council approval), Washington hoped that a bilateral agreement between the two states would provide a new and more secure legal basis for the American presence. However, the Iraqis balked at the original U.S. offer, which would have given American commanders a free hand to order operations without Iraqi approval and exempted all American personnel from Iraqi law. The two sides reached a tentative agreement in October 2008 on a SOFA that would give American forces in Iraq immunity only for acts committed on American military bases and that sets a deadline of the end of 2011 for American withdrawal from the country (though a future Iraqi government could request that the deadline be extended). It remained to be seen as of October 2008 whether the agreement would be approved by the Iraqi parliament.[43]

The speculation about American desires for long-term basing rights in Iraq remains just that—speculation. Given the plethora of American facilities in the Gulf states already (a land base in Kuwait, headquarters of the Fifth Fleet in Bahrain, a large air base in Qatar, access to port and air facilities in the UAE and Oman), it is hard to see why American interests require that Iraq provide more military bases. However, it is highly possible that the United States will have access to military facilities in Iraq as well, if not actual "permanent bases" there. Whether this is an advance for American interests is a matter of debate. Iraq's history with foreign military bases is not a happy one. The British bases in the country became a lightening rod for Iraqi opposition groups questioning the nationalist credentials of the Hashemite monarchy. The monarchy's close association with Great Britain was one of the leading causes of its overthrow in a military coup in 1958. American bases in the country could become a similar millstone around the neck of future Iraqi governments. The Maliki government does not seem to be interested in a permanent American military presence in the country, putting forward a timetable for complete American withdrawal by the end of 2011. If Iraqis do not want the American military in their country, it is hard to see how staying would improve the American strategic position.

There is one group of Iraqis that would be more than happy to host a permanent American military presence—Iraq's Kurds. Given their well-grounded historical fear of strong central governments in Baghdad as well as of their neighbors in Turkey and Iraq, the leadership of the Kurdish Regional Government sees in an American military presence a guarantee of its hard-won autonomy. It is not so clear that an American military presence in Iraqi Kurdistan would serve American interests. It would involve the United States in the festering dispute between the KRG and Baghdad over the borders of the Kurdish autonomous area, most directly in the Kurdish desire to include Kirkuk and its surrounding oil fields. An American military presence in the KRG might act as a restraint on the Kurdish leadership on the issue of independence. U.S. policy has consistently favored the territorial integrity of Iraq, and the influence an American military base in the Kurdish area would give to Washington on Kurdish decision making could be a brake on Kurdish thoughts of independence. An American presence might also act as a restraint on Turkish military intervention in Iraqi Kurdistan, lessening the chances of a regional crisis. However, if a future Kurdish leadership did make the risky choice for independence, an American base there would place the United States squarely in the middle of a major regional conflict, as Baghdad, Ankara, and Tehran could all be counted on to actively resist Kurdish independence.

As an ancillary benefit of Saddam's fall from power, the United States was able to remove the air wing it had stationed in Saudi Arabia since the end of the Gulf War, which had enforced the southern no-fly zone in Iraq. The American military presence in the kingdom became a major element of Osama bin Laden's case against the Saudi regime, so its departure helped to shore up the Saudi regime, which was facing its own domestic challenge from al Qaeda, and thus to strengthen America's strategic position in the region.[44]

Against these strategic advantages, actual and potential, one must weigh the rise of Iranian power that came with the fall of Saddam's regime and the difficulties the United States has had in stabilizing post-Saddam Iraq. For all his faults, Saddam Hussein did act as a buffer against the spread of Iranian influence in the region. He did so in the 1980s during the Iran-Iraq War and, even weakened by the Gulf War and sanctions, he performed the same function in the 1990s. With the fall of Saddam, Iran has been able to extend its influence into Iraq to an unprecedented degree. The Islamic Supreme Council of Iraq, a major element of the ruling coalition in Baghdad, was created by the Iranian government in the 1980s and has been supported by them ever since. Tehran also has influence with the other major Shi'a groups in the government, the Sadrist movement and the Da'wa Party (in its various branches). Iran's influence is not limited to Iraqi Shi'a groups, as Tehran has longstanding ties with the Patriotic Union of Kurdistan, headed by Iraqi president Jalal Talabani. Some have even accused it of supplying weapons to Iraqi Sunni insurgents.[45] Washington recognizes that Iranian influence is now a key to the future of Iraq, grudgingly opening in 2007 a formal avenue for consultations (through the American ambassador in Baghdad) with representatives of a member of Mr. Bush's "axis of evil." With the stabilization of the security situation in Iraq from mid-2007, the more drastic scenarios of the breakup of the country now seem less likely. However, if Iraq were to fragment into small parts, Iran would be the regional state best positioned to benefit, as the mostly Shi'a south of the country would almost inevitably look to Tehran for protection. Even in the context of a united Iraq, Iran will continue to be the major beneficiary of the weakness of the central government. Iran's strong political, economic, social, and sectarian ties with many important players and groups in Iraqi politics mean that its influence in Iraq will be substantial for some time to come.

Iran's increased influence in Iraq has been accompanied by post-Iraq War victories for Iran's regional allies. Hizballah, which like the Islamic Supreme Council was created by Iran, has become the dominant player in Lebanese politics. Although its rivals won a majority in the Lebanese parliamentary election of 2005, Hizballah has been able to frustrate any efforts by the pro-American government to actually rule the country. It initiated the crisis with Israel in the summer of 2006 by kidnapping Israeli soldiers along the border, and it won regional acclaim by standing up to the month-long Israeli offensive that followed. In May 2008 the group's fighters routed militias connected to groups in the government, taking control of swathes of Beirut before retreating to its Shi'a strongholds. Its centrality (in Lebanese politics) was recognized by the majority after the fighting, with the government accepting a deal brokered by Qatar later in May that gave Hizballah an effective veto on government decisions.[46]

Hamas, another nonstate ally of Iran, has also won important victories in the Palestinian community since the Iraq War. It swept a majority of the seats in the Palestinian parliamentary election of January 2006 and formed a new Palestinian government. When tensions between it and the Palestinian nationalist group Fatah, headed by Palestinian President Abbas, came to a head in the summer of 2007, it was the Hamas forces that decisively defeated Fatah and took sole control of Gaza. While both Hizballah and Hamas share the Iranian government's refusal to recognize Israel, their strength on the ground led the Israelis in the summer of 2008 to negotiate with both groups—on a cease-fire with Hamas, brokered by Egypt, and on an exchange of Lebanese prisoners in Israel for the bodies of the two Israeli soldiers captured by Hizballah in the summer of 2006. This recognition by Israel of the on-the-ground power of Iran's regional allies has not, however, lessened Israeli fears about the Iranian nuclear program. The prospect of an Israeli attack on Iranian nuclear installations cannot be discounted, even as the United States in 2008 seemed to be moving away from earlier speculation about a possible American strike on Iran.[47] Such an attack, even if limited to conventional weapons, would most probably lead to Iranian retaliation against American interests in Iraq, the Persian Gulf, and Afghanistan.[48]

The unmistakable sense in 2008 that Iranian influence was growing throughout the Middle East is by no means permanent. If the United States, with all its power, cannot organize the Middle East on its own, Iran will hardly be able to do so. Iran has its own domestic problems and divisions; there is no guarantee that the more aggressive rhetoric of Ahmadinejad will define Iranian policy in the long term. Already balancing alliances within the region are forming against Iran, led by Saudi Arabia and Egypt. But it is hard to deny that the Iraq War, and America's subsequent inability to stabilize Iraq, opened the door to increased Iranian influence in the region. In that sense, the Iraq War had a negative effect on America's strategic position in the Middle East.

CONCLUSION

The evaluation of any important historical event will change over time, as its consequences (or lack thereof) become clearer and as our understanding of the event itself is improved through continued study. It is therefore with some humility that I make this preliminary assessment of the Iraq War's effects on American interests in the Middle East.

I find the balance sheet five-plus years after the fall of Saddam Hussein to be decidedly negative. In terms of America's "new" interests in curbing the spread of weapons of mass destruction, containing terrorism, and spreading democracy, the war certainly led to some achievements, Libyan disarmament and the possibility of democracy in Iraq being the most notable. However, there were a number of setbacks on these issues as well: al Qaeda's campaigns in Iraq and Saudi Arabia, continued Iranian nuclear development, and the success of anti-American groups like Hizballah and Hamas at the ballot box. The absence of WMD in Iraq harmed American credibility on this issue; the violence and chaos that characterized the birth of Iraqi democracy reduced the attractiveness of the democratic model in the region. This mixed record does not justify the blood and treasure expended by the United States in Iraq.

When assessing the war's effects on the "old" agenda of American interests in the Middle East, the balance sheet is even more negative. In the five years since the war, oil prices have climbed to historic highs, with palpable effects on the American and the world economies. The American victory in Iraq did not jump-start the Arab-Israeli peace process. To the contrary, the years following the war saw the strengthening of forces opposed to peace in the Palestinian camp and an absence of any real negotiations on final status issues. Iran's influence in the region grew notably in the aftermath of the war, creating a whole new set of problems for the United States, Israel, and America's Arab allies.

It is hard to avoid the conclusion that the Iraq War was a major strategic blunder for the United States in achieving its interests in the Middle East.

5 THE IRAQ WAR AND THE STATE OF THE U.S. MILITARY

Michael E. O'Hanlon

How have the U.S. armed forces fared after a half-dozen years of intensive operations in Iraq and vicinity? Answering this question is important for understanding the net effects of the Iraq War on American security. It is even more important for knowing how much longer we can sustain the current effort, or anything close to it in scale and intensity.

As a nation, never have we asked so much of so few for so long. As such, the strain on soldiers and marines must be constantly tracked as we reach decisions about how long to sustain roughly thirteen to fourteen brigades in Iraq (the number with which we began 2009), how much to increase our forces in Afghanistan, and how much faster we should increase the overall size of our standing army and Marine Corps (if that is even possible).

In fact, to date, our military has held up reasonably well under the immense strain. By most measures of quality, it is still looking roughly comparable to the early years of the Reagan buildup—if not necessarily as strong and healthy as its typical state of the late Reagan years or the 1990s. Of course there have been huge individual sacrifices, and for many soldiers and marines and their families, things are not good at all. We owe these people more than we can ever say, more than we can ever repay. But at a strategic level, while it would be unrealistic and imprudent to imagine increasing the U.S. presence in Afghanistan faster than we reduce it in Iraq, the state of the force is not so bad as to necessitate an immediate change in our war-fighting approaches.

In this regard, to be as straightforward and clear as possible, I believe that those who argue that the U.S. Army and Marine Corps are now "broken" because of the strains of recent wars are simply wrong. A broken military would not have been able to carry out one of the most remarkable military comebacks in American history in Iraq in 2007–8, by any reasonable definition of the word "broken," to put it plainly. Those who argue in more nuanced fashion that the strains on the force are risky and could still lead to major readiness crises in the future, or that the human costs of the war on American soldiers and marines (not to mention Iraqis) have been excessive and unwarranted, can make reasonable arguments. And those worried about our ability to respond elsewhere also have ample evidence to make their case that Iraq has represented a huge opportunity cost. But those who go so far as to claim the U.S. military today has been rendered fundamentally less capable than before, and to argue that it is now combat "unready" as a result of its recent deployments, cannot sustain that position with available data.

Reaching this provisional verdict on the effects of the Iraq War on the U.S. military is of course not the same thing as commending the Bush administration for its conduct of the war. Nor is it tantamount to saying that the net effects of Operation Iraqi Freedom have been positive for the American ground forces. In fact, when examining how the U.S. armed forces, and particularly the ground forces, have been affected by the last half-dozen years of war, the strains and risks that have been incurred need to be weighed very heavily in any analysis—they have been enormous. That said, there has also been tremendous learning as a result of the wars. A net verdict on how the fighting has affected the overall quality and caliber of the American military is complicated to reach.

The most important area of strain on the military is in its personnel. While there are equipment shortages and maintenance depot queues of equipment due to the ongoing wars, Congress has been sufficiently generous with supplemental appropriations that these situations are not dire. And while normal training patterns for soldiers and marines have been badly disrupted by Iraq and Afghanistan, there can be little doubt that the overall battle toughness of these forces is robust. As of this writing in late 2008, the combat forces were holding up acceptably well at a strategic level despite these strains. But the costs on individuals have been enormous. The strategic risk of having so much of the force committed to one place for so long has been quite considerable. And the ongoing concern that the military may not be able to withstand the current pace and intensity of operations for as long as the war lasts remains a foreboding worry for American national security decision makers.

In short, even if it appears that the strain is tolerable at the moment, future developments could force a change in that assessment. We are definitely running risks, in terms of scenarios we could not easily handle and in terms of the underlying health of the all-volunteer military, that could wind up coming to haunt us. As such, this chapter's bottom line must by necessity be somewhat inconclusive; we will not in fact be sure of just how the Iraq War has affected our military for at least a few more years, and probably more.

This chapter proceeds as follows. It first assesses the broad state of American military readiness today, examining equipment, personnel, and training. Most effects of the Iraq War on these three categories of readiness as traditionally defined are negative. But of course the Iraq War has battle-hardened the force, led to demonstrable improvements in military performance in counterinsurgency and stabilization missions, created a generation of war veterans who will command the American military at varying levels for decades to come, and disabused the American national security establishment of any faddish or facile infatuation with technology while sobering many of those who believed too simplistically that a revolution in military affairs was radically changing warfare.

These benefits of the war merit acknowledgment and serious scrutiny. They are real and significant. And under certain hypothetical future conditions—say, a partial collapse of Pakistan that occurred several years after the most intense phase of the Iraq War had ended—the benefits of having a battle-hardened force trained and tested in stabilization operations could wind up benefiting the United States enormously. In such a place, the United States would not have the luxury of learning on the job as it has in Iraq, or taking three to four years to get its doctrine right. Pakistan's nuclear arsenal would require that any such operation (presumably conducted with the cooperation of at least part of Pakistan's own armed forces as well as other coalition partners) be successful quickly. Some of the key ingredients of the progress in Iraq—the Sunni Awakening, changes in intra-Shi'a politics such as the ceasefires promulgated by Moktada al-Sadr, de-Ba'thification reform and its positive implications for the security forces—were of course specific to that country in their detailed application and implications. But the broad principles of counterinsurgency that were honed in addressing these challenges are of much wider applicability. They include the discriminant and restrained use of force in situations involving innocent civilians, efforts to distinguish "reconciliables" from "irreconciliables" and trying to work with the former where possible (even when they are former adversaries), and the use of American troops to help provide day-to-day security for indigenous populations in partnership with local security forces.

But there are also circumstances in which the military's current commitment to Iraq (and Afghanistan) could greatly hurt the nation. If another major operation were required in the next couple of years, for example, the United States would not have the available ground forces to conduct it on short notice.

This conclusion needs to be put in perspective, however. As Secretary of Defense Robert Gates underscored on September 29, 2008, in a speech at the National Defense University in Washington, DC, the U.S. Air Force and Navy have considerable residual power for many additional contingencies that could arise—be they in Korea, the Taiwan Strait, the Persian Gulf, or elsewhere. These military tools would admittedly be of limited use in some scenarios, such as an operation to stop a genocide in Africa or help stabilize a deteriorating situation in Kashmir or northwestern Pakistan or Southeast Asia. But most such scenarios are either very unlikely to occur, or unlikely to require U.S. military forces to address, or likely to be of less strategic importance to the United States than the wars it is currently fighting. Finally, in a truly grave national crisis, the U.S. ground forces do in fact have several divisions' worth of force structure and equipment that would be deployable within perhaps one to three months of a decision to use them. This would only be possible by asking American troops to make an even more extraordinary sacrifice than they have to date. But in a dire national emergency there is little doubt that they could respond.

Overall, the message here is nuanced. The wars have placed immense strains on the force, but they have not broken the army or Marine Corps in any colloquial or technical sense of the word. There is a chance that could change in the next year or two. But given the expected drawdown in Iraq (likely to be faster and deeper than any buildup in Afghanistan), the chances are high that in strategic and institutional terms at least, the U.S. military will survive these wars and remain quite strong.

MILITARY READINESS AND THE IRAQ WAR

The question of military readiness is a critically important matter in many national security debates and in many American political debates as well.

Readiness has often been a political football. In the 1970s, America's military was alleged—in large part correctly—to have gone "hollow." A substantial force structure existed, but it was not particularly strong within, and it did not hold up very well when called upon to perform. During the mid- to late 1990s, similar allegations about the U.S. military were made as the armed forces were downsized in the aftermath of the cold war.[1] In the first decade of the twenty-first century, as the Iraq and Afghanistan missions have continued relentlessly, many have spoken of a U.S. Army that has become broken.

What do terms like "hollow" and "broken" even mean in the context of military preparedness? And what does "readiness" itself mean?

Readiness refers to prompt and immediate-response capability. It is defined by the Joint Chiefs of Staff as the ability of the armed forces to deploy quickly and perform initially in any military contingencies as they were designed to do.[2]

Readiness is just one of several military planning concerns that strategists and policymakers must emphasize. They also need to worry about longer-term development of military capabilities relevant to expected future threats. Such long-term planning (for what some call "long-term readiness," though that is a confusing use of terminology that is best avoided) can compete with near-term ability to carry out key functions—or readiness. Emphasizing the latter requires lots of money and time for training, for spare parts and fuel and ammunition, for focus on threats or military missions that are already recognized as important. Emphasizing the longer-term, by contrast, tends to require more money and time devoted to research and development, to professional military education, and to experimentation with new war-fighting concepts and technologies.[3]

Short-term readiness can be in competition with long-term preparedness. Dollars spent on R&D cannot be spent on fuel or ammunition; officers' time devoted to running future-oriented exercises and experiments is not available for drilling forces for near-term missions; units trying out new concepts are not as able to practice on more immediate tasks or potential tasks.

Readiness for one mission can also compete with readiness for another. The Balkans wars were seen as distractions from "real" war-fighting priorities and readiness requirements in the 1990s, since formal war plans were more focused on northeast Asia and the Persian Gulf. The Afghanistan war was not anticipated or planned very well before it occurred, in part because of the preoccupation with what were considered more immediate threats requiring that readiness efforts be focused on them. The U.S. military prepared much better for the invasion phase of the Iraq War than for the post-invasion phase, suggesting that readiness considerations had emphasized classic invasion scenarios at the expense of counterinsurgency and stabilization missions. And in the last few years, the ledger has shifted, with the constant preparation for ongoing operations in Iraq and Afghanistan dominating the time and attention of soldiers and marines to the detriment of training for other missions.

Even once one defines readiness fairly narrowly and leaves broader strategic issues for separate debate and analysis, there are challenges in assessing it. The military is always short of certain capabilities as defined by its doctrine and its process for determining military "requirements." How much does one shortfall matter, in a given area of personnel or equipment or training, when other capabilities and other resources are robust? Just as with the debate over metrics in Iraq, it is always possible to find readiness metrics that make a predetermined political case—that seem to suggest that the military is either in fine shape, or by contrast that it is falling apart. It is for such reasons that Richard Betts, a Columbia University professor, subtitled one chapter in his seminal book on the subject of readiness "lies, damn lies, and readiness statistics."[4]

The most dependable way to evaluate readiness is of course real enemies. War is always a major learning experience, and a great judge of capability. Naturally, however, this is not a reliable or desirable way to assess readiness. The downsides are obvious—the possibility of suffering a major defeat before learning what went wrong, not to mention the inherent costs in blood and treasure of combat under any circumstances. But it is still true that the United States employs its military often enough that real operations are significant sources of information and important barometers of preparedness.

A few examples from the American experience of the last three decades can illuminate key issues. In 1980, the United States failed to rescue hostages in Iran, and lost eight servicemen, when an accident during refueling in the Iranian desert led to the cancellation of the mission. Poor coordination among the different military services involved and lack of realistic training may have contributed to the tragedy. In Lebanon in 1983, the U.S. military learned about the importance of force protection, and the difficulty of maintaining neutrality during a peacekeeping mission, when the marine barracks were bombed. In short, it found out it was not ready to protect its forces against the types of threats that presented themselves on that battlefield (which of course foreshadowed the types of suicide truck bombings that became tragically commonplace in the ensuing quarter century). The Kosovo War in 1999 was impressive in many ways and debunked the notion that the U.S. military had somehow been rendered hollow by its post-cold war downsizing. But it also revealed how immobile the army was, when it tried to send a modest number of Apache helicopters to nearby Albania. The Iraq War required major learning, or relearning of past lessons since forgotten, about counterinsurgency operations, with the U.S. military more impressive from 2007 on than in the earlier years of the war.[5]

More positively, in the 1986 bombing of Libya, as well as the 1989 invasion of Panama, Ronald Reagan's military buildup was at least partially vindicated as U.S. forces (and equipment) performed impressively. In the Panama case, improvements in military command and control instituted in the 1986 Goldwater-Nichols act helped ensure a well-directed mission as well.

Waiting for the next war to evaluate a new readiness initiative or take stock of what traditional efforts have accomplished is, however, not a preferred, or a reliable, way to evaluate readiness. As such, other more mundane methods must be employed. They typically begin with dividing the subject into three broad categories: personnel, training, and equipment. Within each of these three umbrella groupings, one can then break things down further. One can look at different subcategories of troops and of various types of military specialists, assessing the capabilities of each key subunit. One can do similar things when evaluating training for various units, as well as the availability and condition of equipment—not only major vehicles but also spare parts and ammunition.

Consider first military personnel matters. Key measures of personnel readiness include the experience and aptitude of typical troops, the availability of individuals with critical specialized skills, and the ability of the military to recruit new members as well as to retain those already in. By 2008, concerns about recruiting trends had begun to be mitigated, as an improving situation in Iraq, shorter tours, and alas a weaker civilian economy combined to make the job of military recruiters easier than it had been for several years.[6]

In recent times, there has been considerable concern in some quarters about a lowering of personnel standards. For example, the military has accepted more recruits with general equivalency degrees (GEDs) rather than high school diplomas; it has enlisted a higher percentage of applicants scoring very low on its aptitude tests; and it has also taken on more individuals over forty years old as first-time military personnel.

Army trends for age and GED degrees have begun to cause considerable concern in the last year or two—though the nature of the problem needs to be kept in perspective. The GED is considered academically equivalent to a high school diploma, and certainly the military can ensure that anyone with such qualifications is up to par by testing them in other ways, too. Moreover, as of 2005, 90 percent of Department of Defense recruits continued to have high school diplomas, comparable to the 1985 figure at the height of the Reagan buildup. And the typical recruit scored better on the Armed Forces Qualification Test (AFQT) in 2005 than in 1985. That said, while figures for the other services have remained good, the army has experienced some problems, with the high school graduation figure for 2005 dipping to about 80 percent (worse than the 1985 figure of 86 percent, though still much better than the typical level of about 55 percent of the 1970s).[7] By 2007, the percentage of high school graduates had declined to slightly more than the 70 percent norm of the 1970s, suggesting a trendline that does need to be arrested and reversed.[8] Thankfully, the figure was back up to 83 percent by 2008.[9]

Recently, there has been a rumor that West Point graduates have been leaving the service at drastically increased rates as soon as their minimal obligations are satisfied. In fact, this appears not to be true. The last year for which data is available as of this writing (the class of 2002, which was eligible to leave the service as of 2007), showed a 68 percent reenlistment rate, only 4 percentage points below the 1990s average.[10] More generally, company grade officers (first and second lieutenants as well as captains) have not been leaving the force at a greater than normal rate either; the average rate during the Iraq War has been less than the average rate of the late 1990s, for example.[11] A similar conclusion is true of majors.[12] Nonetheless, the army is now short several thousand officers in aggregate.[13] This is largely because the army is increasing the number of officers needed as it enlarges the number of brigades in its force structure. In addition, the army did not enlist enough young officers in the early 1990s, meaning that the current pool of officers from which to recruit for midlevel positions is too small.[14]

On another matter, while the number of individuals scoring relatively high on aptitude tests remains better than the 1980s, trends are in the wrong direction.[15] Moral waivers for matters such as criminal history have increased substantially in recent years, with a total of 860 soldiers and marines requiring waivers from convictions for felony crimes in 2007, up by 400 from just the year before. While most of the convictions were for juvenile theft, and the aggregate total is modest compared with the size of the force, only by arresting such trends will the quality of the force be ensured.[16] Again, figures for 2008 were improved, though not yet where they ideally should be.[17]

The most serious issues concern the human costs of war on individuals. There have been many tragedies. These represent huge sacrifices for the people involved, to whom the nation owes a huge debt. And the benefits of the Iraq War may not have been worth these sacrifices. But the key point is that, to date at least, these humanitarian travesties do not add up to a broken military. Most troublesome trends within the ranks of the army and Marine Corps have stabilized in the last couple of years, albeit at higher levels of divorce, suicide, psychological stress, and other such personal tragedies than were experienced before the recent wars.

To be specific, military personnel divorce rates have leveled off somewhat at about 3.5 percent per year, after reaching 3.9 percent in 2004. They are not worse than in the general population, but they are still above the 2.9 percent level of 2003, and they are far greater than they should be.[18] Nevertheless, it is hard to view them as evidence of a military that is going hollow. Rather, they are more appropriately viewed as evidence of a force under very serious strain, but one that is holding together nonetheless, at least for the moment.

Suicide rates reached 17.3 per 100,000 soldiers in the U.S. Army in 2006. This is not far off from the age-adjusted and gender-adjusted average for the U.S. population on the whole (for males, for example, the rate is 17.6 per 100,000), but still much higher than the rate of 9.1 per 100,000 soldiers in 2001. Again, the data are best viewed as reflecting far too many individual human tragedies, and as suggesting an overall military under significant strain—but not as proof of any vicious spiral in which an already bad situation is exponentially worsening. They provide reason for serious worry, but not necessarily for a precipitous strategic action such as premature withdrawal from Iraq.[19]

For one group of soldiers surveyed in 2008, among those who had been to Iraq on three or four separate tours, the fraction displaying signs of post-traumatic stress disorders was 27 percent (in contrast to 12 percent after one tour and 18.5 percent after two). As of early 2008, among the 513,000 active-duty soldiers who have served in Iraq, more than 197,000 had served more than once, and more than 53,000 had deployed three or more times.[20] This is further reason to try to wind the wars down soon. Multiple deployments are worse than single deployments for those who have to carry them out, in more than just the obvious ways. But this situation is probably not sufficient reason to greatly increase the risk of strategic defeat, if another year or two of relative patience can substantially reduce the odds of such an outcome.

There are precedents for the above problems in the army. For example, in the late 1990s there was a shortage of Air Force pilots of more than 10 percent, as no-fly zones over Iraq taxed airmen and airwomen's patience, and high pay rates in the civilian economy enticed many of them to take off their uniforms. This would clearly have been a problem for any operation requiring a large fraction of the force structure, such as a major war; through careful monitoring of the deployment burdens of various units and individuals, however, it was at least temporarily manageable for the challenges of the 1990s. In addition, certain other military specialties were overused, and certain individuals were overdeployed, because the force structure had not been properly constructed for frequent midscale deployments. There were shortages of certain "low density/high demand" military specialties. On top of that, some units were undermanned and had to be reinforced by individuals borrowed from other units when preparing to deploy. This was acceptable on the whole, but led to situations where some people were deployed with a different unit than their own.[21] If their own unit was itself later deployed, the same person might wind up deploying abroad twice in a relatively short time; the military personnel system did not protect them from such inadvertent overuse. This was more a matter of fairness to military personnel, and sustainment of good morale, than a crisis for war-fighting readiness, but it was important to address just the same. Again, the moral of the story is that not all problems with military readiness are of equal concern, though most merit attention and remedial action.

In response to the above cases, therefore, targeted policy interventions usually occurred. For example, pilot bonuses were increased.[22] In addition, in some cases a higher level of future attrition was simply assumed to be likely (especially at a time when a strong civilian economy created many high-paying commercial jobs for pilots), and more military pilots were recruited and trained to compensate. Recruiting and advertising budgets, as well as the number of personnel assigned to the recruiting task, can also be varied; in fact, there is a fairly detailed econometric literature on just how well each type of policy tool tends to work historically (in terms of increasing recruiting or retention per dollar spent).

Additional remedial steps can be considered as well. More military specialties can be rewarded with differential, added pay (rather than linking compensation so linearly to military rank). Because military pay, while never truly enough to compensate those who actively risk their lives for their country, is nonetheless reasonably good by comparison with private sector jobs for individuals of comparable age, experience, and education in the U.S. military, the idea of selective bonuses for certain specialties would seem reasonable. (This is true even without counting retirement pay and noncash benefits in the comparison, which tend to be greater for the military than the private sector.) Equity and fairness considerations need not preclude such an approach of selective, targeted raises and bonuses.[23]

It is also possible to consider modifying military pension plans. The military retirement system is essentially an "all or nothing" operation. Stay in for twenty years and become fully vested and immediately eligible for full benefits; stay in a day less and receive nothing. This approach probably hurts retention for those considering whether to stay in the military as they approach five to ten years of service. That is the period when another few years of military employment promises no accrued pension benefits whatsoever (unless personnel wind up staying the full twenty years), yet when private sector jobs generally would begin to vest them quickly. These types of reforms may be considered simply as a matter of fairness, or of keeping up with the times and the changing nature of the American economy. Yet they may not be given sufficient attention absent a problem in readiness that motivates innovation.[24]

A specific word is in order about the reserve component. In the middle of the decade, Army National Guard forces in particular were used heavily in Iraq and Afghanistan, leading many soldiers to wonder if they had made a good decision to join the reserve component. Since then, however, the use of the reserve component has been reduced substantially, with only one or two brigades at a time deployed of late. Given the ongoing increase in the number of brigades found within the active force (due to the army's restructuring program), and the expected reductions in U.S. military deployments abroad over the coming two years, it should be possible to avoid another "surge" in reserve deployments—and thus to minimize the danger of a deterioration of effective recruiting and retention within the Army National Guard, Army Reserve, and Marine Corps Reserve.

Moving to the subject of training, in the Vietnam and immediate post-Vietnam eras, preparation for combat was not nearly rigorous enough. But great attention was focused on this matter in the 1980s, demanding regimens were developed, resources were amply provided for training, and subsequent military performance was seen to improve greatly. Ever since that period,

Reagan-era benchmarks have remained important in determining proper standards by which forces should be trained—from basic training to specialized training to unit training at main bases to large-formation training at the various weapons schools and combat-training centers.

There are still questions and issues in regard to training, however. One concerns the growing role of simulators. As flight simulators and even tank simulators become much more realistic, to what extent can they replace the need for true training? Military personnel need to work with real weapons, realistic (if simulated) battle spaces, and real ammunition—not only at a technical level, but to acclimate people to the pressures and the fear of combat. That said, do we really know for a fact that tank crews need eight hundred miles a year of driving their vehicles (rather than six hundred, with many more hours on simulators)? Or that pilots need twenty to twenty-four hours in the air per month, the late cold-war norm, rather than today's fourteen to eighteen?[25] These questions underscore the degree to which tracking readiness cannot be purely a technical or an accounting exercise. Judgment is always needed, and as such mistakes are always possible (and sometimes they are not appreciated until a force engages in actual combat). One reasonable guideline is that we should be wary about making rapid, major changes in how we train, absent periodic validation under stressful, realistic circumstances (such as actual wartime operations) that combat skills are remaining strong.

The army and Marine Corps have faced another problem during the Iraq and Afghanistan wars. Soldiers and marines have virtually no time to do anything more than deploy to the theater of combat, return, rest, and then prepare to go back. Generalized training in other types of combat, besides the counterinsurgency and counterterrorism now being carried out in Iraq and Afghanistan, is by necessity being neglected. The assumption is that forces who performed so brilliantly in classic combat in 2003, and who have been so hardened by ongoing combat of a different type since then, will remain proficient for the full range of possible missions for the foreseeable future even without the full range of training as required by official doctrine. But that is an assumption, not an obvious truth. The assumption can be periodically tested by asking modest numbers of troops to be subjected to tough assessments of their skills in other types of combat on the training ranges (even if there is not enough time or there are not enough resources to do so for most formations). But again, there is a level of uncertainty with measuring readiness that is hard to eliminate entirely.

A final issue in training is that it must accurately anticipate the types of fighting American forces may have to conduct. In this sense, the Iraq War has helped reveal huge gaps in preparation that have been largely remedied as a result.

Moving on to equipment, combat units clearly need vehicles in working order, enough ammunition to fight for a reasonable time, and enough spare parts to fill projected demands. The question is not just instantaneous readiness, but ability to sustain operations for some reasonable period.

What is a reasonable period, however? Wars often last longer (or less long) than expected. In addition, assumptions about how long we will have to deploy forces before being obliged to employ them are also scenario-dependent, meaning that readiness metrics for strategic transportation assets and the like are difficult to determine with complete precision.

All things considered, assessing equipment readiness is in the end probably easier than doing so for people or even training. It is generally a question of countable hardware, not human skills. The chief challenge is in assessing the importance of a situation in which equipment inventories drop by a certain moderate amount—say 10 to 15 percent relative to nominal requirements of "mission capable" aircraft or tanks or trucks or ships. At what point does the cohesion of a tank unit suffer in that case, for example? This type of question is particularly hard for larger and more complex units. But everything from training operations to past combat experience provides some guidance, so there is a basis for constructing rules of thumb about "acceptable" and unacceptable levels of shortfall.

In the broadest terms, the wars in Iraq and Afghanistan would NOT seem to have created huge equipment problems for the army. For most major types of vehicles—all classes of helicopters, Abrams tanks and Bradley fighting vehicles, medium-weight trucks—no more than 20 percent of the total inventory has been in the Central Command theater at a time (according to Congressional Budget Office data published in 2007). For some types of equipment, especially new systems, deployment fractions were higher—21 percent for the Stryker medium-weight wheeled combat vehicle, about 25 percent for most heavy trucks, and a whopping 99 percent for up-armored HMMWVs. In addition, the usage rates for these vehicles, while high compared to peacetime norms, were modest compared with their original designs (which envisioned sustained maneuver warfare with much greater amounts of flying and driving). Moreover, by 2007, the Iraq and Afghanistan operations had been ongoing for a sufficiently long period that the army (and presumably the Marine Corps) had found ways to maintain equipment and refurbish it fairly rapidly as it cycled back to the United States (about two-thirds of equipment, worth about $20 billion in aggregate at any given time, does cycle in and out of the combat theater with the unit operating it). For most major fighting vehicles and helicopters, there was no shortage of usable equipment for forces based back in the United States. There *were* notable shortfalls of Strykers and two of seven types of trucks; on the latter point, the degree to which one type of truck could be substituted for another in the event of a new crisis or conflict elsewhere is hard to determine (but there were substantial surpluses in some of the other five categories of trucks, so it is likely some substitution could occur). On balance, it seems safe to conclude that while Iraq and Afghanistan have taxed the equipment inventories of the U.S. ground forces in particular, the far greater strain at this point is on people, not weaponry.[26]

THE POSITIVE ASPECTS OF THE IRAQ EXPERIENCE FOR THE U.S. MILITARY

As tragic as the Iraq War has been in so many ways for so many people, the cold and hard facts of the matter are that militaries exist to fight wars (or at least, to be able to fight them so as to deter conflict) and that they improve by practicing their profession. Training and exercises can be made very realistic to allow many skills to be honed even without fighting. But they cannot create the toughness that comes from surviving combat, and they cannot test skills that the military has failed to establish as training and combat priorities.

Such was the fate of most counterinsurgency and stabilization mission skills until the nation was a couple of years or more into the Iraq conflict. They simply had not been top priorities for the American armed forces. Whatever the lessons of Vietnam may be for others, one of the key lessons of Vietnam for the U.S. military was to avoid counterinsurgency operations. Of course, it was this same tendency that helped cause the frustrations experienced by the United States in Vietnam, since it went into that conflict with an army focused on large-scale battle in Europe rather than the type of combat that was necessary for success in Southeast Asia. But after eight years of frustration in Vietnam, rather than decide to emphasize such missions for possible future operations of similar ilk, the U.S. military reverted to its preferred focus on high-intensity or large-scale combat operations. Desert Storm was the kind of fight it wanted; so was the invasion of Iraq. But a lengthy stabilization campaign was not. This tendency, however mistaken, was at least somewhat understandable during the cold war, when a large Soviet adversary needed to be checked. But it persisted thereafter. And the peace operations of the 1990s in the Balkans in particular, as demanding as they were in many ways, did not truly change this mentality because they did not involve ground combat.[27]

The Afghanistan campaign started to change things, but not fast enough to help much in an Iraq War that began only eighteen months after the first shots were fired in the Afghan theater. Moreover, the Afghan campaign created a new model of warfare in which very modest numbers of American troops could work with foreign partners and leverage high technology to achieve remarkable success, especially in the war's opening months. This was not a model that could be easily translated to Iraq, however, so the benefits of the experience were limited as an educational and teaching tool for the U.S. armed forces.

The Iraq mission gradually forced the American military to adapt, and it is a much different organization than it was only half-dozen years ago. The learning process began with operations by forces commanded by the likes of General Peter Chiarelli in Baghdad in 2004 and Colonel H. R. McMaster in Tall'Afar in northern Iraq in 2005. It accelerated as then Lt. Gen. David Petraeus and others wrote a revised U.S. Army/Marine Corps manual on counterinsurgency back in the United States in 2006.[28] It culminated of course in the so-called surge of 2007–8 in Iraq. That surge should be understood not simply as an increase in American force levels in Iraq, but as a change in basic approach and strategy. While it did benefit greatly from the Sunni Awakening, the al-Sadr ceasefire, and other developments in Iraq, none of these would have worked absent a new focus on protecting the Iraqi population through the combined and concerted efforts of American and Iraqi security forces.[29] That conceptual reorientation of the military mission in Iraq took four or five years to happen. Once it had, the American military arguably became the world's best at so-called low-intensity conflict or counterinsurgency and counterterrorism operations, overtaking the British and Israeli armed forces (which revealed their respective limits in Basra, Iraq, and Lebanon in recent years) in this type of military operation.

Becoming much better, and even arguably the world's best, hardly guarantees future mission success of course. As of late 2008, the war in Afghanistan was demonstrably not going well. America's improved counterinsurgency capabilities were not adequate to compensate for a small and weak Afghan army, a sanctuary for resistance fighters in Pakistan, a resource-deprived and ineffective central Afghan government, and inadequate troop numbers from outside powers that when combined with the limited capacity of the Afghan army and police made for a fundamentally inadequate force posture. U.S. forces have not become miracle workers who can defy the laws of physics or of basic counterinsurgency. In addition, many top-level officers have been resistant to the breakthroughs evident in Iraq and to the corresponding lessons of that progress. Should such officers again gain the upper hand in American defense planning, the lessons of Iraq could be largely lost. But on balance, throughout the officer corps and much of the enlisted ranks, the American ground forces today are enormously more capable of effective counterinsurgency than they were a half-dozen years ago.

Beyond this broad change in attitude, priorities, and capabilities, there have been a few other specific benefits from the Iraq experience as well. For one thing, American military vehicles are now much more survivable against weapons like improvised explosive devices. Up-armored HMMWVs and mine-resistant ambush-protected vehicles (MRAPs) are now found by the many thousands in the American military.[30] Prior to the Iraq War, they were not. In fact, prior to Iraq, the emphasis of the army and Marine Corps had been on making American combat vehicles lighter, more easily deployable, and more dependent on sensor technology to avoid taking the first shot (rather than taking the traditional approach of relying on armor to help survive such shots). The theory behind this move toward lighter ground forces was always subject to question, given the prevalence of simple explosive devices on many of the world's battlefields (as in Lebanon and elsewhere) and the limited ability of sensor technologies to detect incoming weapons in time to counter them in the confines of many battlefield environments.[31] The Iraq War settled the debate, however, or at least redefined it to a considerable extent.

The Iraq War has also given at least some added impetus to creating or expanding a number of other capabilities for the American military and the U.S. government more broadly. Translators are being hired in greater numbers. The role of private military contractors is being refined and better regulated. State Department capabilities for aiding in stabilization and reconstruction operations are being expanded at least modestly.

What is the overall magnitude of these learning experiences? Have they been lessons at the margin, or more fundamental and significant? The evidence points toward the latter interpretation, at least for the style and type of fighting witnessed in Iraq. Simply put, the United States was clearly losing a war for four years that, together with its Iraqi partners, it is now not losing (even if it was not yet demonstrably winning as of late 2008). Iraqi civilian fatality rates were down 75 percent from their immediate presurge levels; ethnic cleansing was down by an even greater amount; local ceasefires were multiplying in Iraq and beginning to give impetus to top-down political compromise as well (reflected as of mid-2008 in major recent progress on budget, pension, amnesty, and provincial powers laws, and potential progress on de-Ba'thification reform). Improvements in American military doctrine and associated performance do not explain all of this progress. But they surely explain a good deal of it and were a necessary element in producing the changed Iraqi environment. To give one more concrete example, while the Sunni Awakening produced many new American allies in places such as al-Anbar Province, the systematic street-by-street and house-by-house actions to roll up al Qaeda cells (and other extremists) required the active cooperation of American military units and Iraqi Security Forces with Awakening Movement fighters. The latter (totaling less than one hundred thousand nationwide) simply did not have the necessary numbers or capabilities to do these sorts of jobs on their own.

CONCLUSION

The Iraq War revealed huge gaps in American military preparedness that have been largely remedied by this point. Whether it is too late to salvage an acceptable outcome in Iraq remains unclear (though there seemed to be ample grounds for hopefulness as of this writing in late 2008). But what the American military has learned it will not forget, and will be of potentially great utility in any future wars involving counterinsurgency, counterterrorism, stabilization, and/or peacekeeping operations.

The U.S. armed forces in general, and the army in particular, may have been allowed the luxury of forgetting how to do these sorts of tasks after Vietnam (if indeed it ever really internalized the basic precepts in the first place). At that moment in history the greater threat remained the unlikely but still plausible possibility of direct conflict against the Soviet Union. Today, with the broader challenges of weak states and terrorist extremism so vivid and so directly threatening to America's interests, it will not be allowed to forget. Nor will it likely want to, since its performance of late in Iraq has been extraordinary, and the outcome there—whatever its character—will likely be much better than it would have otherwise been as a result. In short, even if the overall legacy of the Iraq War is mixed, as seems quite likely, the American military will probably have much to be proud of and will probably see the war in a much more positive overall light than it remembers the Vietnam experience (even if it will likely see it in a worse light than the nation's victories in the world wars).

There are specific circumstances in which the Iraq War could wind up being a clear net negative or net positive for the American military and American national security in general. If war with Iran or North Korea occurs in the next couple of years through no fault (or choice) of the United States—perhaps even because leaders in Tehran or Pyongyang sense an opportunity due to the U.S. commitments in Iraq and Afghanistan—our ongoing presence in Iraq will likely slow any response by ground forces substantially and limit our feasible options even once we do respond. In this situation, Iraq will have clearly cost us. If by contrast a country like Pakistan begins to collapse, and does so *after* most U.S. troops are home from Iraq, the war in the Persian Gulf may wind up having helped us by greatly strengthening our capacities for counterinsurgency, counterterrorism, and stabilization missions.

Leaving aside such very specific (and relatively unlikely) scenarios, what can we say from a broader perspective? To put it bluntly, is the clear improvement in the American military that has resulted from Iraq (and Afghanistan) worth the cost?

That cost should be measured principally in lives lost and permanently compromised (through physical or mental disability, divorce, and other such effects). The other costs from the Iraq War to the military—measured in terms of equipment damaged, training hours squandered, or good military personnel lost from the force due to the excessive operational tempo they experienced while in uniform—are real but not nearly as great. Most are being addressed reasonably well in real time due to the wartime supplementals. And the decisions of many good people not to reenlist (or join the military in the first place), while regrettable, has not yet reached historically unusual proportions.

What is the bottom line? There is no way to say for sure because it depends on how much future demands on the American military will allow us to make use of the lessons learned in Iraq. An investment paid in so much blood has to be measured against the lives saved and blood not spilt in future conflicts, as well as the broader benefits to the nation as a whole. Since these possible future wars have not yet been fought, or even identified, we cannot yet know.

In attempting to offer an answer to the question, we need to reach an estimate of the likelihood of future wars of great significance to the nation requiring those skills that have been developed in the sands along the Tigris and Euphrates. The above-noted Pakistan scenario is one possibility; numerous others could be imagined, not only in Iran but even in the West Bank (after a Mideast peace accord), or Saudi Arabia (after a coup), or Kashmir (after an Indo-Pakistani peace deal on terms that presently seem very unlikely), or elsewhere.

To justify the investment of so many American lives, such a military operation would have to be important indeed. If it could truly consolidate an end to the Arab-Israeli conflict, or help remove Kashmir as a possible spark of all-out war between the two nuclear powers of South Asia, or stabilize a country like Saudi Arabia that provides 15 percent of the world's oil, it might reach that threshold of importance. Most other missions, in my eyes, would not. In other words, however much our risks of failure in a hypothetical future stabilization mission in Somalia or Yemen or Bangladesh or even Indonesia might be mitigated by the Iraq experience, the stakes are not high enough to justify the losses we have suffered over the past half-dozen years in Iraq—at least not when evaluated in this way.

However, these are my subjective views. Others can reasonably disagree. Whatever our present thinking, though, we will presumably someday know the real answer to the question, since in ten or twenty years we will know how the Iraq experience affected our military's performance in the wars and other missions that may have followed.

For now, the one concrete conclusion that can be hazarded is that, given the state of our military today, we should surely get out of Iraq as soon as we reasonably can. At the same time, we need not feel that the U.S. armed forces are so near collapse as to require an immediate and rapid withdrawal regardless of the situation on the ground. With rather high confidence, we can conclude that they are not.

6 THE INTERNATIONAL POLITICAL COSTS OF THE IRAQ WAR

Thomas G. Weiss

Whether September 11, 2001, marked a paradigm shift in international relations, George W. Bush administration's ensuing so called war on terror, and especially its catastrophic pursuit of the Iraq War, have taken a heavy toll. This chapter pays special attention to the often overlooked international political price exacted by the American invasion and occupation of Iraq. Given the ledger's mammoth debit, the administration of Barack Obama faces a bumpy initial road in its foreign relations, but the damage is not irreparable. Indeed, friends and even foes are keen to have Washington resume its leadership role on the world stage. During the honeymoon, President Obama and his team can and must navigate future foreign policy shoals and ameliorate the damage wrought by the Bush administration's mishandling of Iraq.

A state's prestige, moral authority, and overall standing in the world are palpable assets in the pursuit of its national security and foreign policies. In a globalizing world, they can affect, among other things, whether its policies and actions are supported or sabotaged—as the tragic attacks of September 11 demonstrated dramatically. Nearly every country in the world lined up in solidarity behind the United States as it responded to the shocking assaults on its territory. There was a comforting ring to the September 12 headline in *Le Monde*, "Nous sommes tous américains," and close to universal approval at the United Nations.

Yet initial good will and a blank check in Afghanistan disappeared virtually overnight as Washington squandered international sympathy, choosing instead to pursue a largely go-it-alone policy in Iraq after March 2003 (albeit with support from the United Kingdom). The decision alienated traditional allies and exacerbated tensions with long-standing adversaries with specific and negative implications for the war on terrorism in general and the occupation of Iraq in particular.

Since then, the United States has suffered from its unabashed unilateralism. Beginning with the massive demonstrations across the world against the war, subsequent polls suggest that the United States continually lost favor as the Bush administration boasted of its disdain for international organizations, treaties, and global public opinion. From the increasingly tepid response in traditionally allied countries, to outright hostility in the Islamic countries of Asia and the Middle East, the global public's growing distaste for American foreign policy is only part of the story. The Iraq War has inflicted political damage on the United States in numerous other respects as well. What price has the country paid for the war? In particular, what exactly has been the impact of the war on the U.S. place in world politics? Can the damage be repaired? What will it take to do so?

This chapter seeks to answer these questions. The first section analyzes the international political costs of the Iraq War in addition to the better-known economic and military ones. It should be stated at the outset that the international political costs of the Iraq War are inextricably bound up with, and often subsume, the political costs of the Bush administration's foreign policy approaches more generally. Indeed, disaggregating one from the other is a virtually impossible analytical task. The second section examines future challenges facing a multilaterally challenged United States under the new Obama administration and outlines a number of steps that could help mend Washington's threadbare reputation. The concluding section provides a dash of guarded optimism for an American return to the multilateral fold, noting that international organizations have routinely served the national security interests of the United States.

TOWARD A BALANCE SHEET

In many ways, the true costs of the Iraq War are incalculable. Even before the October 2008 global financial and economic meltdown that was linked in part to the Bush administration's mammoth debt, other aspects of the price paid by the United States will not be fully visible for some time. Fareed Zakaria's summary is apt: "The costs have been ruinously high—for Americans, for America's reputation, but especially for Iraqis."[1] This section deals first with those economic and military ones that are at least in part quantifiable. The especially difficult costs to establish, which are the real point of this chapter, are the more controversial and subjective political ones.

Costs to the U.S. Economy and Military

In strictly economic terms, the costs exacted by American actions in Iraq are obvious and dramatic. The record of spending for the war maintained by the Congressional Research Service indicates that Washington expends nearly $4,000 per second in Iraq.[2] This translates into roughly $238,000 per minute, $14 million per hour, $343 million per day, or more than $10 billion each month. If these numbers are combined with monies for ongoing operations in Afghanistan, the totals increase to nearly $5,000 per second, or nearly $12.5 billion each month to fight the Global War on Terror in these two theaters. This total is more than two and a half times the 2007–8 budget for UN peacekeeping operations, for which the total U.S. contribution is about $1 billion.[3] Yet, these figures only cover those amounts requested up-front by the president and approved by Congress.

Research conducted by Joseph Stiglitz and Linda Bilmes suggests that the actual economic costs are far greater than even these distressing-enough official government estimates.[4] First, Defense Department statistics fail to account for monies drawn from their regular operational budget to fight the war in Iraq. Second, Stiglitz and Bilmes point out that any reckoning of costs for Iraq must consider the "time value" of money spent. Given the fact that the war on terrorism has been financed through massive borrowing, dollars spent since 2003 will be paid back with less valuable dollars in the future. Finally, the residual effects of Iraq will continue to have an impact on the domestic economy above and beyond the current recession. The number of soldiers returning from Iraq who are or who will be entitled to compensation and government-administered medical care is staggering. Stiglitz and Bilmes estimate that the long-term health care benefits for returning veterans insured by the government will alone total more than $91 billion in the course of veterans' lives.

The alarming economic figures are compounded in numerous ways by the price paid by the U.S. military. First, and most important, at the outset of 2009 are the more than four thousand lost lives and some sixty-five thousand casualties exacted by the war, not to mention the untold numbers of soldiers returning from battle with shattered psyches. Second, the disastrous handling of the war has created serious difficulties for the military's efforts at attracting new recruits. A third, and not as frequently noticed, problem has been the physical deterioration of the U.S. military's material capabilities. Due to budget constraints, maintenance and replacement for worn-down and destroyed equipment have failed to keep pace with the damaging impact of battle and harsh Iraqi terrain.

Finally, significant investments of blood and treasure for the war in Iraq have the further consequence of diverting American attention and resources away from the real war on terrorism in Afghanistan. Instead of following up their successful military operations against Taliban and al Qaeda forces in fall 2001 with sustained peace-building, the Bush administration turned its sights on Saddam Hussein's Iraq. The decision to wage war against Baghdad not only created a more fertile breeding ground for international terrorism but also left the still-open wounds in Afghanistan to fester. As a result, the Taliban and al Qaeda have reestablished control of significant swathes of Afghan territory.[5] According to U.S. intelligence sources, the elected government of Hamid Karzai currently controls less than one-third of the country, raising fears that Afghanistan is slipping back into the category of failed states.

International Political Costs

Beyond the considerable economic and military costs of going to war against and then occupying Iraq, the Bush administration's decision to overthrow Saddam Hussein has taken its toll in the political realm. Most obviously, American unilateralism has significantly damaged U.S. relations with traditional allies, alienated foreign governments once sympathetic to American aims, and tarnished the United States's reputation worldwide. As James P. Rubin points out, the gap between the United States and its traditional allies "has grown dramatically in the last eight years, primarily as a result of Washington's declaration of independence from the constraints of multilateral diplomacy and its assault on a series of pending and existing international treaty regimes, such as the Kyoto Protocol, the International Criminal Court, the Anti-Ballistic Missile Treaty, the Comprehensive Test Ban Treaty, and the Biological Weapons Convention."[6]

Less apparent have been the Iraq War's deleterious effects on American foreign policy objectives in other areas. The U.S. decision in March 2003 without Security Council approval effectively marginalized the United Nations. While this produced the unintended (in some countries) consequence of lending additional legitimacy to future decisions by the Security Council—

which stood up to the hegemon and survived—it also strained U.S.–UN relations considerably. The 2005 World Summit showcased the damage.

Not only did the summit fail to significantly address issues critical to world politics, but the distractions of Iraq's occupation led to half-baked efforts to establish a Human Rights Council and the failed opportunity to initiate UN secretariat reform along with no agreement on weapons of mass destruction (WMDs), terrorism, and proliferation—all supposedly high priorities for U.S. foreign policy.[7] Taken together, the political costs of Iraq are no less significant than those on the economic and military fronts. The political costs are parsed below.

Damaged Diplomacy and Public Opinion As Edward Luck reminds us, Washington's diplomatic record conveys "mixed messages" to friends and foes alike.[8] The United States has sometimes been the prime mover for new international institutions and norms, but just as often has kept a distance or stood in the way. This historical pattern did not change after September 11, when the challenges of terrorism were cast in high relief. While perhaps some who regretted the lack of U.S. leadership in years past hoped initially that the post-9/11 political environment would trigger more initiatives and a spirit of compromise from the world's remaining superpower, they undoubtedly did not have in mind the war in Iraq.

At the same time, the Bush administration provides an anomalous contrast to the image and actions of the previous administration's "assertive multilateralism," two words not likely to be uttered in the current or a future White House. Clinton administration strikes against Afghanistan and Sudan in 1998 in response to attacks against the *USS Cole* were launched without recourse to the United Nations. The Bush administration, in contrast, went immediately to the world organization after September 11, a multilateral impulse that is usually overlooked.[9] And while the smoke was still rising from Ground Zero, the Security Council rallied behind the United States with its swift passage of Resolution 1368, reaffirming the right to self-defense under Charter Article 51 in response to terrorist acts.

When the White House extended its war on terror with talk about invading Iraq, the president surprised his neoconservative base by appealing to the United Nations. Whether this decision was motivated by tepid public support for war, resistance by the holders of the purse strings in the U.S. Congress, nudging from overseas allies, or coaxing from cabinet officials, Bush's decision to seek Security Council support before March 2003 suggests less of a predilection for unilateralism than demonstrated by the Clinton White House.[10] The president and the secretary of state, Colin Powell, worked to engage the world body, but their efforts were hardly facilitated by other members of the administration. Washington's strained relations with its European allies were weakened by Donald Rumsfeld's blunt public diplomacy. His rhetorical partition of Europe into "old" and "new" halves was received angrily by leaders in Western Europe. Rumsfeld's meaning was clear: the "old" countries of the European Union heartland were "problems" in the defense secretary's eyes because of their opposition to the war. In contrast, Rumsfeld looked eastward and found allies in a new Europe willing to confront twenty-first-century security threats as determined by Washington.

Despite Rumsfeld's slap in the face to Germany and France, his dichotomy at first appeared to be more accurate than perhaps he had intended. To many observers, two Europes had emerged. While the EU's founding members stood in solidarity against American designs on Iraq, their more recently acceded neighbors—Great Britain, Spain, Denmark, the Czech Republic, and a host of Eastern bloc nations—publicly backed the United States.

Yet a closer look suggests more nuance. Public opinion in the United Kingdom and Spain, the two countries most firmly behind Washington, was decidedly against the war. Indeed, publics throughout Western Europe, as well as those in a smattering of Eastern European countries, were unified in their opposition to the war. Public dissatisfaction in the "coalition of the willing" appeared most quickly in Spain. Following the Madrid train bombings one year later in March 2004, Spanish voters ousted the conservative Popular Party government of José María Aznar in favor of Socialist Party candidates. The new prime minister, José Zapatero, quickly followed through on his campaign promise to extract Spanish troops from Iraq.

The period since the start of the war has witnessed other political setbacks as well. Tony Blair, who once enjoyed the highest popularity ratings of any Labor prime minister in British history, stepped down from his post in July 2007 with the Iraq quagmire weighing heavily in his 23 percent approval numbers. His successor, Gordon Brown, has since distanced himself from the previously warm ties between the Bush White House and 10 Downing Street, which unkind media had described as a subservient canine. Similarly in Poland, prime minister Jarosław Kaczyński suffered defeat in his country's November 2007 parliamentary elections due in large part to his zealous support of the war in Iraq. His opponent, Donald Tusk, had campaigned vigorously on a platform promising the withdrawal of all nine hundred Polish soldiers from Iraq. At the same time, Australian voters were deciding to bring the twelve-year rule of Prime Minister John Howard to a close. Howard, a staunch ally of the Bush administration, had previously been censured by the Australian Senate for misleading the public on reasons to invade Iraq.

Public dissatisfaction has weakened the White House's "coalition of the willing" in other ways as well. At the start of operations against Iraq in 2003, the American-led alliance consisted of thirty-eight countries supplying twenty-five thousand troops. Since then, almost half (eighteen countries) have withdrawn their support, thereby reducing the number of non-U.S. military personnel to fewer than fifteen thousand. More countries are expected to follow suit by early 2009. Most damagingly, Great Britain began to draw-down its forces from Iraq in 2007, cutting the number of its soldiers nearly in half. Further planned reductions were temporarily halted in 2008 because of the violent upsurge in Iraq's southern provinces, but Prime Minister Brown hinted that additional cuts would soon be instituted.

The global public's distaste for the war, however, extends far beyond ballot boxes in Europe and Australia. According to data issued by the Pew Global Attitudes Project, international distrust of the United States has intensified across the globe. While the United States continues to enjoy significant popularity in Africa and is held in high regard by majorities of people in Japan and India, the picture in other regions of the world is bleak. Since 2002, negative perceptions of the United States have increased throughout Latin America, Asia, and the Middle East. For instance, majorities of respondents viewed the United States negatively in Bolivia and Brazil, while in Argentina, an overwhelming 72 percent of people polled expressed disdain for American foreign policy behavior since the beginning of the war.

Perhaps not surprisingly, negative perceptions are most appalling in the Muslim countries of the Middle East and Asia. The Pew Project finds that popular opinion of the United States in these areas has steadily dwindled since 2003, reaching rock bottom in Turkey during fall 2007 when American prestige dipped into single digits.[11]

Improved relations with Germany and France resulted from changes in government rather than public attitudes. Nevertheless, recent squabbles between the White House and newly elected governments in Europe over NATO's future in Afghanistan suggest persistent tensions. Indeed, Europe's failure to do more there reflects an enduring wound inflicted by the war in Iraq, one susceptible to further aggravation. Secretary of Defense Robert Gates scolded European allies in January 2008 for conceptually combining the Afghan and Iraqi conflicts and blamed European antipathy toward NATO operations in Afghanistan on their residual anger over Iraq.[12] Allies in Europe reacted angrily to Gates's assertions, leading one prominent German business daily to warn of a "deep tear" in the traditionally strong fabric of the transatlantic alliance.[13]

This is not to suggest that the future of American foreign policy rests on winning global popularity contests. Nor is it the case that U.S. standing in the world is irreparably damaged. On the contrary, as Robert Kagan points out, "Despite the negative opinion polls, most of the world's great powers are drawing closer to the United States geopolitically."[14] Still, negative world opinion highlights the fact that the Bush administration's war on terror, and its foreign policy agenda more widely, are not considered an "international 'public good.'" This problem will continue to plague the next administration in its efforts to drawdown troops and leave behind a stable Iraq, as well as deal effectively in its "other war" in Afghanistan.[15]

U.S.–UN Relations If the run-up to war with Iraq marked a particularly low point for American foreign policy and its reputation abroad, it also signaled a pyrrhic victory of sorts for the United Nations. The Security Council's credibility and legitimacy were the subjects of considerable debate well before September 11. Selectivity and double standards in council deliberations about which conflicts warranted a response, for example, contributed to the sense that the UN organ was simply a conduit for Western, and more particularly Washington's, security interests. Questions abounded. Why persist in Bosnia but withdraw from Rwanda? Why commit so forcefully to Kosovo and not to Sudan or the Democratic Republic of Congo? Such inconsistency had tarnished the UN's reputation as an honest broker.

For some observers, Operation Iraqi Freedom struck the death knell for Security Council legitimacy. According to one view, the council's responsibility to subject the use of force to the strictures of international law had finally crumbled under the pressure of U.S. power. International lawyers such as Michael Glennon argued that while the Security Council's gradual collapse had begun years earlier in the controversy concerning Kosovo, the war in Iraq kicked out the remaining supports propping up the council's dwindling legitimacy.[16]

Other voices expressed a perverse pleasure in the violence engulfing Iraq. Richard Perle, for one, gleefully announced that the Bush administration's decision to march on Baghdad represented the simultaneous downfall of two contemptible forces in world politics, Saddam Hussein and the United Nations. According to Perle, though "the chatterbox on the Hudson will continue to bleat," the "liberal conceit of safety through international law administered through international institutions" would finally be placed behind glass in a museum for failed ideas.[17]

In reality, the U.S. failure to persuade the Security Council to endorse its designs on Iraq in 2003 may have been fortunate. Had American diplomats succeeded, it would have very likely further eclipsed the remnants of Security Council legitimacy. The trumpeting of self-defense as a response to 9/11 was understandable and actually approved by the Security Council. However, the council's blanket authorization for Afghanistan can now be seen as an incentive for the Bush administration to take on Iraq.

Despite considerable public rhetorical muscle-flexing by Bush administration officials concerning the right to preemptive self-defense, arguments presented by the United States to the council in 2003 did not employ this tenuous concept. Instead, U.S. diplomats relied on the legal framework outlined by previous resolutions on Iraq. Washington argued that appropriate enforcement of Security Council Resolutions 678, 687, and 1441 demanded the removal of Saddam Hussein from power, but this narrow line of argument ultimately placed a straight-jacket on American attempts at persuasion. The meaning and interpretation of Resolution 687—the 1991 decision to end the first Gulf War and the centerpiece of the American case—suffocated any hopes of legitimacy. Among other problems, the measures outlined in Resolution 687 to address Iraqi noncompliance do not automatically authorize Chapter VII use of force, contrary to American arguments.[18] When the United States abandoned its hopes for council authorization on Iraq, it effectively sidelined the world body. Yet Iraq highlighted UN resiliency in the face of efforts by the world's remaining superpower to bend the organization to its will and ignore the constraints of international law.

The United States marched to war without the council's approval but nevertheless was obliged to return at several junctures to seek help with the internationalization of the much-contested occupation. In May 2003, Washington sought support for Resolution 1483 recognizing the "coalition of the willing" as Iraq's legitimate governing authority. Again in November it secured

Resolution 1511, calling on the UN to endorse a multinational force to help U.S. troops keep the peace and to return governing control of the country to Iraqis "as soon as practicable." Then again, in early 2004, Washington asked for help in finding a formula to identify an acceptable Iraqi sovereign before June 30. The American military presence continued to operate with Security Council approval until December 31, 2008, after which the U.S.-Iraq Status of Forces Agreement (SOFA) went into effect.

The return of the United States to the United Nations following the invasion of Iraq undoubtedly signals the limits of unilateralism and military force, on the one hand, and the potential value of multilateralism and diplomacy, on the other hand. Clearly, among traditional allies of the United States, there is a desperate desire for better relations with Washington. In May 2007, when France's new president Nicolas Sarkozy met with then secretary of state Condoleezza Rice, she asked, "What can I do for you?" He replied, "Improve your image in the world."[19] Policy matters but so does style and symbolism, which was immediately obvious when Zalmay Khalilzad arrived in New York to assume his duties as the U.S. permanent representative to the UN. Khalilzad was welcomed with open arms by the UN's diplomatic ranks, if for no other reason than he was not John Bolton.

This suggests substantial room for maneuver and improved relations when Washington decides to regain lost ground and to tread more softly at the UN. While there were numerous foreign policy disputes during the presidential campaign, both Barack Obama and John McCain agreed on at least one thing, namely, that more collaboration and partnerships were going to be an essential component of the approach by the 44th president.

Nevertheless, the war in Iraq has had stifling effects on the ability of the United States to act as a "norm carrier" in the ongoing conversations about humanitarian intervention. The use of the Security Council à la carte creates problems for states' seeking more consistency in the application of international norms. Indeed, Iraq is a conversation stopper for many when discussing possible loosening of criteria for intervention, or setting aside the principle of nonintervention. With Bush's and Blair's spurious and ex post facto "humanitarian" justification for invading Iraq, the legitimate idea of humanitarian intervention or the new norm of the responsibility to protect (R2P) has been contaminated by association. As a result, while the genocide in Darfur unfolds unabated, many regard the precedents of the Bush Doctrine so threatening as to require renewing the principle of nonintervention rather than downgrading sovereign prerogatives, even with a humanitarian rationale. The mere mention, for example, by French Foreign Minister Bernard Kouchner of the need to invoke the R2P idea in May 2007 in the face of the Burmese junta's unwillingness to permit access by outside aid workers led to toxic reactions among Asian countries and elsewhere in the Third World. The legacy of the ex post facto humanitarian justifications in Iraq—after those relying upon WMDs and links to al Qaeda were exposed as vacuous—will be with us for some time.

World Summit American actions in Iraq have other implications for U.S.–UN relations beyond the drama of Security Council politics. Indeed, on the occasion of the UN's 60th anniversary at the World Summit in September 2005, the United States missed a critical opportunity to affect the sort of change to which the administration professed commitment. To be sure, blame for the paltry results of the summit cannot be placed solely on the doorstep of the United States and the Iraq War. At the same time, "UN reform" is supposedly a priority of U.S. foreign policy, and the disappointing results partially reflect the Iraq War's ill effects on the international diplomatic arena as well as the pyrotechnics of U.S. Ambassador John Bolton, who arrived at his post and left without receiving Senate confirmation, further poisoning the negotiating atmosphere.

Birthdays are sometimes good moments to take stock. The results of the UN's 50th anniversary in 1995 should have led world leaders and observers to look askance on the prospects for any major overhaul of the UN in 2005, especially without vigorous American leadership. With the United States mired in Iraq, the moment would not allow any dramatic reform. Nonetheless, Secretary-General Kofi Annan decided to stake his legacy on the structural reform of the world organization. The results of the 2005 World Summit suggest that was an unfortunate choice for the 2000 Nobel laureate. Two years earlier, Annan had issued calls for reform, noting the "fork in the road" at which the UN stood. No one was happy: the UN could not impede U.S. hegemony, and the UN would not approve action against Saddam Hussein.

Annan asked sixteen former senior government officials—his High-level Panel on Threats, Challenges and Change (HLP)—to describe what ailed the UN and propose a way forward. The blue-ribbon panel's December 2004 report, *A More Secure World: Our Shared Responsibility*, contains a laundry-list of recommendations, which I have unkindly dubbed the "101 Dalmatians." It offered a "grand bargain" to sell to that elusive international community, in which opinions about what constitutes progress in world politics vary widely.[20] In March 2005, the specific language of packages and grand bargains was dropped, but the HLP's concept and propositions were essentially endorsed by Kofi Annan's own distillation of priorities for action at the summit, *In Larger Freedom: Towards Development, Security and Human Rights for All.*[21]

In many ways, creating the High-level Panel and convening the summit were attempts, according to a host of diplomats, "to keep Washington in the tent." The Bush administration had wandered away from the world organization—somehow, "my way or the highway" was not conducive to conversations with the UN diplomatic corps. Clearly, the present moment is historically unparalleled. There is no precedent for America's current military, economic, and cultural predominance—what former French foreign minister Hubert Védrine dubbed the *hyper-puissance.*[22] As a result, much contemporary UN debate can be compared with the Roman senate's effort to control the emperor. What exactly is the meaning of a collective security organization in a world so dominated by American power?

The heads of state and government signed off on the *2005 World Summit Outcome Document* after much last-minute brinkmanship,[23] but "a once-in-a-generation opportunity to reform and revive the United Nations has been squandered,"[24] said the lead editorial from the *New York Times.* Hostility toward the United States, and its decision to go to war with Iraq, played a large role in the dismal results. Once seen as a window of opportunity to revisit the United Nations in light of changes in world politics since San Francisco, instead negotiations exposed the very debilitating political and bureaucratic conflicts that regularly paralyze the organization. Ironically, the negotiations displayed in the limelight the indecisiveness and pettiness that the summit was supposedly convened to address and exacerbated by Washington's isolation as a result of the war in Iraq.

The only real advances at the summit were the creation of a Peace-building Commission,[25] and a definitive if somewhat lukewarm endorsement of the emerging norm of the responsibility to protect individuals from mass atrocities.[26] But on issues close to the heart of U.S. foreign policy, virtually nothing took place. This reality in large measure represents the fall-out from the Iraq War.

Surely a concern with weapons of mass destruction in a post-9/11 world is a priority for U.S. foreign policy, but the summit's final document is silent on "disarmament and non-proliferation," a victim of last-minute horse trading—and aptly dubbed a "disgrace" by Annan.[27] This priority for the United States undoubtedly was doomed for the same reasons that the Nonproliferation Treaty negotiations are in crisis—nuclear countries wanted to get commitments from nonnuclear countries, but the latter wanted disarmament from the former in exchange.[28] Even the unsuccessful pursuit of such weapons by Saddam Hussein provided a perverse demonstration effect as to why proliferation is perceived to have benefits.

Little progress was evident on terrorism, a topic that has moved front and center, at UN headquarters and elsewhere. Discussions there traditionally failed even to formulate a definition of "terrorism."[29] There always have been two main sticking points. The first was captured by the expression "your terrorist is my freedom fighter"—that is, many developing countries justify armed violence by those fighting for national liberation. The second was whether "state terrorism" should be included in any definition agreed by the vast majority of member states—the use of force by Israeli and more recently U.S. forces, for many, is mentioned in the same breath as suicide bombers.

Significantly, the HLP confronted head-on these traditional stumbling blocks: "Attacks that specifically target innocent civilians and non-combatants must be condemned clearly and unequivocally by all."[30] The secretary-general chimed in, "The proposal has clear moral force."[31] The summit's final text lacks, however, any clear definition of terrorism; for the first time in UN history the heads of state and government at least issued an unqualified condemnation. They agreed to "strongly condemn terrorism in all forms and manifestations, committed by whomever, wherever and for whatever purposes."[32] However, the final text eliminated earlier and clearer language that making targets of civilians could not be justified in exchange for dropping an exemption for movements resisting occupation.

Two other issues of central importance to Washington—human rights and reform of the secretariat—also were harmed by the blowback from the war in Iraq and the continuing occupation. The creation of the Human Rights Council (HRC), for instance, was a purported priority for U.S. foreign policy, but the United States failed to take the lead, no doubt because of human rights humiliations in Abu Ghraib and the military holding facility at Guantánamo Bay. With activists and government leaders openly questioning U.S. commitment to human rights protections in its Global War on Terror (GWOT), the war in Iraq provided an unsuitable backdrop for the assertion of American leadership on the human rights front. As a result, what initially promised to be a propitious opportunity—supplanting the dysfunctional Commission on Human Rights (CHR) with a more effective body—proved to be another opportunity lost because the former standard bearer had dropped the standard.

Created in 1946, the commission functioned until 2006 when it was replaced by the Human Rights Council, which supposedly would be an improvement.[33] During the CHR's lifetime, many of the most egregious human rights villains not only were elected but spent most of their energy protecting their own performance from scrutiny by being on the inside. A number of developing countries opposed certain initiatives because they elevated either solidarity among themselves (and their collective desire to fend off criticism as unacceptable intervention) or the principle of state sovereignty over protection.

While such repressive governments as Cuba and Saudi Arabia were often given the nod by their regional caucuses, the election of Libya as chair of the CHR in 2002 was the most alarming indication that sovereign states did what they wished, regardless of commonly understood human rights standards. According to UN tradition, it was "Africa's turn" to hold the presidency of the commission, and Libya was elected over the protests of the United States and other Western governments. For many states, especially in the global South, state sovereignty or cultural solidarity routinely trump UN efforts to protect rights. Indeed, election to the CHR was highly sought as one way to set the agenda and avoid criticism.

Will the Human Rights Council, created in 2006 after controversy at the World Summit, be any different from its flawed predecessor? The elected members of the CHR in 2005 included Sudan, at the same time that its government was pursuing slow-motion genocide in Darfur, and Zimbabwe, while it was bulldozing the houses of seven hundred thousand suspected opposition supporters and rounding up journalists and other critics. The High-level Panel recognized the CHR's "eroding credibility and professionalism" and noted that "states have sought membership of the commission not to strengthen human rights but to protect themselves against criticism or to criticize others." However, its recommendation was counterintuitive in dealing with the litany of embarrassments: universal membership instead of "only" one-quarter of the members.

The secretary-general, in his only serious dissent from the HLP's recommendations, proposed that member states "replace the Commission on Human Rights with a smaller standing Human Rights Council." The World Summit's leaders argued about whether the new council might one day become a principal organ, like the Security Council and the Economic and

Social Council (ECOSOC), and review the human rights of all members, not just those selected for special scrutiny. Views on the ultimate size still ranged from a more businesslike twenty to thirty up to fifty, virtually the same size as the commission.

World leaders at the 2005 World Summit failed to agree on the details, but at least resolved to create a Human Rights Council as a subsidiary of the General Assembly, which would decide its "mandate, modalities, functions, size, composition, membership, working methods and procedures."[34] The proposal that members be chosen by a two-thirds vote of the General Assembly was eliminated as well as the possibility that it might someday be transformed into a principal organ. Protracted negotiations continued until March 2006 when the General Assembly decided finally about the new council's mandate and composition. The first members were elected by the General Assembly in May 2006, and the council convened in Geneva for the first time in mid-June.

Some were disgruntled because the mandate given to the new council was mainly promotional and involved no clear protection role. Others were displeased because the number of members of the new council had decreased while others thought the body still was too large. There was criticism that membership was subject only to a simple majority vote instead of the more stringent two-thirds requirement.[35]

The performance by the Human Rights Council requires time to evaluate more definitively—even if we have already passed the half-way point of the five-year evaluation period specified by the General Assembly—but the preeminence of sovereignty rather than human rights is clear. Nevertheless, for the first session in June 2006, hopes were high but results proved disappointing. The HRC condemned Israel nine times, but condemned no other country. Both Kofi Annan and Ban Ki-moon questioned why the HRC could single out Israel but ignore Sudan, North Korea, and Myanmar.

The fact that the new council meets at least three times a year for ten weeks was a step forward in terms of making human rights an ongoing concern rather than being relegated to a single circumscribed session for three weeks each year. That all members may be subject to an evaluation of their own records is a potentially powerful symbolic indication that all states' records should be open to independent review and not shielded by claims of sovereignty.

The Universal Periodic Review (UPR)—a scrutiny of all HRC member states—was designed to be a key feature of the new institution, but no reviews were accomplished in the first two years. Finally in April 2008, the agreed procedure for conducting UPRs once every four years went into effect. As terms are for only three years and states are ineligible for reelection after two consecutive terms, a government facing an embarrassing review could simply not run for office. Moreover, the involvement of government-appointed experts is still being discussed, clearly not the way to ensure an independent evaluation.

The inaugural assessment evaluated human rights protections in an even assortment of sixteen countries, reviewing information for the countries under consideration from a host of sources, including NGO testimony, treaty bodies, and academic research. Results at the time of writing remain unclear. However, the efficiency of the first round suggests that the council will meet its goal of reviewing the human rights record of forty-eight countries each year. If the schedule is maintained, the HRC will assess the records of all 192 member states within the allotted four-year time frame. At the same time, the new "culture" is that neither governments nor NGOs criticize by name government policy—hardly a step forward. Also, a special session can be convened by a mere majority vote of the General Assembly, which means that the more than 130 member states that are also members of the Non-Aligned Movement will be able to call for special scrutiny of Israel at almost any time.

Special "rapporteurs," or independent experts, have been used over the years to highlight the precarious human rights situation in particular countries or of crosscutting themes (for instance, on summary executions or indigenous peoples). But the June 2007 session of the HRC voted to terminate the mandates for the special rapporteurs for Cuba and Belarus as part of a more general attack on transparency and a defense of sovereign prerogatives. Human Rights Watch, for one, expressed grave concern about the selection process for the forty-one human rights experts or working groups focusing on particular themes, such as violence against women and arbitrary detention, and on the situations in specific countries, including Myanmar and Sudan. In the future, these experts will be appointed from a published roster of "qualified candidates," but the selection process itself includes a disquieting decision-making role for a committee appointed by the council's regional groups, another recipe for sovereignty rather than human rights considerations to be the top priority.[36]

While the modest reduction in numbers and the simple-majority election procedure in the HRC were disappointing in relationship to earlier possibilities, other measures might nonetheless help. One advance was the actual election campaign, which was designed to discourage the worst human rights offenders from being candidates. Rather than backroom horse trading, there was a more open election process. As a result, certain countries (for example, the United States, Sudan, Libya, Vietnam, Syria, Nepal, Egypt, Zimbabwe, Uzbekistan, North Korea, and Belarus) did not bother running, and others (sixty-four countries ran for the forty-seven seats in its first year) had to agree to place their own records on the table as part of the campaign. This approach could help attenuate the worst aspects of egregious human rights violators' shielding themselves from criticism by serving on the HRC. Their sovereignty, in short, provides less cover.

The fact that the United States was not a candidate in 2006, 2007, and 2008 keeps the former standard bearer for human rights on the sidelines while permitting the election of such other human rights "champions" as China, Russia, Egypt, Saudi Arabia, Pakistan, and Cuba. Washington's refusal to run doubtless emanates from two interrelated factors, both providing further evidence of Iraq's damage to U.S. foreign policy. First, the torture of Iraqi prisoners at the hands of U.S. military officers in Abu Ghraib, compounded by accusations of abuse in Guantánamo Bay, raised uncomfortable questions that the White House surely did not want scrutinized any further. Second, given these disturbing revelations—and international hostility toward the Bush administration more broadly—the possibility that the United States would not be elected to the newly established council resurrected the haunting embarrassment of its ouster from the CHR in 2001.

Nevertheless, John Bolton may have been correct when explaining why Washington was opting out: "We want a butterfly. We're not going to put lipstick on a caterpillar and declare it a success."[37] Unfortunately, the residue from the war in Iraq meant that Washington was missing in action without an official position to point out that the larvae remained in the cocoon and even a caterpillar requires nourishment to become a butterfly.

Finally, toning up the UN secretariat was supposedly of the utmost significance to the Bush administration. But Washington's hostility and the legacy from the unilateral pursuit of the war in Iraq also made this objective impossible. Scandals surrounding the oil-for-food program that fed Iraqis during years of UN sanctions, not to mention sexual exploitation by a few UN officials, troops, and civilians in peacekeeping missions, are scars on the UN secretariat and its member states. They demonstrate serious flaws in the central administration, which is too often inefficient, politicized, corrupt, and in desperate need of repair.

As a result of pressures from Washington and other Western capitals, the secretary-general appointed an independent commission to explore the allegations of mismanagement. The preface to a more public report on oil-for-food management was authored by Paul Volcker, the former chair of the Federal Reserve Board, and it contains language that could have been written by a Beltway neocon: "The inescapable conclusion from the Committee's work is that the United Nations Organization needs thoroughgoing reform—and it needs it urgently."[38] The oil-for-food findings about the results from cat-and-mouse dealings with Saddam Hussein's Iraq are not an aberration. Such problems are endemic, though solving them may require much more attention from member states, especially the most powerful. Again, this requires Washington's participation, not isolation.

What were the main management challenges for U.S. foreign policy at the UN as the world organization prepared for the post-Kofi Annan era and remain so for his successor, Secretary-General Ban Ki-moon? The most essential one proceeds from the need to change the way that the international civil service and its chief executive do business. As such, it is necessary to go substantially beyond the formulaic language in the World Summit's final document "to enhance the effective management of the United Nations."[39]

A 1997 innovation by Annan consisted of naming the first deputy secretary-general. But this deputy, rather than acting as an all-purpose stand-in, needs a new job description. He or she should be an independent manager acting as chief operating officer for the organization. In this way, the management buck would stop just short of the secretary-general, who should remain the UN's chief politician, diplomat, and mediator.

The Volcker team proposed that the deputy, like the secretary-general, be nominated by the Security Council and approved by the General Assembly. Such a formality is unwise as it would require amending the UN Charter. But the objective is imperative and could be accommodated by having the council informally endorse the nominee, who would have "clear authority for planning and for personnel practices that emphasize professional and administrative talent over political convenience."[40]

The HLP and the secretary-general proposed, and the summit agreed, to consider a one-time buy-out to cut dead wood from the permanent staff, and Annan indicated willingness to do so. The more pertinent task, whether or not any buy-out occurs, lies in gathering new wood. Recruitment should return to the idealistic origins of the League of Nations and early

UN secretariats: competence should be the highest consideration rather than geographical origins, gender, and age—the various justifications for cronyism that are now shamelessly used in filling both junior and senior positions. But even if certain affirmative-action measures continue, the onus should be placed on governments demanding positions in the organization to nominate only their most professionally qualified and experienced candidates—not just those close to the boss who fancy life in New York or Paris. Significant talent exists in the developing world, unrecognized and unrewarded, waiting to be tapped.

To be fair, both *A More Secure World* and *In Larger Freedom* indicated the need for substantial changes in the way that the secretariat operates and its resources are allocated. Indeed, observers often overlook the fact that Annan instituted significant managerial and technical improvements shortly after assuming the mantle in 1997 and again at the beginning of his second term in 2002. One that has made a difference to more effectively integrating UN efforts and sharing opinions and information has been the introduction of a loosely defined "cabinet" system, with regular high-level meetings among senior officials in the secretariat, agencies, funds, and programs. Ban Ki-moon should be given a longer leash than is usually allowed by member states, with a commitment to permit him to act the way that the chief executive of virtually any corporation operates.

Nonetheless, the all-important Third World bloc refused to authorize more flexibility to the 38th floor (the executive suites on the top floor of the UN's headquarters) because it would move power away from the General Assembly, where by virtue of their numbers they can call the shots. Here again, the fall-out from the Iraq War is palpable, although developing countries have long favored the assembly chamber where they can make use of their overwhelming numbers.

Ironically, John Bolton's approach during the World Summit, which provoked considerable animosity and led to reopening contentious issues, strengthened the opposition to increased discretionary authority for the secretary-general. A relatively small number of developing countries blocked agreement by the September 2005 gathering on just this type of management reform, which they viewed as a subterfuge. They argued that if more discretionary authority and power of the purse were placed in the senior UN administration, it would be more subject to Western (and especially American) influence. Clearly the residue of Iraq remained in New York.

FUTURE CHALLENGES

Everyone is desperate for the United States to return to the multilateral fold. The present is an unparalleled multilateral-cum-unilateral moment—the United States is global in reach and power, but the United Nations has the legitimacy that reflects its universal membership. It is the forum of choice for policy formulation and norm entrepreneurship that is necessary when aspiring to universal relevance and application. Before the war on Iraq, the "hyper-power" was already spending more on its military than the next fifteen to twenty-five countries (depending on who was counting); with additional appropriations for Afghanistan and Iraq, Washington now spends more than the rest of the world's militaries combined.[41]

The sobering experiences in occupied Afghanistan and Iraq have highlighted the limits of American military power, however. The $750 billion in annual expenditures evidently purchase insufficient armor for the emperor to wear. As crises continue to unfold in the Middle East and Central Asia, in Africa and Asia, current American military expenditures will not suffice to meet future challenges.

As for the other elements of power—economics and culture—the United States remains preponderant with the combination of its annual GDP of nearly $14 trillion, the global reach of its entertainment industry, and its capacity for technological innovation. The extent to which the rest of the world was affected by the 2008 U.S. financial and economic crisis highlights the continued preponderance of the United States. It will doubtless stay the major player in international relations even in Fareed Zakaria's "post-American world" with the continued rise of China, India, and the European Union.[42] While Joseph Nye and other proponents of "soft power" outline possibilities for a different kind of influence, what is at stake here is the context within which to use the tools of hard and soft power.[43] Such recognition requires acknowledgment of the comparative advantage for many tasks of multilateralism.

One reflection of this reality, albeit on a different scale, was Washington's decision to give up control of tsunami-relief efforts to the UN in early 2005. After a slow start with a four-country support team, the White House understood that it simply could not deliver a sufficiently coordinated response, which suggests an incipient realization of limits of unilateralism. Most Americans would acknowledge that when it comes to the spotting, warning, and managing of international health hazards—the severe acute respiratory syndrome (SARS) in 2003, avian flu more recently, and AIDS perennially—the

World Health Organization (WHO) is indispensable. The monitoring of international crime statistics and the narcotics trade, the policing of nuclear power, and numerous other important global functions are also based within the UN system. Whatever the left-over rhetoric from the Bush administration, it is hard to imagine that the United Nations will not become much more appealing already in 2009 and the years ahead.

Washington's current short list for the UN should include not only post-conflict reconstruction in Afghanistan and Iraq but also fighting terrorism (sharing information and the fight against money laundering), confronting infectious diseases, pursuing environmental sustainability, monitoring human rights, providing humanitarian aid, rescheduling debt, and fostering trade. Ironically, these very items figured in President Bush's opening address to the World Summit on September 14, 2005.[44] Yet, the continued inability to understand the fallout from Iraq prevented the Bush administration from coming to the obvious conclusion that multilateral approaches hold possibilities that unilateral ones do not.

President Obama will have to reverse course by making amends with certain symbolic gestures and, hopefully, some substantive compromises as well. Indeed, some would not be very costly and would signal the beginnings of significant change in style and content in the White House. Given the widespread distaste for the content and style of the Bush administration, both friends and foes will no doubt give the benefit of the doubt to the next occupant of the White House.

The Obama administration could begin by taking the lead in responding to the threat of global climate change. Backed by overwhelming popular opinion in both the United States and abroad that global warming poses a major threat to world security, the new administration could spearhead international efforts to tackle this looming challenge. The Nobel Prize-winning Intergovernmental Panel of Climate Change (the IPCC, which shared the award with Al Gore, who received the honor for his documentary, *An Inconvenient Truth*) has outlined a number of bold initiatives to combat the potentially catastrophic adverse consequences of environmental degradation.[45] Instead of standing on the sidelines and preventing international cooperation as it did in Bali, the United States could and should fill the leadership void.

The United States could also once again become a champion of human rights by building on its decision to close Guantánamo and return to the rule of law, especially by rather quickly making an about-face on its policy toward the International Criminal Court (ICC). Dissatisfaction with the institutional shortcomings of both criminal tribunals for the former Yugoslavia and Rwanda, respectively, demonstrated to many the need for a permanent court. In response, the Rome Statute on the ICC was signed in 1998 and entered into force four years later with the requisite sixty ratifications. Anyone who commits crimes under the statute after July 1, 2002, is liable for prosecution. Thus far, the United States has refused to become a party to the statute.

Government lawyers have argued that the court exposes U.S. soldiers and politicians to the possibility of politically motivated prosecutions, but such a scenario in reality is an empty threat since the ICC can only act if a country does not have legal measures in place, and the Security Council also can veto cases. In response to the Rome Statute's ratification in 2002, the United States has aggressively pursued a host of bilateral agreements with its allies and others that circumvent the ICC's jurisdiction. Particularly, Washington has demanded that other countries refuse to surrender American nationals if requested by the court and has provided incentives to sign bilateral agreements to that effect.

The United States could set aside these bilateral agreements in favor of joining the international consensus that international judicial pursuit should be the most common response to large-scale atrocities.[46] Indeed, Washington did not stand in the way for Darfur because Security Council Resolution 1564 established the International Commission of Inquiry on Darfur, which identified perpetrators and asked the ICC to prosecute unnamed Sudanese war criminals. More action of this sort would signal to the world that the United States is prepared to take the lead in doing away with the tradition of ad hoc responses to massive human rights violations. Washington led the charge in 1948 and at several junctures subsequently, but then in 2001 the Bush administration took the unprecedented step of "unsigning" the Rome statute in a gratuitously hostile gesture. Even if the Senate were not to ratify the treaty, at least the Obama administration could "resign" the treaty and move toward being the rhetorical standard bearer for the rule of international law instead of a pariah.

In addition, the fallout from Iraq has also meant that humanitarian intervention is no longer on the side of the angels for fear that Washington can manipulate it and strengthen its rationale for preemptive strikes against rogue states and terrorists. The emerging norm of the responsibility to protect has been contaminated by association with the Bush administration's spurious "humanitarian" justifications for invading Iraq after the supposed links to Iraq and the possession of WMDs were exposed as vacuous. The UK's position as ally has been even more damaging. In March 2004, Tony Blair offered the most worrisome example of abuse of R2P when he applied it retroactively to Iraq. "We surely have a duty and a right to prevent this threat materializing," Blair announced, "and we surely have a responsibility to act when a nation's people are subjected to a regime such as Saddam's."[47]

With the possible exception of the prevention of genocide after World War Two, no idea has moved faster or farther in the international normative arena than R2P. Yet the notion that the rights of human beings trump state sovereignty, while radiating briefly across the international political horizon, is now overshadowed as the United States tied down its military in Afghanistan and Iraq and the latter morphed into a vague humanitarian intervention. Because the United States cannot commit significant political and military resources to human protection, political will and the operational capacity for humanitarian intervention have evaporated. Yet the cosmopolitan logic underpinning R2P is uniquely compelling for international relations "given the fact that sovereignty is one of the few principles that has universal appeal among national elites and mass publics."[48]

The Obama team could build by using a report from a bi-partisan Genocide Prevention Task Force led by Madeleine Albright and William Cohen.[49] We have witnessed a values breakthrough of sorts: the responsibility to protect qualifies as emerging customary law after centuries of more or less passive and mindless acceptance of the proposition that state sovereignty was a license to kill. Susan Rice, having been part of the Clinton administration's lamentable decision that kept the United States out of Rwanda in 1994, has expressed clearly the need for Washington not to repeat that mistake and to take the lead in conscience-shocking situations. With the leading candidates being Darfur, the Democratic Republic of the Congo, and Zimbabwe, John Prendergast of the "Enough" project calls the combination of the African specialist Rice along with Secretary of State Hilary Clinton and National Security Adviser General James Jones a "dream team" to prevent genocide.[50] Let's hope that candidate Obama's article in *Foreign Affairs* becomes a touchstone in that he asserted the use of "military force in circumstances beyond self-defense" and specifically listed the need to "confront mass atrocities."[51]

Most importantly for this discussion, the Obama administration faces clear imperatives with regard to Iraq. First, it must pursue a phased but rapid withdrawal with a target date of sixteen months or the spring of 2010 as Obama promised throughout his campaign. But the new president must do so while also working to involve a genuinely multilateral coalition to ensure regional stability in the years ahead. The United States has no other option than to say "yes" to participating in international military and peace-building operations in Iraq and Afghanistan.[52] If it does so with responsibility and in concert with allies, the United States will demonstrate to the world that while the size of the debit for the Bush administration's balance sheet is gigantic and negative, it is not insurmountable.

CONCLUSION

What future lies ahead for the Obama administration six years after the start of war in Iraq and so-called victory was declared? To what extent could it be compared to "a glass at least half full," Kofi Annan's summary of the 2005 World Summit?[53] Whether the U.S. presence and power are overrated and will wane in the coming years remains to be seen. But nothing is irreversible. And learning is possible and desirable because, as Joseph Nye observes, "the world's only superpower can't go it alone."[54]

Despite the missteps of the past eight years, the resulting damage can be repaired. Indeed, simply having a new face in the White House will have a positive impact on American foreign policy. Much anti-American sentiment derives more from the Bush administration's policies and style than from the outright rejection of the United States. "Washington needs to understand that generating international public support for its view of the world is a core element of power," writes Fareed Zakaria, "not merely an exercise in public relations."[55] There are, of course, times when the United States will have to ignore the objections of even long-standing allies, but as the unlikely combination of Ivo Daalder and Robert Kagan notes, "their disagreement should weigh heavily in our decision making—at the very least prompting us to re-examine our assumptions and assessments carefully."[56]

A good place to begin is the United Nations itself. Another arrogant leader, Charles de Gaulle, dismissed the United Nations as *le machin* (the thing) in favor of the real red meat of international relations, Realpolitik. Indeed, "the thing" has proved useful to even George Bush, and American power and the Obama administration's view on international cooperation will circumscribe the United States's role in global affairs and will dominate future UN affairs. Not surprisingly, in a twenty-five-page swan song in *Foreign Affairs* in mid-2008, then secretary of state Condoleezza Rice made no mention of the United Nations.[57] Yet as Ahmed Rashid usefully reminds us in his controversial examination of contemporary foreign policy, given the current threats to international peace and security, including "civil wars, ethnic cleansing, terrorism, proliferation of weapons of mass destruction, organized crime, disease, poverty, and mass starvation . . . the role of a multinational organization such as the UN is indispensable."[58]

In nominating his confidante Susan Rice as ambassador to the United Nations, Barack Obama enunciated his "belief that the UN is an indispensable—and imperfect—forum." By naming a seasoned academic and policy analyst who has his ear and by restoring the post's cabinet status, Obama not only announced that the United States has rejoined the world and is ready to reengage with all member states, but also that the United Nations would be essential to U.S. foreign policy during his administration. He also acknowledged what is evident to most people on the planet who were not in the ideological bubble of the Bush administration, namely "that the global challenges we face demand global institutions that work."[59]

Certainly, there are those who disagree. No doubt this chapter has done little to dispel the beliefs of those who are skeptical of the UN system, or of those who see it as an obstacle to foreign policy pursuits in the national interest. Still, it is critical to underscore that there is no danger that any U.S. administration would permit the UN or any other international institution to stand in the way of its pursuit of vital national interests. At the same time, it is possible on virtually every issue to accommodate the reasonable concerns of other states while preserving the vital interests of U.S. foreign policy. Indeed, compromise may in fact be the most effective route to optimizing the pursuit of such interests. "The goodwill accrued along the way yields leverage to seek support on other matters or to fend off pressure on bottom-line US concerns," argues David Shorr.[60] If "unilateralism and multilateralism are best understood as two ends of a continuum,"[61] the Obama administration will profit from reasoned strategic considerations and substantive issues that might optimize prospects for "tactical multilateralism."[62] In short, pundits too often overlook how the UN system serves American interests and gives Washington cause to proceed with international acquiescence, if not jubilant support.

In this context Ted Sorensen, a former speechwriter for President John F. Kennedy, asks, "What is more unrealistic than to believe that this country can unilaterally decide the fate of others, without a decent respect for the opinions of mankind, or for the judgment of world institutions and our traditional allies?"[63] For his part, Princeton University's John Ikenberry points to a striking irony: "The worst unilateral impulses coming out of the Bush administration are so harshly criticized around the world because so many countries have accepted the multilateral vision of international order that the United States has articulated over most of the twentieth century."[64]

The reality of U.S. power means that if the United Nations and multilateral cooperation are to have a chance of working, let alone flourish, the globe's remaining superpower, if that term is still apt, must be on board. "In a world marked by enormous tumult and change and at a time when America's international standing and strategic position are at an historic nadir," writes a team from the Center for a New American Security, "it is vital to chart a new direction for America's global role"[65]

In thinking about exerting strategic leadership in the twenty-first century, this group seems to have forgotten a crucial fact that probably also is not in the minds of many readers—namely, that the United States raced to be the first country to ratify the UN Charter, winning Senate approval on July 28, 1945, barely a month after the ink dried on the signatures by the fifty-one countries present in San Francisco. The United States certainly was as preponderant on the international stage then as it is now. The world organization was not the creation of pie-in-the-sky idealists. As one historian notes, "Its wartime architects bequeathed us this system as a realist necessity vital in times of trial, not as a liberal accessory to be discarded when the going gets rough."[66]

Looking back on a "remarkable generation of leaders and public servants," Sir Brian Urquhart remembers, "They were pragmatic idealists more concerned about the future of humanity than the outcome of the next election; and they understood that finding solutions to postwar problems was much more important than being popular with one or another part of the American electorate."[67]

Could that same far-sighted political commitment dawn again? A substantial contribution to improving the heavily negative balance sheet from the Bush administration's pursuit of the Iraq War would be the articulation of such a vision from the very outset of the Obama administration.

7 THE IRAQ WAR AND U.S. PUBLIC OPINION

Clay Ramsay

The decline in American public support for the Iraq War is surely the best-known fact about U.S. public opinion in recent years. In an April 2003 ABC/Washington Post poll, 70 percent thought that "all in all, considering the costs to the United States versus the benefits . . . the war with Iraq was worth fighting," while only 27 percent disagreed. By June 2008, however, just 34 percent believed the war was worth fighting, while 63 percent did not.

It is only natural that such a broad shift would bring in its train a set of assumptions in the policy community about how the public will view U.S. national security in the years to come. This chapter seeks to bring the body of publicly available survey research to bear on these assumptions, in order to learn what has changed in the broad worldview held by majorities and what has not.

The policy community's expectation at such a juncture is generally that the public will go into a phase of isolationism, or at least of relative disengagement from world affairs. "Isolationism" is an important but vague term that is marked by its origins in the 1920s, but is now used in many different ways. This chapter operationalizes isolationism (as well as "engagement") as a set of discrete attitudes and preferences. To each of these it applies measures, in the form of poll questions asked in exactly the same words at intervals between 2002 and 2006 (and some more recently). Some of these survey questions have been asked for much longer, while a few were first asked early in the war.

Although this emphasis on trendline questions may seem narrow, it is the only reliable way to ascertain movement in public opinion, and so only a few nontrendline questions have been included for illustration. Polls by the Chicago Council on Global Affairs (CCGA, formerly the Chicago Council on Foreign Relations), the Pew Research Institute, and the German Marshall Fund (GMF) are dominant in what follows, because all three have been faithful guardians of trendlines important for students of security and foreign policy.[1]

Overall, this review of the evidence indicates that:

- The public's broad majority orientation toward multilateralism is virtually unchanged, and in some regards a little strengthened. Its evaluation of broad foreign policy goals is fundamentally the same, though showing less intensity than in the immediate post-9/11 years. Its perceptions of threats to the United States have generally returned to the levels of the 1990s—levels that were more elevated than is often thought.
- The public rejects the idea of preventive war as a tool of policy and is much more alive to the distinction between preventive war and preemptive war in the face of an imminent attack. It is considerably less willing to undertake a war that is related to assuring the oil supply. While there is still viable majority support for activities meant to promote democracy abroad, there is a new wariness about the use of force to do so. However, there is still strong majority support for military action against terrorists who are nonstate actors.
- Support for foreign aid dropped in 2004 but recovered in succeeding years. Majorities remain willing to contribute U.S. troops to UN peacekeeping operations or humanitarian missions, both in principle and in some specific instances; signs of fatigue are surprisingly low. The public has been disappointed with the UN's performance, but a majority looks on the institution favorably nonetheless. A large majority would like to see the UN reinforced and the United States more willing to make policy decisions within the UN.

FREQUENTLY VOICED ASSUMPTIONS ABOUT THE IRAQ WAR'S EFFECTS ON PUBLIC OPINION

In the media and among foreign policy observers, it is frequently assumed that as a result of the Iraq War, isolationism is rising among the American public and will be strong enough to set the tone for a few years. Some prominent researchers and commentators have at times been categorical on this.

For example, Andrew Kohut, director of the Pew Research Center, commented on several occasions on a 2005 Pew poll finding that received much press. In that poll, 42 percent of Americans said, "The United States should mind its own business internationally and let other countries take care of themselves"—up from 30 percent in 2002. In November 2005 Kohut said, "What's striking is the common thread, both the opinion leaders favoring a less assertive role for the United States and the public's isolationist views. This particular period of time marks a transition from the post-9/11 era."[2] The following year, Kohut drew back from describing the public as isolationist:

> There is no sign that most Americans want the United States to turn its back on the world or that anti-foreign sentiment in this country is rising. Discontent with Mr. Bush's policies, notably on Iraq, has led to widespread public frustration. And while it has also created more isolationists, they remain a minority. . . . America's current mood is less a rejection of the rest of the world than it is a deep concern about terrorism and a growing wariness about America's own assertive foreign policy. In particular, there is little potential support for the use of force against Iran. And more generally, the American experience in Iraq has reduced support for preemptive wars.[3]

By March 2008, however, Kohut had returned to his earlier tone, writing, "Disillusionment with the Iraq war has ushered in a rise in isolationist sentiment comparable to that of the mid-1970s following the Vietnam war. . . . A rise in isolationism has signaled a diminished public appetite for the assertive national security policy of the Bush years and, in general, a less internationalist outlook."[4]

Kohut may have shifted back to his earlier view because it found agreement among other prominent observers of foreign policy. Thus Charles Kupchan, a senior fellow at the Council on Foreign Relations, stated, "There seems to be a turning inward across the American spectrum . . . an inevitable consequence of Iraq."[5] Similarly Peter Beinart, editor of the *New Republic*, wrote, "While September 11 merely intensified an old mood [which, in Beinart's argument, began with the Gulf War in 1991], Iraq is producing a new one. Public isolationism has jumped sharply since 2002. . . . In the years to come, if the isolationist mood deepens, future presidents may find themselves unable to act early and aggressively against foreign threats." Beinart's piece appeared in the *Washington Post*, whose editors titled it "The Isolation Pendulum: Expect a Cyclical U.S. Retreat From World Affairs After the Iraq War."[6]

To be sure, the belief in a return of isolationism in the public has not been universal. *New York Times* columnist David Brooks has dissented, saying, "The bulk of the evidence suggests there is no rising tide of isolationism in this country, even with the bloodshed in Iraq. . . . The rest of the evidence shows high engagement in foreign affairs. Public support for multilateral action remains phenomenally strong. Support for foreign aid is higher than it's been." However, Brooks argued in the same piece that a new anti-Arabism had resulted from the Iraq War: "The belief that while most of the world is chugging toward a globally integrated future . . . the Arab countries . . . just have to be walled off so they don't hurt us again. People won't express such quasi-racial views directly to pollsters, but the attitude shows up."[7] Thus Brooks offered a substitute for the isolationism theory, but thought no hard evidence would be found for it.

DEFINING TERMS

The term "isolationism" provides a shorthand that allows observers to think simplistically about the public. The public is pictured as either leaning forward in support for U.S. engagement in world affairs, or "turning inward" and disengaging from the world. In fact, it fits the evidence better to view the public as distinguishing among different kinds, levels, and motives of engagement on different international issues.

For clarity's sake, I will break down support for engagement into a number of components, some general (philosophy of engagement), others concrete (specific forms of engagement). Each component can be tested empirically, because public opinion surveys have asked questions about that component more than once, creating time series or "trendlines." In the best cases, the trendline begins in 2002, a little before the Iraq War, and continues into 2007 or 2008—and there are many of these best cases available. In some other cases, the trendline begins early in the war and continues long enough to be worth attention. In every instance, the poll trendline bears usefully on the question of how the Iraq War experience has affected the public over time as it looks at America's role in the world.

A *philosophy of engagement* encompasses a view of how the United States should best relate to the world, in terms of the classical compass marks of isolationism, multilateralism, and unilateralism. It also involves adherence to broad foreign policy goals for the long term as well as a coherent set of perceptions about real or potential dangers to the United States's vital interests.

CCGA has asked the public to rate the importance of a set of goals, in some cases repeatedly for decades. It is reasonable to think that a change in the public's orientation would show up in these measures. The goals examined here are:

- Maintaining superior military power
- Combating international terrorism
- Preventing the spread of nuclear weapons
- Strengthening the United Nations
- Protecting weaker nations against foreign aggression
- Helping to bring a democratic form of government to other nations

Specific *forms of engagement* are the possible "breakpoints" where policymakers choose to invest resources and take risks, but the public may refuse majority support. Much discussion of public opinion that revolves endlessly around the public's general orientation—multilateralist, unilateralist, or isolationist—in fact derives its highly charged quality from anxiety over these breakpoints, where policymakers know it is possible for the public to leave them high and dry.

The following list gives eight forms of engagement for which one or more trendlines offer measures of support:

1. *Preventive* military action against a state (that is, where an attack by another country is *not* imminent, but is thought to be possible sometime in the future);
2. *Preemptive* military action against a state (that is, where an attack by another country *does* appear to be imminent);
3. Military action to ensure the oil supply;
4. Military action to install or reinstall a democratic government in another country;
5. Military action that takes place in another country, but is targeted at a violent nonstate actor—for example, a terrorist group;
6. Using U.S. troops for humanitarian purposes;
7. Providing general support for the UN, building the UN's capacities, and contributing troops to peacekeeping operations;
8. Support for foreign aid.

Finally, it is widely acknowledged that world public opinion played an extraordinary role in the U.S. debate leading up to the 2003 invasion and has continued to impede American attempts to make the Iraq War a less unilateral effort. There is excellent trend data tracking the American public's awareness of the world public's attitudes toward the United States and its policies, and this data will be examined as an aspect of public opinion on national security policy.[8]

THE PUBLIC'S RESPONSES TO QUESTIONS ON PHILOSOPHY OF ENGAGEMENT

General Measures of Isolationism

A venerable measure of isolationism, dating back to 1945, is a question that asks: "Do you think it will be best for the future of this country if we take an active part in world affairs or if we stay out of world affairs?"[9] Since 1986, support for taking an active part has typically been in the 60–70 percent range. In 2002, CCGA found 71 percent in favor of taking an active part and 25 percent for staying out. "Taking an active part" was 67 percent in 2004 and 69 percent in 2006, declining to 63 percent in 2008. The German Marshall Fund, asking the same question within the first three years of the Iraq War, recorded a decline from a higher level—from 79 percent in 2004 to 72 percent in 2005.[10] Taken together, these findings suggest only a mild inflection away from engagement.

In December 2006 the Pew Research Center asked a similar question, in which respondents could "completely or mostly" agree or disagree with the flat statement: "It's best for the future of our country to be active in world affairs." Asked this way, support for engagement was higher, with 90 percent agreeing in 2003 and 86 percent in 2006. However, those who said they *completely* agreed dropped eight points—from 50 to 42 percent.

Another venerable question that has excited so much comment—"Please tell me whether you agree or disagree . . . The U.S. should mind its own business internationally and let other countries get along as best they can on their own"—has a history of getting assent from roughly one-third to one-half of Americans. It has fluctuated in this zone of approval since 1972 (back in the 1960s, only about one-quarter agreed).

The sentence hitches together two phrases that differ in their implications—the first discreet, the second uncharitable—but add up to proposing relations that diplomats used to call "correct." Asked on four occasions in the 1990s, on average 38 percent agreed and 55 percent disagreed.[11] In January 2000—with the United States at peace—Gallup found 46 percent agreeing and 50 percent disagreeing with the statement, higher than what Pew had found when it asked the same question in March 1999 during the run-up to the war in Kosovo (35 percent agreed, 57 percent disagreed). In December 2002, with UN inspectors preparing to enter Iraq, agreement was down to 30 percent (Pew), and it was about the same (33 percent) in March 2003, days before the war began. The rise of agreement by nine points to 42 percent in October 2005 was the catalyst for new expectations of isolationism's return. Pew and CBS both asked the same question in December 2006, and while Pew found 42 percent, CBS found a majority agreeing (52 percent). After this wide discrepancy, the question has not been asked again as of this writing. While the question does not seem to be a very sensitive instrument, it is plausible to assume that fatigue with the Iraq War contributed to a rise in agreement.

Another long-time trend question has a more unilateralist than isolationist accent. Respondents are asked whether they agree or disagree that "since the U.S. is the most powerful nation in the world, we should go our own way in international matters, not worrying too much about whether other countries agree with us or not." This has a special relevance in the Iraq context, where the United States and Britain went to war without obtaining a UN Security Council resolution authorizing the invasion. In December 2002 Pew found 72 percent disagreeing and only 25 percent agreeing with the statement. In March 2003, the month of the invasion, *Newsweek* found disagreement at 62 percent and agreement up to one-third (33 percent). By July 2004 disagreement had nudged back up to 65 percent, with agreement down to 28 percent (Pew), and in December 2006 disagreement was at 68 percent. It seems that the moment of going to war had a short-term effect of bolstering a minority view that the United States should "go its own way," but this effect was short-lived.

It is interesting that those who think Americans are becoming more isolationist do not consider a different question, which asks respondents whether they agree that "the United States is playing the role of world policeman more than it should be." On this question—which addresses not isolationism per se, but whether the United States should act as a dominant, hegemonic world leader—large majorities agree, and agreement has grown since the war began. In 2000 the Election Issues Survey found 68 percent agreeing and 28 percent disagreeing. When CCGA asked it again in 2002, 65 percent agreed and a higher 34 percent disagreed. In 2004, however, agreement rose to 80 percent and has remained just below that level (2007, 76 percent; 2008, 77 percent). Apparently, the Iraq War has increased those agreeing with the already popular proposition that the United States overdoes the world policeman role.

Many of the same people who reject the world policeman role would say, though, that the United States should nonetheless "exert strong leadership in world affairs." The German Marshall Fund regularly asks how desirable it is for the United States to do this. In 2002, 83 percent thought it desirable or very desirable, in 2007 84 percent did, as did 80 percent in 2008. However, the number calling this "*very* desirable" has varied. In 2002 41 percent said it was very desirable; immediately after the 2004 election, 49 percent said this;[12] after dropping slightly for the next two years, in 2007, a higher 53 percent called U.S. leadership very desirable, but in 2008 this view was down to 43 percent—near the average level for this decade.

When respondents are offered three alternatives so that more possibilities are aired, their responses over time are even more stable than in the questions just discussed. In 2002, 2004, and 2006, CCGA offered three formulations of a preferred U.S. role in the world. "The U.S. should withdraw from most efforts to solve international problems" garnered 10–14 percent. "As the sole remaining superpower, the U.S. should continue to be the preeminent world leader in solving international problems" garnered 7–10 percent. The remainder—75–79 percent—went to the view that "the U.S. should do its share to solve international problems together with other countries." None of the fluctuations are large enough to be statistically meaningful.

Overall, regarding general questions about U.S. engagement that give respondents a chance to express isolationist sentiments, the Iraq War experience has left discernible traces, but they are slight. The lack of signs of a shift in philosophy on the public's part suggests that in supporting a war in 2003 with little allied and no UN Security Council support, the public thought it was supporting a "one-off," a single necessary exception to its sense of the general rule that the United States should avoid going it alone.

Foreign Policy Goals

Overall, the public has shown stability in its views coupled with an easing of the intensity shown in the first term of the Bush administration. In 2004 fewer people were willing to call so many goals "*very* important," and this is better interpreted as a regaining of perspective than as a turning inward and away from the world.

In 2002, "maintaining superior military power worldwide" was called a very important goal by two-thirds (67 percent). Only 28 percent called it somewhat important, and only 5 percent said it was not an important goal at all. Support for this goal was at a higher level than it had been in the 1990s (59 percent "very important" in 1998). In 2004, however, those calling this goal very important dropped sharply to just half (50 percent). Those calling it somewhat important rose 13 points to 41 percent. In 2006 support for the goal recovered mildly, with 55 percent now calling it "very important" and 36 percent "somewhat important." Results in 2008 were virtually the same (57 percent very important, 36 percent somewhat important). It could be said that opinion on maintaining military power had gone through a sort of correction, bringing support back to the levels of the 1990s. The Iraq War may have increased the numbers thinking that the role of military power is overemphasized.

The goal of "combating international terrorism" received nearly universal support in 2002, with 91 percent calling it very important and 7 percent somewhat important. The intensity of these views clearly derived from the experience of the September 11 attacks, because in 1998 a lower 79 percent called the goal very important. By 2004, this was 71 percent, and there it remained in 2006 (72 percent). The year 2008 has seen a new drop to 67 percent. Thus two-thirds currently call combating international terrorism very important—high, but below the levels prior to the start of the Iraq War, or even those of the late 1990s.

"Preventing the spread of nuclear weapons" elicited 86 percent calling it very important in 2002 (somewhat important, 12 percent). (This was similar to responses in the 1990s: 84 percent called this very important in 1990, as did 82 percent in 1994 and 1998.) By 2004, after a year of the Iraq War, 73 percent called preventing the spread of nuclear weapons very important, where it remained in 2006 and 2008 (74 percent, 73 percent). With the 25 percent calling it somewhat important, a near-unanimous 95 percent said in 2008 that it was an important goal.

Despite the Bush administration's disinterest in the UN, the goal of "strengthening the United Nations" was actually at a high-water mark among the public in 2002, with 55 percent calling it "very important"—the highest recorded by CCGA since 1974, and 10 points higher than in 1998. Thirty-three percent called it somewhat important; just 12 percent said it was not an important goal. In 2004—after the bruising experience with the Security Council over Iraq—only 38 percent called strengthening the UN an important goal, a 17-point drop. By 2006, 40 percent saw it as very important, 39 percent as somewhat important, and 19 percent as not important; 2008 was statistically identical (39 percent very, 40 percent somewhat). (Other poll questions show concretely what measures majorities would support to strengthen the UN; a section is devoted to this below.)

It is intriguing that a goal deeply imbued with the history of U.S. foreign policy rhetoric—"Protecting weaker nations against foreign aggression"—has always gotten a wary reception. In 2002 only 35 percent called it a very important goal, while 56 percent called it somewhat important (not important: 8 percent). This was a "traditional" level of assent, very similar to that in 1998, 1990, and 1986. In 2004 support for the goal dropped, with just 18 percent calling it "very important"—a historic low. In 2006 support recovered somewhat, with 22 percent calling the goal very important, 65 percent somewhat important, and 11 percent not important. In this case as well, attitudes in 2008 are like those of 2006 (24 percent very important, 63 percent somewhat important).

"Helping to bring a democratic form of government to other nations" is an ambiguous phrase that embraces everything from invasion and occupation to activities like those of ex-president Jimmy Carter. Historically, the public has always treated this goal somewhat gingerly: its highest support was 30 percent calling it very important in 1986, and in 1998 29 percent said so. In 2002, only 24 percent called it very important, but 59 percent called it somewhat important (not important: 16 percent). In 2004—after the Bush administration had largely abandoned the premise of Iraqi weapons of mass destruction and migrated to the argument that the invasion was an exercise in bringing democracy to the Middle East—only 14 percent called bringing democracy a very important goal. The number calling it somewhat important was unchanged (58 percent), but those saying it was not important had grown 11 points to 27 percent. In 2006, results were statistically no different. 2008 saw a slight recovery: 17 percent called bringing democracy very important, 59 percent somewhat important, and a lesser 23 percent not important.

This finding is confirmed by the German Marshall Fund's polling, which asked a simpler question beginning in 2005: "Do you think it should or should not be the role of the United States to help establish democracy in other countries?" In 2005, 52 percent said yes and 41 percent no; in 2006 responses were divided (45 percent and 48 percent); and in 2007 only 37 percent said yes, and a 56 percent majority said no; 2008 results were statistically identical (38 percent yes, 56 percent no). The "yes" and "no" levels in this GMF question align roughly with the "favor" and "oppose" levels in questions asked about the Iraq War in media polls over the same years, which suggests respondents are interpreting the GMF question's wording concretely in terms of Iraq.

Most of these goals show the same pattern: a clear drop in the intensity of public support for the goal, but no real change in the shape of the underlying majority attitude toward it. A kind of pause was registered in 2004 toward the maintenance of military supremacy, and especially toward democracy promotion—at least as this was now understood. At the same time the goals of combating international terrorism and preventing the spread of nuclear weapons remained in 2008 goals that around seven in ten Americans called very important. To interpret the measures as signs of increasing public fatigue is problematic because most recovered a bit in 2006 and remained stable in 2008, while increasing fatigue should logically show further declines in support.

Perceptions of International Threats to the United States

A philosophy of engagement also involves having a coherent set of perceptions about real or potential dangers to the United States's vital interests. Here again the CCGA surveys are the most informative for our purpose because of the lengths of their trendlines. CCGA has given respondents "a list of possible threats to the vital interest of the United States in the next 10 years" and has asked whether each is "a critical threat, an important but not critical threat, or not an important threat at all."

International terrorism has been seen as a critical threat by a large majority since CCGA first began asking about it in 1994. In that year—the year after the first bombing of the World Trade Center—69 percent of the public saw international terrorism as a critical threat (with 25 percent calling it important but not critical). It should be noted how far ahead of the policy elite the public was on this issue. In 1994 only 33 percent of CCGA's sample of foreign policy leaders saw international terrorism as a critical threat (58 percent said it was important but not critical).

By 1998, 84 percent of the public saw international terrorism as a critical threat; thus, although the 9/11 attacks were obviously a shock, they did not create a new public attitude. In 2002 this view was a near-unanimous 91 percent. In 2004, however, there was a 10–point drop (to 81 percent) in those who saw international terrorism as a critical threat—a level that remained stable in 2006. Thus the levels of public concern returned to about what they were in the 1990s—which, at the time, were higher than is often thought. These fluctuations in the size of an overwhelming majority view can be reasonably attributed to the Iraq War's impact.

"The possibility of unfriendly countries becoming nuclear powers" is another threat CCGA asks about, and its relevance to the Bush administration's case for going to war with Iraq is obvious. The number viewing this as a critical threat dropped sharply (19 points) between 2002 and 2004. However, the levels of concern have been high throughout: 85 percent calling the threat critical in 2002, 66 percent in 2004, and 69 percent in 2006. Those thinking this is not an important threat at all have never exceeded 5 percent.

"Islamic fundamentalism" might be imagined to form a cluster for the public with the threats just discussed, but in fact it has not. In 1994 and 1998, only 33–38 percent called it a critical threat, and another 33–36 percent called it important but not critical. In the summer of 2002, less than a year after the experience of the 9/11 attacks, 61 percent saw it as critical, but in 2004 concern about "Islamic fundamentalism" had returned to 38 percent seeing it as a critical threat and 43 percent as important but not critical. There was a slight rise in 2006 (43 percent critical, 41 percent important). It appears that over the whole period, the public has distinguished Islamic fundamentalism as a politico-religious current from the issue of terrorism, while still regarding it with concern. Here is a case of the public distinguishing sharply between kinds of threats. The Iraq War's effect is perhaps discernible in the quick drop from the elevated levels in 2002 of those calling Islamic fundamentalism a critical threat.

It is useful to bring in, for comparison, a different potential threat of a classical great-power type. Concerns about "the development of China as a world power" were moderate in 1990, when the cold war was ending but the Soviet Union still existed; higher from 1994 through 2002; and then dropped 16 points in 2004, returning to the late cold war level. Forty percent called the rise of China a critical threat in 1990, 56–57 percent did in 1994, 1998, and 2002, and 40 percent did in 2004.[13] Although China's rise is a very different type of threat, the pattern of fewer respondents calling it critical in 2004 than in 2002 still holds.

The difficulties encountered in Iraq and the absence of weapons of mass destruction there led the public to get its anxieties back into proportion. The data on perceptions of threats in 2006 still showed a majority seeing a world with many dangers. However, this majority's size has returned to about that of the pre-9/11 period.

THE PUBLIC'S RESPONSES TO QUESTIONS ON FORMS OF ENGAGEMENT

Attitudes Toward Preventive or Preemptive Military Action

It is unfortunate that the data requires us to consider preventive and preemptive military action in the same section because the two are quite different, and many arguments favoring the Iraq War relied on conflating the two. The distinction between preventive war (attacking a country that is developing into a potential adversary) and preemptive war (a military response to clear evidence of an imminent attack) is obviously not one in which all Americans have been schooled. However, the most informative poll questions on the subject present both types of war and ask respondents to judge their relative propriety.

The Bush administration made the claim that Saddam Hussein's Iraq presented both a long- and a short-term danger. National security advisor Condoleeza Rice's famous comment about whether Iraq had a nuclear weapons program—"There will always be some uncertainty . . . [but] we don't want the smoking gun to be a mushroom cloud"—was a perfect conflation of the case for preventive war ("uncertainty") with the case for preemptive war ("mushroom cloud").[14]

Six months after the invasion, the Program on International Policy Attitudes (PIPA) asked a complex poll question in an effort to understand whether and how the public made such distinctions. In November 2003, respondents were offered four alternatives as follows (emphases below have been added):

> For some time there have been debates about when, as a rule, countries have the right to overthrow the government of another country. For each of the following please indicate which position is closest to yours.
>
> a. Countries have the right to overthrow another government if they have strong evidence that the other country is acquiring weapons of mass destruction that could be used to attack them at *some point in the future.*
>
> b. Countries have the right to overthrow another government only if they have strong evidence that they are in *imminent* danger of being attacked with weapons of mass destruction by the other country.
>
> c. Countries have the right to overthrow another government only if the other country attacks them first.
>
> d. Countries have the right to use military force to stop another country from invading, but this does not give them the right to overthrow the invading country's government.

Three in ten (31 percent) chose position (a) that justified preventive war. Four in ten (41 percent) chose position (b) that justified preemptive war but rejected preventive war. Only one in ten (9 percent) chose position (c) that justified defensive war waged until the overthrow of the enemy government, while rejecting preemptive war. Another 15 percent, however, chose defensive war strictly limited to repelling an invasion (d). Thus 24 percent altogether rejected preemptive war, even in the face of an imminent attack. Two-thirds (65 percent) rejected preventive war.

In 2004, CCGA asked a similar question, with three choices instead of four. CCGA's question ran as follows:

> Which best describes the conditions under which you think countries, on their own, should have the right to go to war with another country they believe may pose a threat to them?
>
> a. If they have strong evidence that the other country is acquiring weapons of mass destruction that could be used against them at some point in the future.
>
> b. Only if they have strong evidence that they are in imminent danger of being attacked by the other country.
>
> c. Only if the other country attacks them first.

The CCGA question is roughly comparable to the earlier PIPA question. In summer 2004, less than one-fifth (17 percent) now chose the position that justified preventive war (a)—down from 31 percent. Now more than half (53 percent) chose the position that justified preemptive war but rejected preventive war (b)—up from 41 percent. The final option (c) garnered 24 percent—exactly as many as chose (c) plus (d) in PIPA's 2003 question. Thus 77 percent now rejected preventive war.

It appears that from fall 2003 to summer 2004, Americans who accepted preventive war as a legitimate option dropped by almost half; those who accepted preemptive war but rejected preventive war rose by about one-quarter; and the numbers who insisted on strictly defined defensive war as the only legitimate option remained the same. This is a dramatic change in a short time, and it can be fairly attributed to the effects of the Iraq War.

Attitudes Toward Military Action to Ensure the Oil Supply

A classic accusation made about the Iraq War by some opponents (as well as about the Gulf War before it) is that it was a "war for oil." Helpfully, CCGA began asking in 2002: "Would you favor or oppose the use of U.S. troops to ensure the oil supply?" From 2002 through 2006, willingness to see U.S. troops deployed for this purpose dropped by 20 points—from 65 to 45 percent. Opposition grew from 30 to 49 percent in the same period.[15] Regrettably, there is no trendline before 2002 because this would give us a pre-9/11 test level of support, but with what we have, it seems reasonable that both the invasion experience and the mounting costs have lowered the base of support for military action that is clearly related to assuring the supply of oil.

Attitudes Toward Military Action to Install a Democratic Government

Although there are trendlines that measure change in the support for the general idea of establishing democracy in other countries, most of them begin in 2004—that is, just after the key moment of change that we have seen in other measures.

Only one question (from CCGA) links such efforts explicitly to using military force. In 2004, 63 percent opposed "the use of U.S. troops to install democratic governments in states where dictators rule"; only 30 percent were in favor. Results in 2006 showed slightly more opposition (up to 66 percent) but the same level of minority support (29 percent).

PIPA asked a few questions in 2004 and 2005 to test arguments the Bush administration was then making. In December 2004, 59 percent disagreed that "the U.S. has the right and even the responsibility to overthrow dictatorships and help their people build a democracy" (agree: 34 percent). In September 2005, PIPA found that only 19 percent of Americans thought "the goal of overthrowing Iraq's authoritarian government and establishing a democracy was by itself a good enough reason to go to war with Iraq." Seventy-four percent disagreed, including 60 percent of Republicans—levels that suggested many supporters of the Iraq War could not stomach the democratization rationale and still held to a security-based rationale for the war. The same study asked whether "the experience in Iraq [has] made you feel better or worse about the possibility of using military force to bring about democracy in the future?" Seventy-two percent said the experience had made them feel worse about this option (better: 19 percent).

Attitudes Toward Military Action Against Terrorist Groups

In 1998, 2002, and 2004, CCGA asked respondents about a range of measures that could be undertaken "to combat international terrorism." (It did not ask this series in 2006.) One of the Bush administration's accusations against

Saddam Hussein's regime was that it worked closely with al Qaeda—an accusation that has been discredited by various blue-ribbon commissions and is no longer accepted by most experts. Thus it is worthwhile to look for a shift in public opinion in 2004, as support for U.S. strikes abroad on terrorist nonstate actors might conceivably have frayed as a result of the Iraq experience.

In 1998, 74 percent favored "U.S. air strikes against terrorist training camps and other facilities"; in 2002 this was up to 87 percent; in 2004 it dropped negligibly to 83 percent. "Attacks by U.S. ground troops" on the same objectives were favored in 1998 by a relatively low 57 percent; in 2002 this was 84 percent; and in 2004 it dropped to 76 percent, with 20 percent opposed. In 2002 CCGA also proposed "toppling unfriendly regimes that support terrorist groups threatening the U.S." as another measure to combat international terrorism (actually an excellent description of the war in Afghanistan in 2001). Seventy-three percent supported this, with 24 percent opposed. In 2004 support fell six points to 67 percent (28 percent opposed)—a drop reasonably attributable to the Iraq War.

Of course these are very general questions, bound together by the premise that terrorist groups would be the targets of military action. Nonetheless, it appears that support in principle for direct attacks on nonstate actors—or even on state patrons they might have—diminished little in the first year after the Iraq invasion.

Attitudes Toward Using U.S. Troops for Humanitarian Purposes

Since the Iraq War has been presented intermittently by the Bush administration as a humanitarian undertaking—first, because Saddam Hussein was guilty of documented crimes against humanity, and later, because the rising violence between Shi'a and Sunni would overwhelm Iraq if U.S. forces were not kept there—one could imagine less public openness to any new opportunities to make sacrifices in other humanitarian crises. Overall, though, the Iraq War has brought only a little wear and tear on the public's willingness to intervene in genocidal situations.

CCGA first asked in 2002 whether respondents would favor or oppose deploying U.S. troops "to stop a government from committing genocide and killing large numbers of its own people." In 2002, 77 percent favored this type of use of American troops; in 2004, it was 75 percent; in 2006, 71 percent; and in 2008, 69 percent—only an eight-point drop in six years. Similarly, Pew asked in September 2001 (before the attacks) and then in October 2005 whether "protecting groups or nations that are threatened with genocide" should have "top priority," "some priority," or "no priority at all." In 2001, 49 percent gave this top priority, and 41 percent some priority; in 2005 46 percent gave it top, and 39 percent some priority. Those wanting no priority were just 5 percent in both years (nonresponses did grow from 5 to 10 percent).

Lines of questioning that only started after the Iraq War began do hint at growing fatigue. In 2004, 72 percent told CCGA that they were willing to use U.S. troops "to deal with humanitarian crises," with 25 percent opposed; in 2006 this was down to 66 percent (28 percent opposed). PIPA asked three times in 2004–5 about contributing U.S. troops to a UN peacekeeping force in Darfur. In July 2004 57 percent supported contributing troops, as did 60 percent in December, but support fell to 54 percent in June 2005. These drops, though real, do not exceed six points and do not suggest any effect on the public's broader commitment to its values regarding genocide. A comparable question asked by CCGA in 2006 and 2008 found 65 and 62 percent, respectively, favoring the use of U.S. troops as "part of an international peacekeeping force to stop the killing in Darfur."

Attitudes Toward Strengthening the UN, Improving Its Peacekeeping Capacities, and Contributing Troops

Beyond the undoubted importance of contributing a share of troops to some UN peacekeeping operations, we should also consider the public's willingness to invest in the UN's capacity to conduct peacekeeping—a capacity that has been overstretched at several points in its history. Some poll measures show a definite negative impact from the Iraq experience—especially those that evaluate the UN's general performance. At the same time, though, in other questions that focus on actual willingness to invest in the UN's capacities and allow it a major role in world decision making, majority support is considerable and little affected by the Iraq War.

In brief, the public remains disappointed with the UN's performance, but a majority looks on the institution favorably nonetheless. A large majority would like to see the UN reinforced, with more peacekeeping resources of its own, and with the United States more willing to make decisions collaboratively in the UN.

A venerable trendline question, asked most frequently by Gallup, says, "Do you think the United Nations is doing a good job or a poor job in trying to solve the problems it has had to face?" In February 2002, 58 percent gave the

UN a good rating and 36 percent a poor rating. By September 2002—when the Bush administration's will to proceed first collided with opposition in France and Germany—the "good" rating was down to 40 percent and the "poor" rating up to 50 percent (CBS). In January 2003, once UN inspectors had arrived on the ground in Iraq, a 50 percent plurality gave the UN a good rating (42 percent poor), and this mildly positive view held through February. In March came the administration's failure to gain UN Security Council approval to invade Iraq; the "good" rating now fell to 37 percent (58 percent "poor"). Here it held steady until the beginning of 2006, when it dropped a bit further to 30 percent (64 percent "poor"). This is one of the rare instances where an attitude impacted by the Iraq experience did not either find a plateau, or recover somewhat after 2004.

Throughout this time, however, favorable attitudes toward the United Nations in general were higher than ratings of its performance. In the simplest and most frequently asked question, "Would you say your overall opinion of the United Nations is very favorable, mostly favorable, mostly unfavorable, or very unfavorable?" favorable ratings of the UN remained at majority levels from February 2003 through May 2005—at 65–68 percent in the month before the war began, then fluctuating in a 55–66 percent range afterward.[16] From October 2005 through April 2007, however, favorable views dropped into a lower range—48 to 61 percent—perhaps affected by unfolding news about past corruption in the Iraq oil-for-food program.[17]

A few trend questions that ask what role the UN should have in world decision making were first asked in 2004, a time of much speculation about whether the organization would go into a complete eclipse.

In November 2004 BBC World Service asked whether it would be a mainly positive or negative trend if the UN "becomes significantly more powerful in world affairs." Fifty-nine percent called this a positive trend, a figure which rose to 66 percent when WorldPublicOpinion.org repeated the question in December 2006. CCGA asked in summer 2004 whether respondents agreed or disagreed that "when dealing with international problems, the US should be more willing to make decisions within the United Nations, even if this means that the United States will somehow have to go along with a policy that is not its first choice." Two-thirds (66 percent) agreed, and just 29 percent disagreed. In 2006 this majority declined to 60 percent and in 2008 to 52 percent. This decline indicates some frustration with the UN, but it is not accompanied by less willingness to endow the UN with more resources.

When presented with the idea of seriously expanding the UN's peacekeeping capacity, seven in ten Americans have supported this idea in the years following the Iraq invasion. CCGA asked in 2004 and 2006 whether respondents would favor or oppose "having a standing UN peacekeeping force selected, trained and commanded by the United Nations"; 72–74 percent favored the idea, with only 20–24 percent opposed. In 2008 support remained stable at 70 percent. More broadly, 68 percent agreed in an October 2006 PIPA question that "for the US to move away from its role as world policeman and reduce the burden of its large defense budget, the US should invest in efforts to strengthen the UN's ability to deal with potential conflicts in the world" (28 percent disagreed). This is only a little lower than the 73 percent majority in 1995, the other occasion the question was asked.

It would be reasonable to assume that the burden of maintaining the Iraq War would preclude for the public any idea of contributing U.S. troops to a UN peacekeeping operation—at least in conditions short of genocide or other extreme humanitarian emergencies, as we have seen above. CCGA has asked at intervals since 1994, "In general, when the United States is asked to be part of a United Nations international peacekeeping force in a troubled part of the world, do you think we should take part or should not take part?" The 1990s saw growing majority support for responding to such a request by providing troops: 51 percent in 1994, 57 percent in 1998, and 64 percent in 2002. In 2004 support rose again to 78 percent; however, the trendline is not perfect, because in 2004 the respondent was unable to offer the response "it depends on circumstances." In earlier years, 16 percent on average answered "it depends," so had this option been available in 2004, support might have been around 62 percent.

Support for contributing to given UN peacekeeping operations can be expected to vary with the values evoked by the conflict situation and the mission's prospects for success. However, since the burden of the Iraq War has had no impact on responses to this trend question, it seems logical that later, when that burden is lessened or removed, majority support in principle will remain substantial.

Thus in the years after the Iraq invasion, the public has shown discrimination in its different views of the UN's performance, the UN's general value as an institution, and the UN's future role and capacities. This capacity of the public to discriminate has been a difficult point for students of public opinion to convey to others in the policy community. In the future, a successful U.S. recovery from the international costs of the Iraq War will entail recasting how the United States works within the UN. For American public opinion as well, a future administration's ability to gain support for its foreign policy will depend in part on understanding that even Americans who are critical of the UN tend to wish it more active and effective.

Attitudes Toward Foreign Aid

Since the Iraq War is also an exercise in development and nation-building, in which USAID is an active participant, it would be reasonable to expect that public attitudes toward foreign aid would be affected by this aspect of the Iraq experience. Overall, support for foreign aid in general did dip in 2004, only to recover in succeeding years.

A foreign policy goal that CCGA has asked about since 1974 is "helping to improve the standards of living of less developed nations." Each time since 1974, more than 70 percent have called this an important goal, though those calling it "very important" have never risen above 39 percent. In 2002, 82 percent called it an important goal (29 percent very important); in 2004 this fell to 72 percent (18 percent very important); and in 2006 it returned to 82 percent (22 percent very important).

Pew asked nearly the same question in 2001 (just before the 9/11 attacks) and once more in 2005. In 2001, 86 percent gave "helping improve the living standards in developing nations" a "top priority" (25 percent) or "some priority" (61 percent). In 2005, 89 percent gave it either a top priority (31 percent) or some priority (57 percent). Since Pew's 2005 measure is a little higher than that of 2001, this pattern accords well with the one shown in CCGA's polls—a dip in 2004 followed by a recovery.

There has always been more public interest in the goal of "combating world hunger," which has been seen as important by 90 percent or more; from 1974 through 2002, majorities called it "very important" (CCGA). In 2002 94 percent called combating world hunger an important goal (very important, 54 percent). In 2004 this dropped to 90 percent, with only 43 percent calling it very important; in 2006 it was 91 percent, and the numbers calling it very important recovered to 48 percent. The year 2008 showed no meaningful change (91 percent important, 46 percent very). During 2002–6, only 14–21 percent said it was *not* important to help developing countries, and only 6–9 percent said it was not important to combat world hunger.

The German Marshall Fund asked, beginning in 2005, respondents' views on "providing development assistance to poor countries." In 2005, 68 percent of Americans were favorable to this (21 percent very favorable); in 2006, a higher 72 percent (28 percent very favorable); and in 2007, a lower 66 percent (28 percent very favorable). Those unfavorable toward assistance remained in a narrow 25–30 percent range.

In 2007 GMF offered a list of seven kinds of donors and asked "who . . . should have the primary responsibility for delivering development assistance." The greatest number (37 percent) preferred multilateral institutions—"international organizations like the World Bank and the United Nations" (a preference shared, incidentally, by the European countries polled). In second place, about equal numbers of Americans preferred NGOs (18 percent) or the U.S. government (17 percent) for this task.

Overall, support for foreign aid has experienced only a light impact from the strain of the Iraq War. These questions do not go deep enough to locate signs of the large overestimates that most Americans have long made about how much foreign aid the United States gives. Much past research has established that a large majority assumes that foreign aid makes up 10 to 20 percent of the federal budget; if asked whether 1 percent of the budget (the actual level) would be an appropriate expenditure, a large majority endorses it.[18] It seems probable that any news Americans hear about Iraq would tend to reinforce this misperception because U.S. economic aid to reconstruct Iraq is substantial and often featured in the news. But strictly from the standpoint of measurable change over time, Americans' support for foreign aid seems to be surviving the Iraq experience fairly well.

Awareness of World Public Opinion Regarding the United States

This inquiry has found a good many changes that were minor and brief, and a few that were more substantial in its search for the Iraq War's effects on the public's larger foreign policy views. But there is another area in which change was substantial and meaningful: the public's perceptions of how world opinion regarded the United States and its foreign policy.

From November 2002 to July 2003, PIPA made repeated measurements of this perception, so we are fortunate to have a trendline that covers the key months of the launching of the Iraq War. PIPA asked, "Thinking now about the rest of the world, on average, how do you think people in other countries would rate how well the US is managing its foreign policy? Please answer on a scale of 0 to 10, with 0 being very poorly and 10 being very well."

In November 2002—a month of great stress over Iraq at the UN Security

Council—half of Americans thought the rest of the world would give U.S. foreign policy at least a 5 (20 percent) or higher (6–10: 30 percent). Only 45 percent perceived, more correctly, that the world's judgment might lie in the 0–4 range. In January 2003 those perceiving a negative judgment rose to 50 percent, then to 55 percent in February, and then stayed in this range in March (52 percent). The next poll was conducted from April 18 to 22, the very moment of the fall of Baghdad, which many thought would consolidate victory and improve the world's view of the invasion. Now only 34 percent thought the rest of the world would give U.S. foreign policy a rating between 0 and 4, and a 62 percent majority thought it would give a 5 (19 percent) or higher (43 percent).

Two months after the fall of Baghdad, however, a majority returned to the assessment that the rest of the world judged U.S. foreign policy negatively. In June 2003, 54 percent thought most would give it a 0–4 rating—about as many as had thought this in February and March; in July, 56 percent thought so. This question shows that many Americans were aware of the extent of world disapproval before the war began; then they hoped that a rapid, successful conclusion would stem this disapproval, but soon they realized that the Iraq War would be a continuing source of negative reactions to the United States.

In March 2003 PIPA began asking a different trendline question that cut closer to the bone because it asked directly about the war: "Thinking about how all the people in the world feel about the US going to war with Iraq, do you think the majority of people favor it, the majority of people oppose it, or views are evenly balanced?" PIPA asked this question nine times from March 2003 to March 2006. Since the question offers a middle position, it is a good measure of how many felt confident that the world overall either mostly favored or mostly opposed the war.

At the opening of the war in March 2003, 31 percent thought a world majority favored the Iraq War, 35 percent thought a majority opposed it, and 31 percent thought the two views were evenly balanced. Never again did more than 27 percent think the world viewed the war favorably. The percentage thinking a world majority *opposed* the war rose until it reached 53 percent by October 2004. Apparently, however, it did not grow into a robust majority, because in March 2006 it was 49 percent. Those saying the world public's views were evenly balanced generally held between 30 and 33 percent (March 2003–October 2004), but in March 2006 they were down to 28 percent. When the question was last asked (March 2006), only one-fifth—21 percent—thought a world majority favored the war; half (49 percent) thought a world majority opposed it; and just over one-quarter (28 percent) believed there was no majority view at the world level.

Another trendline question, this time by Pew, began in July 2004; it asks about the general reputation of the United States in the world. Respondents are asked whether "compared to the past . . . the US is more respected by other countries these days, less respected by other countries, or as respected as it has been in the past." Respondents who said the United States is less respected now were asked whether this is a major problem, a minor problem, or not a problem at all.[19]

The majority that thinks the United States is less respected than in the past has varied little from July 2004 to May 2008, but judgments about the importance of the problem have changed. From 2004 through 2006, 65–67 percent said the United States is now less respected; in May 2008 this was up to 71 percent. But more importantly, the numbers calling this a major problem for the country have grown from four in ten to a clear majority. In July 2004, 23 percent of the whole sample thought this loss of respect was only a minor problem; another 20 percent said there was the same amount of respect as before; and 10 percent said the country was now actually more respected abroad. Taken together, 63 percent were unconcerned for various reasons. By May 2008, 56 percent of the whole sample thought loss of respect for the United States was real and a major problem. Those calling it a minor problem had dropped by half, down to 14 percent; another 18 percent said there was the same respect as before; and 7 percent said the country was now more respected. Taken together, only 39 percent were unconcerned by the problem.[20]

These three measures point to public attitudes that have changed gradually but powerfully during the course of the war with Iraq. Beliefs about the direction of world public opinion on the United States and its policies have steadily altered over time. It seems probable that the length and inconclusive quality of the Iraq War are important factors in this change.

CONCLUSIONS

What can we conclude from this examination of the trend data? The underlying structure of attitudes about the role of the United States in the world has been modified very little by the Iraq War. Americans' philosophy of engagement, and the role they would like to see the United States take in the world, have changed least of all. However, the rush of events in 2003 and early 2004—the Bush administration's struggle with the UN Security Council, the success of the first month of military operations, the rise of the insurgency, the absence of weapons of mass destruction, and the shift to a democratization rationale—impacted a range of public attitudes about forms of engagement sharply and briefly in 2004. The public has discriminated among different kinds, levels, and motives of engagement on international issues and has taken care not to throw the baby out with the bathwater. Most measures of these attitudes recovered by 2006, but a few did not, and they are signals of what has changed when the public looks now at foreign policy.

A majority in the public is now on guard against the idea of preventive war and likely to resist any project that looks like a preventive war. At the same time, in a situation where a truly imminent threat is objectively present—and widely recognized as such outside the United States as well—it would be possible to marshal support for preemptive military action, especially if this action had UN sanction.

The more closely a potential military action is related to the oil supply, the lower its initial base of support in the American public is likely to be in the current climate. Since the 1991 Gulf War policy practitioners have largely anticipated this, and arguments made to the public in favor of a military action have almost always avoided making a connection to oil. This habit will stand practitioners in good stead in coming years.

The public's concern over whether any proposed military action is truly multilateral was always great, but this has only been heightened by the Iraq War. The multilateral nature of a military effort will be both more necessary and more difficult to demonstrate to the public's satisfaction.

The public has long been willing to see the United States contribute a share of troops to peacekeeping operations, but the UN aegis for these operations has probably become even more important than it was in the past. Although the public has issues with the UN's performance, the UN hallmark provides more assurance of participating in a truly multilateral effort than is otherwise available. The Iraq experience of a slowly dissolving ad hoc coalition has driven this home.

The greatest change brought about by the Iraq War is actually the American public's much greater awareness of world public opinion about the United States. Policy practitioners are likely to find that in the next debate over a possible military action, world public opinion—as well as what Americans think—will be an inescapable factor, present in the debate from the begin-

ning, affecting how the American public evaluates the options put before it. Elites will have more difficulty controlling the terms of the debate than they did in 2003, and the potential cost of losing world support will rank higher with the public.

Having mentioned what has changed, it is equally important to understand what remains the same. The public's philosophy of engagement is no different than it was before the Iraq War. The public remains somewhat more multilateralist than the norm in U.S. foreign policy itself. It remains supportive of a robust defense, though many more now think that the role of military power has been overemphasized in recent years. If the public had full information about the size of the defense budget and its proportion of the federal budget, it could probably support significant cuts in aspects of defense spending, if these accompanied adaptations to current threats.[21]

Large majorities do continue to see important threats to the United States; these majorities are just not as large as they were in the two years after the 9/11 attacks. In particular, willingness to conduct military operations against *nonstate actors* practicing terrorism has not been affected by the Iraq experience.

Democracy promotion has been given a bad name by the Iraq experience, and support for aggressive versions of it is unlikely to return anytime soon. However, the traditional forms of support and education meant to strengthen democratic practices in other countries have about the same underlying support as they had before the war.

Support for foreign aid among Americans is essentially what it was before the Iraq War—strong where the principle is concerned, colored by overestimations of how much aid the United States gives, and also conditioned by low expectations regarding effectiveness. These strengths and weaknesses are virtually unchanged by the war experience.

Everything considered, these effects do not put very serious constraints on U.S. policymakers. Yet the policy community may find it hard to live within them. In the eighteen years since the end of the cold war some bad habits have developed. The cold-war period is remembered as one of greater American hegemony than it really was, and the aspects of U.S.-Soviet condominium that also characterized that time appear dimly in the rear-view mirror. The 1990s, which logically from a realist perspective might have been a time of careful consolidation of hegemony in every dimension of hard and soft power, was in fact a time of relative disinvestment. To name two examples, opportunities were lost to assist Russia more generously as it went through a painful restructuring of its economy and institutions, and the United States's infrastructure for its public diplomacy was judged unnecessary and dismantled. The hazy recollection of how American hegemony actually worked in past decades has fostered grandiose expectations on the elite's part that sometimes collide with the parameters set by the public.

For political leaders and the policy community to live within the constraints of public opinion, however, they would not need to go very far. They would have to:

- drop preventive war as a policy alternative;
- develop a concerted energy policy that can give the impression that military options in the Middle East are *not* a mainstay of American strategic planning about energy;
- take multilateral organizations, especially the United Nations, seriously and view them as candidates for long-term investments; and
- realize that world public opinion has become much more of a force than in the past due to globalization and the ongoing information revolution.

It would be entirely possible for the Obama administration and for the policy elite in general to make these four adjustments—if they convince themselves that all four are indispensable.

8 ARE WE SAFER NOW?

Peter J. Dombrowski and John S. Duffield

> *Senator John W. Warner (R-VA): "Are you able to say at this time, if we continue what you have laid before the Congress here as a strategy, do you feel that that is making America safer? Does that make America safer?"*
>
> *General David H. Petraeus: "I don't know, actually. I have not sat down and sorted it out in my own mind."*[1]

POSING THE RIGHT QUESTION

During the long debate over the Iraq War, the value of the war to the United States has often been assessed largely in terms of the actual or projected progress within Iraq itself. When the situation within Iraq looked good or as though it would improve, proponents of the war felt vindicated. When things were going badly or looked like they would get worse, critics of the war felt the same.

For experts, including the policymakers, diplomats, and generals responsible for U.S. operations and policy in Iraq, the war's trends and outcomes may provide appropriate standards by which to judge the success of their efforts. But for the American government as a whole, charged with promoting U.S. national security in general, they are not sufficient. The president and his advisors bear much wider responsibilities—they must consider not only the success of the Iraq War itself but also the impact of the war on the full-range of international challenges, threats, and opportunities facing the United States.

Thus, for the American people, as for the Republican senator from Virginia, the paramount question is not whether we are winning in Iraq, but whether the United States is more secure today for having undertaken the war than it would have been had the Bush administration chosen another course of action. It is whether, given competing demands on limited U.S. national security resources, some if not all of the blood and treasure devoted to Iraq could have been better spent in the pursuit of other pressing national security goals or husbanded for future national security challenges (not to mention used to address urgent domestic needs). In short, after six years of U.S. military intervention in Iraq, are we safer?

As discussed in Chapter 1, it is easy to understand why many people are not interested in or would rather avoid addressing this question. But we believe that it is essential to do so. Bush administration positions aside, the issues of what American interests were and are at stake in Iraq remain in dispute to this day. In the near to intermediate term, the challenge is largely one of coping with state and nonstate threats, as represented by Iran and al Qaeda, respectively. In the intermediate to long run, U.S. interests involve the resolution of several deadly and long-standing conflicts in the Middle East, including the Arab-Israeli conflict, Shi'a-Sunni disputes, and the struggle for dominance between Arabs and their non-Arab neighbors such as Iranians and Turks. Sometimes forgotten but always in the thoughts of the geopolitically minded is access to and control over global energy supplies, including Persian Gulf petroleum and natural gas. How the Iraq War has furthered such enduring interests and the declared objectives of the Bush administration will go a long way toward determining its overall impact on U.S. national security, especially if we can account for the various unintended consequences of the war and the sacrifices—human, financial, political, moral, and so forth—that have accompanied the war effort.[2]

Consequently, this concluding chapter offers specific answers to the question of whether we are safer now. It begins with a review of the original expectations of the broader consequences of the war for U.S. national security. Building on the preceding chapters, we then offer our own comprehensive assessment of the benefits and costs of the war. We complement this assessment with a counterfactual analysis of the likely consequences of other courses of action that the Bush administration might plausibly have pursued. Would the United States be more secure today if President Bush had not chosen to invade Iraq the way the U.S. military did in March 2003? We conclude with a discussion of the lessons of the war for future U.S. policy in Iraq and beyond.

INITIAL EXPECTATIONS

Before summarizing the costs and benefits of the war, it is worth revisiting the nation's original expectations about the consequences of invading Iraq. The Bush administration argued that a war would eliminate a serious threat to the United States and its interests, would have a number of other benefits for U.S. national security, and would cost the American people little or nothing. Above all, senior administration officials repeatedly claimed that Iraq possessed chemical and biological weapons, was actively seeking the means to manufacture nuclear weapons, and would acquire nuclear weapons soon. Moreover, they maintained that Saddam Hussein posed a credible threat to use these weapons of mass destruction (WMD) against American forces and allies and to share them with terrorist groups like al Qaeda.[3] By March 2003 if not before, President Bush and his staff were convinced that Saddam would not disarm as required by the United Nations. Speaking at a press conference just two weeks before the invasion, President Bush remarked, "The world needs him [Saddam] to answer a single question: Has the Iraqi regime fully and unconditionally disarmed, as required by Resolution 1441, or has it not?"[4] Contrary to the judgment of several key allies, the UN weapons inspectors, and the rhetoric of the Iraqi regime, President Bush decided that the answer was "no" and that the time to act was at hand.

In the months preceding the war, the U.S. government and its supporters offered a wide range of additional reasons for invading Iraq above and beyond the president's focus on Iraqi weapons of mass destruction and ties to international terrorists. In Chapter 4, F. Gregory Gause summarizes the list quite well: to support nonproliferation, to prosecute the war on terror, to promote democracy, to help resolve the Arab-Israeli conflict, and to maintain a strategic position in the region largely defined in terms of access to oil.[5] For example, administration supporters argued that a war could lead to a proverbial virtuous cycle of peace in the entire Middle East. As President Bush mused at the American Enterprise Institute in early 2003, "A liberated Iraq can show the power of freedom to transform that vital region," and a new democratic government in Iraq "would serve as a dramatic and inspiring example."[6] As late as March 2005, following elections in Iraq and in the Palestinian territories, a U.S. government official lauded the "snowball effect" of democratization on the region.[7]

In addition to justifying the war on a variety of national security grounds, the Bush administration minimized the potential costs of the war and the possible unintended consequences of an invasion. Government officials universally painted a picture of a quick and inexpensive victory, with American forces handing over power to a friendly Iraqi regime in a matter of months.[8] Indeed, Vice President Dick Cheney famously claimed that the war would virtually pay for itself through increased oil revenues as Iraqi fields were brought back on line. When Lawrence Lindsey, the president's chief economic advisor, casually suggested a potential price tag of as much as $200 billion, this figure was roundly criticized by others in the administration, and Lindsey was subsequently dismissed.[9] Later, the head of the Office of Management and Budget estimated that a war with Iraq would cost only $50 to $60 billion.[10] Although the assessment that an invasion would be relatively cheap was not a reason in and of itself for choosing war, it did play an important role in convincing experts and the public that a cost-benefit analysis of the war would be highly favorable.

Not everyone shared these upbeat expectations, however. To the contrary, many people outside the government questioned the Bush administration's portrayal of the generally positive consequences of a war with Iraq. Some were skeptical of the administration's claims about the benefits that would accrue from deposing Saddam Hussein. They argued that the threat posed by Iraq was greatly exaggerated; that it did not possess a significant arsenal of WMD; that if it did, Iraq could be deterred from using them; that it lacked meaningful ties to al Qaeda and other anti-American terrorist groups; and that it would in any case never provide terrorists with WMD.[11]

At the same time, a number of experts suggested that the costs of a war would be much higher than the Bush administration claimed. Some focused on the likely economic consequences. Perhaps the most thorough analysis was conducted by Yale University economist William Nordhaus. Considering both the costs of military operations and those for subsequent occupation and peacekeeping, reconstruction and nation-building, and humanitarian assistance efforts, he estimated that U.S. government outlays in the first decade following the initiation of hostilities could amount to anywhere from $151 billion (2002 dollars) in the event of a short and favorable war to $755 billion in the case of a protracted and unfavorable conflict. If the possible impact on oil markets and macroeconomic effects were included, the total costs to the United States could range from $99 to $1,924 billion.[12]

Others pointed to an array of possible negative consequences outside Iraq. For example, Brent Scowcroft, who had served as national security advisor to President George H. W. Bush, feared that an attack on Iraq would set back the war on terror by diverting attention and resources, undermining international cooperation, and provoking outrage against the United States in the Arab world.[13] Former secretary of state James Baker warned that unilateral action would damage U.S. relations with practically all Arab countries and even many of the United States's traditional allies in Europe and elsewhere.[14] In what was perhaps the most prescient analysis, Steven Miller of Harvard University summarized these and a number of other concerns, including how a war could jeopardize a range of significant American interests and undermine the overall position of the United States in the world. "Even if the military campaign goes as the Bush administration hopes and is easy and cheap," he judged, "these other considerations may weigh so heavily in the scales that they would lead to the conclusion that the net impact of the war was negative."[15]

In sum, as the Bush administration prepared, under a cloak of operational secrecy, to attack Iraq, supporters of launching a war against Saddam Hussein's regime publically minimized the costs and maximized the potential benefits of a war while critics discounted the potential benefits and envisioned much higher costs. As many of the contributors to this volume have already demonstrated, much of the debate during the ebbs and flows of the war itself followed a similar pattern. Bush administration officials and their political supporters interpreted developments in Iraq through the lenses of ideology, neoconservative security policy beliefs, and political necessity; as such, their assessments remained strikingly upbeat even in the face of bad news from commanders in the field, Iraqi officials themselves, and the criticisms of key American allies. In a similar fashion, critics often reflexively discounted so-called good news such as al Qaeda figures killed, falling levels of violence, restored services, and periods when the entire Middle East appeared to be heading in a positive direction. With the passage of time, official reports, leaked data, and insider accounts by key participants have allowed us to evaluate these claims and counterclaims more carefully.

THE BALANCE SHEET: OUR OVERALL ASSESSMENT

The contributors to this volume have provided detailed accounts of some of the most important national security issue areas affected by the Iraq War. While not comprehensive by any means, taken as a whole, they provide a solid basis for drawing more general conclusions about how the Iraq War has affected U.S. national security and how it is likely to continue to do so in the coming years. In the following pages, we draw on the preceding chapters to offer our own overall assessment of the consequences of the war for U.S. national security, both in and outside Iraq, since March 2003.

As discussed in Chapter 1 and reflected in the presentation of the other chapters, we have divided the national security consequences of the Iraq War into two broad categories. The first concerns the effects of the war on the overall security environment faced by the United States. To what degree and in what ways has it furthered or impeded the achievement of other important goals of U.S. national security policy? The second concerns the impact of the war on the instruments and resources of U.S. national security policy. To what degree has it increased or reduced the ability of the United States to address the principal challenges to its interests?

Our assessment follows this structure as well. Before proceeding, however, we wish to make clear that our analysis is limited to those consequences of direct relevance to U.S. national security. We do not consider the costs to the people of Iraq in terms of lives lost, disrupted, or otherwise irrevocably altered, although these costs (as well as possible benefits) may well color U.S.-Iraq relations well into the future. By the same token, we do not assess the broader impact of the war on the international system or international law, which has arguably seen a significant setback to the emerging norms of humanitarian intervention,[16] and perhaps, an emerging norm supportive of preemptive action.[17]

Challenges to U.S. National Security Interests

We first consider the overall impact of the Iraq War on the security environment. To make this assessment, we must consider both the nature and magnitude of the challenges faced by the United States before the war and how those challenges have changed as a result of the war. Put differently, we must ask how and to what degree the war helped or hindered U.S. efforts to deal with the full spectrum of threats that existed to the United States and its national security interests. In this regard, it is important to exclude changes in threats, such as those potentially posed by the rise of China and the resurgence of Russian power, that are at most indirectly related to the war. In approaching this subject, we will further differentiate between the threat posed by Iraq and other relevant challenges.

The Iraqi Threat How has the war changed the threat posed by Iraq to the United States and its national security interests? Before the war, as is well known, the administration maintained that Iraq represented a grave, perhaps imminent threat that could not be effectively addressed through other means. By this account, Saddam Hussein was a brutal dictator who would stop at nothing to achieve his ends, both at home and abroad. Iraq possessed significant stockpiles of chemical and biological weapons and was actively seeking to acquire a nuclear capability, a long-sought goal that was nearly within its grasp. Iraq had significant ties with international terrorist organizations like al Qaeda and might provide such groups with WMD that could then be used against the United States and its allies.

As is also now well known, this portrait of the threat was greatly exaggerated.[18] Thus the benefits to U.S. national security derived from replacing Saddam's regime are necessarily much less than had been expected, claimed, or promised in that regard. Iraq possessed no meaningful stockpiles of WMD, and it was nowhere near acquiring nuclear weapons. Virtually all of its proscribed weapons had been destroyed years before, and it had made little or no effort to reconstitute its once-advanced nuclear program. As Ivo Daalder and James Lindsay summarized just two years after Saddam's statue fell, "It was clear that his regime had not constituted an imminent threat to the United States. . . . Whatever Saddam's desires, by the time the war started he did not have the capability to threaten his own people or his neighbors, let alone the US, with chemical, biological, or nuclear weapons."[19]

Likewise, Iraq had no significant ties with al Qaeda or any other significant terrorist organization that posed a threat to the United States. To the contrary, Saddam Hussein was distrustful of al Qaeda and viewed Islamic extremists as a threat to his regime. Thus the nightmare scenario that Saddam Hussein might give WMD to al Qaeda or other terrorists bent on attacking the United States was far-fetched.

Instead, the greatest contribution to U.S. national security resulted from the removal of Saddam Hussein himself from power. Gone is the tyrant who threatened and occasionally attacked other countries in the region, with the potential to create havoc on world energy markets. Nor is there much chance that his regime or something similar could be reconstituted. Saddam was executed and his sons killed, and a revival of Saddamist thinking seems highly unlikely. Even the Ba'th Party, which originally espoused a program and ideology that was attractive to some elements in Iraq and elsewhere, has little resonance today. Instead, they have been replaced by a fledgling, multiparty democracy that holds out the promise of a stable domestic order based on the rule of law and peaceful, if not necessarily friendly, relations with all its neighbors. Although the cost of toppling Saddam's regime has been high, the United States did what it said it would do and ensured that little would remain for diehards to rally around when it mandated the de-Ba'thification of the Iraqi military and government and facilitated the speedy trial and execution of Saddam by the Iraqi people themselves.

Nevertheless, the United States remains short of achieving the overarching goal articulated by the Bush administration: "an Iraq that has territorial integrity, a government that is democratic and pluralistic, a nation where the human rights of every ethnic and religious group are recognized and protected."[20] Moreover, the situation in Iraq remains fluid and the long-term political outcome uncertain. As General David Petraeus, then commander of coalition forces in Iraq and the person most responsible for implementing the "surge," warned in August 2008, "It's not durable yet. It's not self-sustaining. . . . There is still a lot of work to be done."[21] Likewise, his successor, General Ray Odierno, cautioned in September 2008 that the recent security gains remained "fragile and reversible."[22]

Thus while there are some reasons to be hopeful that Iraq will emerge united, stable, peaceful, democratic, and even an ally in the war on terror, a number of less desirable scenarios remain plausible, including partition, civil war, widespread repression, and state collapse.[23] Even simply maintaining the post-"surge" status quo as of late 2008 had numerous drawbacks. U.S. and Iraqi forces maintained only a tenuous hold over some parts of the country, a comprehensive political settlement among the various parties, tribes, religious groups, and ethnicities remained elusive, and other countries and nationals continued to meddle in Iraqi affairs with relative impunity. As Peter Galbraith has asked, "Is this a victory?" His assessment concludes that by late 2008, "George W. Bush has put the United States on the side of undemocratic Iraqis who are Iran's allies."[24] If this were to be the long-run state of affairs in Iraq, the outcome of the war would have to be judged severely. Neither Iraq nor the region would remain peaceful and, if U.S. troops were not present, real potential existed for Iraq to emerge as a hotbed of anti-Americanism, not to mention a breeding ground for future terrorists.

Challenges Beyond Iraq While the reduction in the threat posed by Iraq to U.S. national security was modest, especially in comparison with the expectations raised by the Bush administration, a central theme of this book is that the war has tended to exacerbate the other national security challenges facing the United States, in some cases substantially. This is true whether one looks at hostile states, nonstate actors, or the general international security environment.

In the case of state-based threats, the principal effects have occurred in the area of nonproliferation. Before the war, the United States faced potential proliferation threats from North Korea, Iran, Libya, and Syria (in addition to

Iraq). As Joseph Cirincione points out in Chapter 3, the war may have contributed measurably to Libya's decision to abandon its WMD programs and prompted some concessions on Iran's part. But the war did nothing to dissuade North Korea or Syria from pursuing their nuclear programs. And the failure of the Bush administration to follow up on Iran's initial hints of flexibility arguably contributed to the subsequent acceleration of that country's nuclear program. With its attention largely devoted to Iraq, the United States has not been able to convince Iran to halt its nuclear program either by leading an effective international coalition or by credibly threatening to use force.

Given Cirincione's overall assessment it is hard to disagree with his suggestion that the United States should adopt a more comprehensive nonproliferation strategy. Such a strategy would not eschew entirely the use of force, even outside the UN framework. It would, however, place much more emphasis on obtaining international cooperation by playing a leading and legitimating role for a revitalized multilateral approach to nonproliferation.

So far as nonstate threats are concerned, the principal impact of the war has been to impede, if not set back, progress in the war on terror. As Steven Simon shows in Chapter 2, the war has increased the potential terrorist threat to the United States and its interests in several ways. First, it has diverted critical resources, such as special-operations forces, intelligence assets, remotely piloted vehicles, and even combat units, from the critical theater in Central Asia, where the Taliban and al Qaeda have enjoyed a resurgence. It has provided a propaganda victory for jihadists, stirring up even more anti-Americanism in the Muslim and Arab communities that have served as recruiting grounds for terrorist organizations. In Miller's words, "The Iraq intervention [gave] radical Islamist polemicists continuing ammunition for their assertions that the United States wishes to dominate Arab lands, covets the region's oil, despoils Islamic holy sites, and is indifferent to the loss of Muslim lives and the suffering of Muslim populations."[25] Within Iraq itself, the war at least temporarily created a vacuum in which terrorist groups could train and experiment with new tactics. Likewise, Gause argues that the war did more to increase than to diminish the strength of terrorists in the region. To be sure, the United States itself has not experienced another large-scale terrorist attack on its homeland or significant interests outside Iraq and Afghanistan, but this is not a solid foundation on which to base a claim of success.

Not least important has been the impact of the war on the more general security environment. Here we focus on just three aspects: the spread of democracy, the stability of the Middle East, and U.S. energy security. Although the cultivation of democracy can serve several purposes, it has often been regarded as a way to promote U.S. national security, at least in the long term. Mature democracies are more stable, less conflict prone, and thus less likely to pose a threat to United States and its allies. Indeed, democracies are more likely to be U.S. allies or coalition partners.

While some progress has been made in Iraq, the war has tended to undercut the long-standing U.S. goal of promoting democracy, at least as a way of enhancing U.S. national security. This has certainly been the case in the Middle East, where the Bush administration expected or at least claimed that the establishment of a democracy in Iraq would set in motion a democratic wave throughout the region. As Gause notes in Chapter 4, what democratic reforms have taken place within the Middle East, especially in the form of elections, have tended to empower Islamist groups that complicate U.S. policy. Further, the initial enthusiasm for reforms in several other countries in the region quickly waned. The war has in fact been followed by less U.S. pressure on autocratic Arab leaders in the region, and Arab leaders have been able to use the war to reinforce their long-standing message about the perils of rapid democratic change. Even among more sympathetic Arab governments, the spillover problems of the war have caused them to feel less latitude to try political openings, and it has complicated the lives of pro-democracy Arabs by inflaming anti-U.S. sentiment. The idea of liberal democracy has become somewhat tainted by association with the highly unpopular intervention in Iraq. As Thomas Carothers and Marina Ottaway have argued elsewhere, there is considerable skepticism about U.S. intentions among Arab publics because the United States started pushing the democracy agenda at the same time that it began to prepare for war in Iraq. Thus democracy promotion is seen as a smokescreen for removing regimes that the United States does not like and replacing them with regimes willing to protect American interests.[26]

Such setbacks to the democracy-promotion agenda were not limited to the Middle East. The Bush administration's absorption with the Iraq War in particular and the Middle East in general has caused officials to neglect democracy promotion in other areas. It has also meant less funds were available for democracy promotion elsewhere. According to Carothers, U.S. democracy funds for other regions remained largely unchanged or even decreased in the 2000s. Insofar as the war reduced the standing of the United States in other areas, it narrowed the space for productive engagement. The war may also have caused a significant drop in U.S. public support for democracy promotion: one poll registered a steady decline from 52 percent in 2005, to 45 percent in 2006, and then to just 37 in 2007.[27]

To date, then, the Iraq War has not led at the macrolevel to the virtuous cycle of democratization and stabilization in the Middle East and beyond that some claimed during the debates leading up to and during the war. Whether greater progress would have been made in the absence of an invasion, the long-standing inability of the United States to defeat Iraqi insurgents or to establish a credible national government with a working national economy undoubtedly harmed the prospects for stability in the region. Overall, the threats to American interests in the Middle East have either not been ameliorated or have been made worse by U.S. involvement in Iraq. Iran remains a threat to U.S. interests not only because of its nuclear ambitions but also through its ability to export political instability to Iraq, Lebanon, the Palestinian territories, and perhaps farther afield, to threaten its neighbors directly with conventional forces or intermediate-range missiles, and, at least according to some analysts, to endanger energy infrastructure and transportation in and around the Persian Gulf. Indeed, by removing Saddam from power and failing to create quickly an effective central government in place of the Ba'thist regime, the United States disrupted a delicate balance in the region and elevated Iran to the position of regional hegemon.[28] By allowing the Iraqi Kurds to maintain a semiautonomous region in northern Iraq that provides money and a safe haven to ethnic partners in Turkey, the chaos in Iraq has created the potential for sharp disputes between Turkey and the United States that could, among other things, undermine one of the key means of access to Iraq and the wider Middle East—the American base at Incirlik.[29] Meanwhile, some argue, Arab-Israeli relations have festered in the absence of more aggressive American leadership. Worse, allegations (however highly disputed) that Israel has exercised undue influence over American decisions on Iraq have given Palestinians, Arabs in general, and terrorist groups such as Hamas, Hizballah, and al Qaeda still another reason to resist American efforts to bring peace to the region.[30]

Perhaps most difficult, but still important, to assess is the impact of the war on U.S. energy security. To address this issue, it is useful to distinguish between the short- and long-term effects, and between the impact on Iraq itself as an oil exporter and the broader consequences for the region, which remains central to the health of world energy markets.

As a result of the war, Iraq's abilities to produce and export oil have no longer been constrained by the policies of Saddam Hussein and UN sanctions. Saddam had occasionally manipulated Iraqi oil production and exports in a vain attempt to exert pressure on the United States and other targets. More importantly, the sanctions imposed by the UN after the Gulf War prevented Iraq from obtaining the latest technology, spare parts, and foreign investment for its oil fields. Thus through the 1990s and into the 2000s, Iraq's oil production remained well below its substantial potential, and the end of Saddam's regime raised the prospect that this potential could finally be realized, either by an Iraqi national oil company, foreign investors, or both.[31]

The short-term impact of the war on U.S. energy security, however, was generally negative, largely because it at least temporarily disrupted Iraq's ability to produce and export oil. During the invasion itself, a number of critical facilities were not secured and thus were subject to widespread looting. Subsequently, the oil infrastructure was the target of hundreds of acts of sabotage, many of which were directed at Iraq's key export pipelines. As a result, both Iraqi oil production and exports dropped and remained below prewar levels of about 2.5 million barrels per day (MBD) and 2.0 MBD, respectively, through 2007, with the latter falling to as little as 1 MBD in 2004.[32]

In turn, the suppression and volatility of Iraqi oil exports occasioned by the war was undeniably a factor in the rapid rise of world oil prices to record levels in the mid- to late 2000s. Just before the war, futures markets predicted that the price of light sweet crude would remain between $20 and $30 for at least the next few years, while the actual price jumped to several times that amount.[33] Just how large a contribution the Iraq War made to this price rise is difficult to say, given all the other possible causes, such as rapidly growing demand in China and other developing countries and supply disruptions in other oil-producing countries like Nigeria and Venezuela. But economists Joseph Stiglitz and Linda Bilmes have described it as "the single most important factor contributing to the soaring prices" and have estimated its contribution to the increased price of oil at somewhere between at least $5 and $10 per barrel.[34] Some experts have put the figure even higher, depending on assumptions about how high Iraqi production levels might have risen in the absence of a war.[35] To the associated economic costs of higher oil prices one might add how they have helped to empower and embolden several states, particularly Russia, Iran, and Venezuela, that have challenged U.S. security interests in recent years.

The longer-term impact of the war on U.S. energy security is even more difficult to ascertain. Now that the security situation in Iraq has improved, production is back to prewar levels and poised to rise even higher. According to reports in mid-2008, Iraq aimed nearly to double its output from 2.5 MBD to 4.5 MBD in the next five years.[36] If Iraq is successful in doing so, it could help to ease pressure on world oil markets, although changes in aggregate global demand are likely to have a larger impact. Indeed, a confluence of events, including already declining consumption and the global financial crisis caused oil prices to fall dramatically in the fall of 2008.

Nevertheless, it is probably still too early to assume a major increase in Iraqi oil production and exports, as significant obstacles still remain. The potential for a reversal of the recent positive security trends remains very real. Moreover, the government has not yet passed a national hydrocarbon law, which is essential to unlocking the potential for foreign investment. And the important oil export route through Turkey remains subject to interruption as a result of potential tensions between that country and the Kurdish regional government.

The long-term impact of the war on U.S. energy security will also depend to a significant extent on its broader impact on the stability of region, which is likely to be mixed at best. On the positive side of the ledger, the war removed the long-standing threat posed by Iraq to its neighbors, at least for the foreseeable future. But it has also introduced significant new tensions and potential causes of instability. Some U.S. generals now fear that Iraq itself could become a potential victim of a resurgent Iran, especially as the U.S. military presence diminishes over time.[37] How these new dynamics will play out, and with what implications for energy production and exports, will likely take years to discern.

The Impact of the War on U.S. National Security Resources

Perhaps most dramatic of all has been the impact of the war on the resources available for the purpose of promoting U.S. national security. Here, with the possible exception of some domestic reforms affecting the national security and intelligence communities, we find that the effects have been largely negative.

A logical place to begin is with the human and economic costs to the United States, which have been high. Five and a half years after the war began, more than four thousand U.S. military personnel had perished in Iraq, and

approximately seven times that number had been wounded, many seriously.[38] By some estimates, hundreds of thousands of Iraq War veterans have suffered from serious mental, physical, and social problems, such as suicide, depression, posttraumatic stress disorder, alcoholism, and broken marriages.[39] Untold additional numbers of Americans working for private contractors have suffered similar fates.

In the meantime, the budgetary costs have continued to mount. Through mid-2008, Congress had appropriated $660 billion for military operations in Iraq. To this can be added costs due to the war that are hidden in the general defense budget or elsewhere in the federal budget. Stiglitz and Bilmes have estimated that one-quarter of the cumulative $600 billion in increased Department of Defense (DOD) spending since the invasion of Iraq should be attributed to the war. They also calculate that it will cost $250 to $375 billion to replace and repair damaged military equipment. They put the future disability and health-care costs of veterans from the Iraq and Afghanistan wars at between $400 and $700 billion. Beyond that are the costs of future military operations in Iraq and elsewhere in the region that have not yet been budgeted for.[40]

Stiglitz and Bilmes have put the ultimate price tag for the war at between $2.7 trillion (counting only budgetary costs) and $5 trillion (including total economic costs). These overall estimates, and especially their inclusion of interest payments on the national debt, the cost to the economy, and the macroeconomic impact of war, have been criticized as exaggerated.[41] But it is already clear that the Iraq War will be the most expensive conflict since World War Two. A much more conservative estimate by former DOD official Lawrence Korb projected total costs through 2017 at between $1 and $1.5 trillion.[42]

In Chapter 5, Michael O'Hanlon provides a detailed description of the high costs of the war to the U.S. armed forces. He argues that personnel readiness has been most negatively affected as reflected in such measures as lower personnel standards and the large numbers of returning soldiers suffering posttraumatic stress disorder as a result of frequent and repeated deployments. Training, especially for types of combat other than those being carried out in Iraq and Afghanistan, has suffered as well for lack of time. In O'Hanlon's view, however, the war has not created huge equipment problems for active forces, which have found ways to maintain and refurbish most types of equipment fairly rapidly thanks in part to generous funding by Congress.

Overall, O'Hanlon finds that the U.S. military has held up reasonably well despite the immense strain and the individual sacrifices that have been made.

We might note, however, that some other respected military analysts have arrived at less sanguine conclusions. Korb has described the regular ground forces as stretched to the breaking point, and former DOD official Michèle Flournoy has testified that most nondeployed units in the army and Marine Corps are essentially unready in terms of personnel, equipment, and training. To this must be added the tremendous strain that was placed for a time on the National Guard and Reserves and the cannibalization of prepositioned stocks overseas.[43]

One bright spot, as O'Hanlon rightly notes, is the greatly increased capacity of the armed forces for counterinsurgency, counterterrorism, and stability operations. Under the guidance of Generals James Amos and David Petraeus, for example, the U.S. Army and Marine Corps revised their joint counterinsurgency manual to reflect recent experience as well as the wisdom accumulated from U.S. and foreign counterinsurgency campaigns in the last century.[44] As a result of the war, the U.S. military has arguably become the world's best at low-intensity conflict, and it boasts a generation of experienced war veterans who will hold leadership positions for years to come. In addition, at least the early stages of the war confirmed the extraordinary combat power of the U.S. military in traditional operations, and subsequent developments demonstrated its resiliency under difficult conditions. Nevertheless, the prolonged inability of U.S. forces to prevail also revealed the limitations and inadequacies of American military power.[45] Whether these benefits will have been worth the costs to the underlying health of the all-volunteer force will depend greatly on what types of military challenges the United States faces in the future. There may in fact be few situations for which the enhanced capabilities are relevant, and their existence may tempt future presidents to employ the military instrument more often than is necessary or desirable. Not least important, any experiential and reputational gains have been purchased at the price of being much less ready to deal with other scenarios that might have arisen.

A less tangible but still important resource is the respect and moral authority that the United States enjoys overseas. As Thomas Weiss shows in Chapter 6, these assets declined substantially in the wake of the war. Whether the result of the Bush administration's decision to invade Iraq without clear legal authority or its subsequent conduct of the war and occupation, which featured substantial civilian casualties and prisoner abuses, Weiss carefully documents the degree to which the Bush administration was unable to achieve its goals within the UN. To this we would add the widespread lack of support for U.S. policies by even traditional allies, as exemplified by the limited contributions of troops to postconflict stabilization operations in Iraq that presumably served the interest of the entire international community, as well as the difficulties that the Bush administration faced in promoting its agenda, such as the deployment of a missile-defense system and further membership enlargement, in NATO.

Perhaps the most concrete indication of the damage to America's international standing were the dramatic declines that took place in public attitudes toward the United States in many countries and regions of the world. As one early survey concluded, the war in Iraq had a major impact on international public opinion, which moved generally "from post-9/11 sympathy to post-Iraq antipathy or at least to disappointment."[46] Not surprisingly, anti-American sentiments reached their highest levels in Arab and Muslim countries. A 2006–7 survey of public opinion in four Muslim countries conducted by the Program on International Policy Attitudes found that, on average, only 15 percent of respondents had a favorable view of the current U.S. government.[47] According to an accompanying analysis, "There now seems to be a perception that the US has entered into a war against Islam itself."[48]

But opinions toward the United States also plummeted in what has traditionally been more friendly territory. According to the Pew Global Attitudes Project survey, for example, the percentage of people in Britain who said they viewed the United States favorably dropped from 75 percent in 2002 to 58 percent in 2004 and remained between 51 percent and 56 percent for the next four years. In Germany, the number fell from 60 percent in 2002 to 45 percent in 2003, and then declined more or less steadily by another 15 percentage points during the next five years.[49] Likewise, a series of polls conducted by the German Marshall Fund of the United States found that the percentage of Europeans expressing the view that U.S. leadership in world affairs was desirable dropped from 64 percent in 2002 to 36 percent in 2004, where it stayed for the next several years.[50]

The only good news is that the worst seems to be over. The image of the United States improved slightly in roughly half of the countries surveyed by the Pew project between 2007 and 2008 and seemed likely to show further improvements following the change in administration in 2009.[51] One reason is that many Europeans at least drew a distinction between the policies of the Bush administration and the United States in general.[52]

Possibly one of the more surprising findings of this study is the limited impact the Iraq War has had on American public opinion about U.S. national

security policy. Judging by the remarks of some public opinion leaders and self-identified strategic thinkers, it is easy to get the impression that the United States is and should be responding to the war with increasing isolation and perhaps even a revulsion against military power. In fact, however, as Clay Ramsay shows in Chapter 7, Americans remain supportive of international engagement and believe that the nation should play an active role in resolving international problems. Where the public appears to have turned away from specific forms of engagement, especially preventive war and military action to promote democracy, the Iraq War has cast considerable doubt on the utility of such actions anyway. Thus a potentially more important development on the domestic front is the possibility of significant institutional reforms as a result of the war.

Even the Bush administration was forced to admit, albeit belatedly, that the rush to war and the subsequent prosecution of the war left much to be desired. Congress, after a remarkable period of quiescence, eventually roused itself to hold oversight hearing on various dimensions of the conflict.[53] Numerous groups outside the government have taken advantage of the alleged failures in Iraq to offer proposals to reform the national security structures of the United States, including extensive organizational changes to the Department of Defense, the military services, and the various government departments and agencies involved in formulating and executing international affairs since the Goldwater-Nichols Defense Reorganization Act of 1986.[54] From the internal initiatives of the Bush administration and the outside pressures of Congress and the wider national security community emerged a series of reforms.

Perhaps the most serious and sustained to date is the effort to restructure U.S. intelligence collection, analysis, and dissemination. The post-9/11 years were already a dark time for the American intelligence community as a result of dissatisfaction with its handling of the terrorist threat. But the Iraq War further damaged the reputation of the American intelligence agencies both at home and abroad. First, it has been increasingly clear that intelligence community allowed itself to be brow beaten and manipulated by a president and his staff determined to go to war. Reports of mobile laboratories, aluminum tubes necessary for nuclear processing, the acquisition of yellow cake from Niger, and a host of other mini-scandals left the impression that the Bush administration sought—and eventually got—any justification for the war that it wanted rather than a sound assessment of the threat posed by Saddam's regime. Second, it appears that wartime intelligence has not been especially effective either. As the insurgency heated up in 2003, policymakers and the military itself appear to have been surprised at the nature and extent of Iraqi resistance, not to mention the adaptability of al Qaeda in Iraq to the challenge of facing an occupation force. What makes this especially surprising is that if the CIA and other intelligence agencies failed to address adequately the questions of Iraqi WMD in the run up to the war, they were "prescient" in anticipating that "strife, terrorism, and instability" would follow the invasion.[55] In his book *Fiasco*, Thomas Ricks, a *Washington Post* reporter, catalogs a long list of failures in the country, ranging from ineffective use of human intelligence (HUMINT) to a focus on foreign terrorists rather than homegrown insurgents to, perhaps most sadly, counterproductive intelligence-gathering techniques (including everything from torture to the failure to question individuals in a timely fashion) at places like Abu Ghraib.[56]

The result has been that the highly publicized and repeated failures of intelligence prior to and during the Iraq War coupled with preexisting criticisms to force reform on a set of institutions and practices notoriously resistant to change. The centerpiece of intelligence reform under the Bush administration was the Reform and Terrorism Prevention Act of 2004 passed, at least in part, in response to the findings of the National Commission on Terrorist Attacks Upon the United States (popularly known as the 9/11 Commission). Among other things this act created a new position, the director of national intelligence, to lead the entire intelligence community, advise the president on all intelligence matters, and be responsible for acquiring major intelligence-collections systems. During this period and beyond, however, the specific intelligence shortfalls of the Iraq War, including the invasion and conduct, also received a great deal of attention, especially from Congress. Considerable impetus to this effort was provided by the December 2006 report of the Iraq Study Group, which concluded that the various intelligence agencies "are not doing enough to map the insurgency, dissect it, and understand it on a national and provincial level. The analytic community's knowledge of the organization, leadership, financing, and operations of militias, as well as their relationship to government security forces, also falls far short of what policy makers need to know."[57]

The potential importance of intelligence community reforms brought about by the Iraq War (and the prior failure of 9/11) for the future of U.S. national security cannot be overstated. The ability to assess threats ranging from so-called rogue states like Iran and North Korea to China, a potential near-peer competitor, is the responsibility of the intelligence community writ large. Threat assessments are a critical input to national security planning and to the development of grand strategy. If the foundations of the planning process—judgments about threat and indeed the nature of the international security environment—are outright wrong or seriously mistaken, decision makers will, at best, rely solely on personal experience, closely held prejudices, and lessons of history that may or may not be applicable. And, at the tactical and operational levels, the production of "actionable" intelligence that gives the military and law-enforcement agencies the ability to thwart terrorists and proliferators is at least as critical as net assessment of adversaries and potential adversaries. As important as institutional reforms in the intelligence community might be, however, experience suggests that they may not be sufficient or long lasting; some analyses suggest that previous reform efforts have failed at least in part through a mix of bureaucratic, organizational, and political factors.[58]

Summary

We find that, on balance, the costs of the Iraq War have outweighed the benefits. To be sure, the threat posed by Iraq to American interests was reduced through the removal of Saddam Hussein and his Ba'th Party from power. Given the absence of weapons of mass destruction and ties to hostile terrorist organizations like al Qaeda, however, the war resulted in much less of an improvement in U.S. national security than was promised by the Bush administration, and the long-term political outcome in the country remains unclear. Thus even if Iraq emerges as a stable state that poses no threats to U.S. national security interests, the many substantial costs that the United States has incurred will still outweigh the gains from eliminating Saddam Hussein and his regime.

Beyond Iraq, the war has tended to exacerbate the national security challenges faced by the United States, in some cases significantly. Overall, it has done little to reduce the nuclear-proliferation risk, and probably made it worse, as exemplified by developments in North Korea and Iran. It has impeded progress in the broader war on terror. It has undercut U.S. efforts to promote democracy. It has created new sources of instability in the Middle East. And it has tended to reduce U.S. energy security since the war began and possibly well into the future.

Perhaps even more striking have been the war's effects on U.S. national security resources, which have been largely negative. The substantial human and budgetary costs have been much remarked upon, as have the tremendous strains on the U.S. military. What gains the army and Marine Corps have made in their ability to conduct nontraditional military operations have been purchased at an exceedingly high price in terms of readiness and strategic risk. In the meantime, the United States has suffered a tremendous decline in its international standing and moral authority, as measured most readily by public opinion polls. Although some valuable domestic institutional reforms, especially of the intelligence community, may eventually result from the debacle, it is too soon to tell for sure, and there are good reasons to be skeptical.

COUNTERFACTUAL ANALYSIS

Simply comparing the costs and benefits of the Iraq War can provide only a partial answer to the question that motivates this chapter, "Are we safer now?" We must also compare the net costs and benefits of the war with those of the alternative courses of action that the Bush administration might have pursued. Just because the costs of the war may have been so high and the benefits so questionable does not mean that going to war when and how the United States did was not the best option.

It is not, of course, possible to rerun history. Consequently, we can never know for sure what might have happened if the Bush administration had chosen a different path. But that does not leave us without any basis of comparison. Rather, we can employ thought experiments to identify the likely consequences of alternative courses of action, using what is known as counterfactual analysis. This tool focuses on contingency—that is, on actions or inactions located within a specific timeline that, had they been taken or not taken, would have changed the course of many events to follow. When executed effectively, it offers unique strengths over other approaches.

To be sure, by attempting to address our overarching questions with a counterfactual analysis, we are treading on controversial ground. Although the humanities and social sciences have witnessed a number of books and articles on this technique in the past two decades, it is an approach that has not yet found widespread application.[59] One reason is that counterfactual analysis is difficult to do well. Most obviously, there is no way to determine whether the hypothesized outcomes would really have occurred. How instructive such mental experiments are depends entirely on the plausibility of the assumptions employed and the care with which they are executed.

But the existence of such obstacles does not render counterfactual analysis entirely unhelpful. To the contrary, there are ways to reduce, if not eliminate, the risk that it will yield misleading results. Above all, we must insist that the alternative scenarios to be explored are as plausible as possible. Perhaps the most relevant injunction in this regard is the "minimal-rewrite-of-history rule," whereby we alter as few established historical facts as possible.[60] This rule would militate against, for example, assuming that Al Gore won the 2000 presidential election, that Dick Cheney suffered a disabling heart attack in early 2001, or that the terrorist attacks of September 11 never took place.

In the remainder of this section, we explore two sets of counterfactuals. First, and perhaps most importantly, we consider what might have happened if the Bush administration had chosen at least to defer the initiation of major combat operations and perhaps to forego them altogether. Second, we examine the likely consequences of different ways in which the administration might have prosecuted the war and occupation, once the decision to invade in March 2003 without explicit UN Security Council authorization and with little international support had been made.

War Initiation: Choosing the Right Counterfactuals

It is not especially difficult to envision a different course of action for the United States in Iraq. Famously, Iraq was a "war of choice, not necessity, and one driven by ideas, not merely interests."[61] These ideas included regime change, democratization, and the imagined virtuous cycle of using successful change in Iraq to jumpstart the spread of democracy across the region. While commentators from across the political spectrum agreed on the desirability of promoting these ideas and American values more generally, they disagreed often vehemently on the question of feasibility. There were clearly other options.

The first critical decision that one must make in constructing counterfactuals concerns the precise point in time at which the alternative scenarios to be explored should diverge from the historical record. In the case of the decision to go to war, there would seem to be two main options. One would be to assume that the administration decided against even stepping up the rhetoric and pressing for action against Iraq and to examine instead a hypothetical continuation of the previous U.S. policy of deterrence and containment. The other would be to assume that the administration had increased the pressure on Iraq in the form of achieving renewed UN inspections and the preinvasion American military buildup but had deferred a final decision to go to war in order to afford the inspections and diplomacy more time.

The former approach represents a somewhat easier challenge, as the costs and benefits of previous U.S. policy, other than the risk that Iraq might have possessed or been able to acquire WMD, are relatively well understood. Indeed, it is the basis of most of the counterfactual analysis that has already been conducted, both before and since the start of the war. We find this scenario, however, to be much less plausible, for at least two related reasons. First, it is easy to imagine that the Bush administration would, under any circumstances, have eventually grown frustrated with the status quo and decided to take more forceful action, especially as international support for the existing UN sanctions continued to erode. Second, after 9/11, the administration seemed bent on doing something about Iraq. Yet it did not become clear until early 2003 just how much international support—and resistance—the United States might encounter. Certainly by March of that year, it seemed evident to many that the costs of more or less unilateral action in terms of international reactions would be high while a potentially more effective alternative to previous U.S. policy in the form of continued intrusive UN inspections and the potential for additional UN sanctions had been put in place. Thus we will limit our analysis to the second approach. A final reason is that one of the likely outcomes would have been very similar to a reversion to the previous containment-deterrence regime.

What might have happened if the Bush administration, when faced with strong international resistance and criticism, had decided to defer war for at least several months? We find four alternative scenarios to be the most plausible. One is in most respects very similar to what actually transpired and thus merits only a brief discussion. In that case, continued UN inspections would have failed to produce a significant shift in the positions of any of the major actors and the Bush administration would have decided to go to war with a very similar coalition. As a result, the overall costs and benefits would have been very similar, although there may also have been some noteworthy differences. The principal additional costs to the United States would have been those associated with maintaining the forces already deployed to the region and possibly additional units on a war footing and overcoming whatever additional defensive preparations Saddam Hussein would have been able to make. A delay might also have produced some significant benefits, however. It would have allowed the Bush administration to optimize its invasion force—as it was, the 4th Infantry Division was delayed in its arrival in the theater because of a political dispute with Turkey—and to prepare more thoroughly for the stabilization phase of military operations.[62] There is no guarantee, however, that the administration would have avoided the critical mistakes that plagued the subsequent occupation. In addition, continued UN inspections might have allayed fears that Iraq would respond to an attack with chemical and biological weapons, thereby simplifying U.S. military planning and operations.

Of greater interest then are three other scenarios, which we regard as equally plausible. The first of these is what we call "Multilateral Invasion." In this counterfactual, the UN inspectors would have encountered a significant degree of resistance, noncooperation, obstruction, evasion, and/or defiance. Even if Iraq had possessed no significant numbers of WMD or weapons programs, Saddam Hussein may nevertheless have taken actions that made it appear as though his regime had something to hide. As a result, the United States would have been able to garner much greater international support for, and face less resistance to, the use of force to enforce the relevant UN Security Council resolutions and disarm Iraq. A UN Security Council resolution authorizing the use of force may have remained beyond the reach of the Bush administration, but an invasion would have enjoyed much greater international legitimacy.[63]

At the other end of the spectrum of most plausible possibilities is what we call the "Clean Bill of Health" scenario. In this case, the continuation of UN inspections would have eventually demonstrated with increasing certainty that Iraq lacked meaningful arsenals of WMD or the programs to build them, as turned out to be the case.[64] As a result, the Bush administration, however reluctantly, would have had to stand down its potential invasion force and to acquiesce in lifting many of the sanctions and restrictions that the UN had imposed on Iraq. Nevertheless, the administration might well have insisted on the establishment of some international safeguards to ensure that Iraq did not once again acquire WMD or seek to do so at a future date. And it might well have continued to maintain forces in the Persian Gulf comparable in size and capability to those in place prior to the preinvasion buildup to deter and possibly defend against future attacks by Iran and Iraq on U.S. allies and other interests in the region.[65]

It is important to note that the plausibility of this second scenario does not depend entirely on hindsight. Even if many national intelligence agencies had previously believed that Iraq possessed chemical and biological weapons and had some semblance of a nuclear weapons program, by mid-March 2003 this view was becoming increasingly questionable. As Daalder and Lindsay argue,

"A few months of additional inspections would likely have allowed the UN to reach the same conclusion the Iraq Survey Group arrived at almost two years later—that Saddam had effectively disarmed in the early 1990s."[66]

Somewhere between these two alternatives lies what we call the "Return to Containment" scenario. In this case, even several more months of UN inspections would not have resulted in an international consensus on whether Iraq was in compliance with the UN Security Council resolutions. Because of continued international opposition as well as the additional doubts about Iraq's WMD capabilities and programs that further inspections might have sown, however, the Bush administration would have decided to defer launching an invasion. Instead, it would have done what it could to maintain and shore up the existing regime of sanctions and inspections. Not only does such a scenario seem plausible, but it is very similar to the types of counterfactual thought experiments that have in fact been conducted, which attempt to compare the war to a continuation of the previous U.S. policy of containment and deterrence.

The Impact on U.S. National Security Resources

To evaluate the likely costs and benefits of these hypothetical alternatives, we employ the same framework that we used to organize the actual costs and benefits of the war, although in reverse order. We begin with the possible effects on the resources of U.S. national security policy and only then turn to an examination of the likely impact on the security challenges facing the United States, first outside and then from Iraq.

We find that any of these alternatives would probably have been less costly than the course of action actually pursued. To be sure, as in the delayed, largely unilateral invasion scenario discussed above, there would have been at least one set of additional economic, military, and political (both domestic and international) costs: those of continuing and maintaining the buildup of U.S. forces in the region for at least a few additional months. But these additional costs would have been more than outweighed by the substantial cost reductions associated with these alternative scenarios.

The "Multilateral Invasion" and "Clean Bill of Health" Scenarios The costs of the Multilateral Invasion scenario would have clearly been lower across the board. There would have been much less damage to the overall international political standing of the United States. In this regard, the costs, such as they were, would have been somewhat comparable in magnitude to those incurred during the 1991 Gulf War. Indeed, the United States might have gained in stature by affirming its commitment to, or at least avoiding a break with, the multilateralist norms and expectations of the world community.

Likewise, the material and human costs to the United States would have been reduced as other countries assumed a larger share of the burden. The United States would have been able to benefit from larger allied troop contributions during the invasion, as it did during the Gulf War, and especially during the occupation. That said, the military contribution of coalition members in that earlier conflict is sometimes overestimated. Of the 956,600 troops involved in the Gulf War, 697,000 were American.[67] The United States and Britain provided the bulk of the fighting forces, the so-called point of the spear, while the forces of other nations were assigned largely noncombat roles due to problems with interoperability and, in many cases, an unwillingness to engage in real fighting.

Nevertheless, a more truly multilateral occupation force would likely have enjoyed greater legitimacy in the eyes of the Iraqis, thereby reducing some of the challenges faced by American forces. In addition, an occupation that was multilateral from the outset might have avoided some of the mistakes made by the U.S. occupation authorities, especially if given additional months to plan. To be sure, one could question the staying power of additional partners if the security situation had nevertheless deteriorated as it did, judging by the number of existing coalition members that actually did pull troops out of Iraq or severely circumscribe their operations in the face of losses or more strenuous operating conditions. And a more multilateral military operation would have suffered from greater inefficiencies. But the United States might have been able to exercise a good deal of leadership and control over at least the initial phase of operations, much as it had done in Afghanistan.

Arguably, the costs to the United States in terms of resources in the Clean Bill of Health scenario would have been even lower. The international political costs of even grudging U.S. acceptance of the negative findings of the inspectors would have been much less than those actually incurred. The United States would have demonstrated its willingness, even as the lone superpower, to follow the norms and rules of the various international institutions it helped create while at the same time listening to the advice and judgments of key friends and allies. Its claim to legitimate authority within the international system would thereby have been strengthened. And while the United States would likely have maintained some forces in the Persian Gulf, indeed perhaps nearly as many as had been in place before the prewar buildup, the operating costs of those forces would have been much reduced. One effective "cost" of this scenario (as well as of the Return to Containment scenario) is that the U.S. military would never have gained the valuable experience in counterinsurgency, counterterrorism, and stabilization operations that it has acquired in Iraq, although at a considerable price.

The "Return to Containment" Scenario This leaves the costs to U.S. national security resources of the final scenario, Return to Containment, to be examined. Of the three scenarios considered, this one would have generated perhaps the greatest international political costs insofar as the United States would have continued to earn the ire of many in the Arab and Muslim worlds and to appear to be acting in defiance of the views of much of the international community. At the same time, though, these political costs would have been lower than those actually generated by the war.

As for the other impacts on U.S. resources, University of Chicago economists Steven Davis, Kevin Murphy, and Robert Topel have written two papers, one released in March 2003 and the other in early 2006, that attempt to quantify the costs of a policy of continued containment. They have argued that the economic costs of containment would have been comparable, and possibly greater, in size to those actually incurred by the war.[68]

In their 2003 paper, Davis, Murphy, and Topel estimated the discounted present value of containment at $380 billion in 2003 dollars. This amount dwarfed what they viewed as a conservatively high estimate of the costs of war, which they put at $125 billion. In their 2006 paper, they offered a slightly lower estimate of the direct costs of containment of nearly $300 billion. This figure fell roughly in the middle of their estimates of the costs implied by preinvasion views of the likely course of the Iraq intervention, which now ranged from $100 to $870 billion.

How did Davis, Murphy, and Topel arrive at these figures? They began by assuming that the United States would continue to devote approximately twenty-eight to thirty thousand troops, thirty naval vessels, and two hundred military aircraft to the task of containing Iraq. They also assumed an annual average cost per person deployed of $226,000–250,000 and derived capital costs (operations and depreciation) of $4.6–5.4 billion per year. Using these and several other assumptions, they arrived at an annual direct price tag for containment of $11.3–14.5 billion, including both labor and capital costs. Then, assuming an annual discount (or interest) rate of 2 percent and—optimistically in their view—a 3 percent annual probability that Iraq would undergo a regime change that removed the threat to the United States, they calculated the total long-term cost. The principal difference between the 2003 and 2006 estimates followed from the assumption in the earlier paper that the United States would have to devote approximately 50 percent more effort in order for containment to be successful. Varying this assumption across both papers, the estimated direct costs of containment would range from about $250 to $450 billion.

Clearly, these estimates of the costs of pursuing something like the pre-Iraq War policy of containment are lower than the actual financial costs of the war. And there are good reasons to believe that they are exaggerated. The principal problem with these estimates is that they fail to focus on just the marginal costs of containment. The calculations are based on the size of most if not all of the U.S. forces in the region. Yet at least some, and perhaps many, of these forces would have been in the region anyway in order to contain Iran and protect U.S. national security interests more generally. And even if they had not been in the region, many, and perhaps most, of these forces would exist anyway. Thus a more apposite approach would be to consider only the incremental costs of stationing U.S. troops in the region and the additional costs of military operations, such as the enforcement of the no-fly zones, implementation of the maritime embargo, and military exercises, which were specifically undertaken for the purpose of containing Iraq. Elsewhere, we have estimated these marginal costs to be on the order of only a few billion dollars per year.[69]

The Impact on Challenges Beyond Iraq

What impact might the pursuit of alternative policies have had on the achievement of other U.S. national security objectives? In constructing counterfactuals, one must pay careful attention to the opportunity costs. How could the money, lives, and political capital that were expended on the Iraq War have been otherwise used to promote U.S. national security? Overall, we would argue, the war has tended to make the other national security threats and challenges that the United States faces more difficult and intractable. At the same time, it has diverted and depleted resources that could have been devoted to addressing these other threats and challenges. These effects are perhaps most apparent in four areas: the war on terror, nuclear nonproliferation, U.S. national security interests in the Middle East, and the ability of the United States to respond with appropriate military force to other crises across the globe.

The Iraq War was intended in part to strike a blow against international terrorists that threatened the United States. If the Bush administration had pursued a different course of action, however, the terrorist threat to the United States would arguably be much less than it is now. If the United States had not invaded Iraq, or had done so only with much more international support, it would have had more resources to devote to the war on terror elsewhere. The Bush administration began to divert critical military and intelligence assets from Afghanistan by early 2002, and the Afghanistan theater has remained relatively starved of resources ever since. In addition, it is difficult to imagine that anti-American sentiments in the Muslim world would have intensified as much as they have if the administration had chosen one of the counterfactual alternatives described above. In none of the other scenarios would the types of conditions in Iraq that have provided opportunities for the recruitment and training of terrorists have been created to the same extent, if at all.

The war was also intended in part to deliver a wake up call to other potential proliferators, such as Iran and North Korea, prompting them to desist in their efforts to acquire nuclear weapons. In the case of Iran, as discussed by Joseph Cirincione, this strategy may have succeeded, at least temporarily. Following the invasion, Iran momentarily evidenced a much greater willingness to make concessions. But the Bush administration failed to seize this seeming opportunity to negotiate an end to Iran's nuclear program, perhaps precisely because it was emboldened by its initial easy success in Iraq.

In the case of North Korea, however, the war was not followed by any signs of willingness to compromise by the Kim regime and, in combination with the administration's confrontational approach, may have had just the opposite effect. By tying down so many U.S. forces in Iraq, moreover, it greatly limited the coercive potential on which the administration's nonproliferation strategy was largely based. Although the effects of the war are difficult to disentangle from those of the administration's tendency to demand unilateral concessions before even beginning negotiations, it is likely that greater restraint on the part of the Bush administration toward Iraq would have been more productive in terms of preventing proliferation.

Third, it was argued that the war could trigger a wave of democratization in the Middle East. It has tended, however, to have the opposite effect, discrediting democracy in the region by associating it with internal instability and conflict. If the Bush administration had refrained from a unilateral war, it seems likely that democracy promotion would have remained a more viable, if perhaps still problematic, strategy than it is today. Certainly, a multilateral invasion would likely have been more successful at establishing a peaceful, democratic political order in Iraq, which could have served as a source of inspiration for reformers and as a model for other states in the region.

Although oil was conspicuously absent from the reasons offered by the administration for war, it should have been clear that any U.S. policy toward Iraq would have major implications for oil production in the Persian Gulf and world energy markets more generally. And at least in the short- to medium-term, the effect of the war was to disrupt Iraqi oil production and destabilize energy markets. Whether a comparable disruption as a result of Iraqi actions against its neighbors would have occurred under the Return to Containment scenario would have depended on the success of containment. But, arguably, a multilateral invasion would have produced a more favorable outcome in this regard. Likewise, under the Clean Bill of Health scenario, Iraq would presumably have been able to increase investment in the oil sector, resulting in higher levels of production.

Finally, under all of the alternative scenarios, the United States would have maintained a greater capacity to respond to other contingencies with military force when called for. Fortunately, outside of Afghanistan, the constraints that the war has placed on U.S. military capabilities were never laid bare by a serious crisis. But recent events have provided at least one cautionary example.

In August 2008, just as United States was negotiating a withdrawal schedule with the Iraqi government, long-simmering tensions between the Republic of Georgia and Russia erupted in a shooting war.[70] As Russian tanks rolled through South Ossetia and other parts of Georgia, President Bush and other senior officials warned Russia to stand down and threatened negative consequences for Russo-American relations. The Bush administration was not only concerned for the broader geopolitical ramifications of Russia's actions but also protective of Georgia in particular, given its close relations with the Georgian president, past support for the Georgian military, and sponsorship of Georgia for NATO membership. But as opinion leaders observed repeatedly during the crisis, the United States was simply not prepared to give Georgia more than symbolic support and humanitarian aid because the nation's military resources were already spread so thin as a result of the ongoing operations in Afghanistan and Iraq. Whether a more robust, possibly militarized, response would have been desirable is debatable. Clearly, however, had the United States not chosen to invade Iraq or had done so in a way more conducive to conserving American military resources, the Bush administration would have had more options available in responding to the Russian actions.

The Impact on the Threat Posed by Iraq

Perhaps the greatest uncertainty surrounds the issue of whether Iraq would have posed more or less of a threat to the United States should the Bush administration have chosen another course of action, especially a reversion to something like the previous policy of containment. How effective would alternative approaches have been at dealing with the Iraqi threat?

Arguably, a multilateral invasion would have resulted in a lower level of threat. As with the actual war, Saddam Hussein and his regime would have been eliminated. Presumably, moreover, the following occupation would have gone more smoothly and been more successful in establishing a stable, democratic regime in Iraq. At a minimum, greater international participation would probably have helped the U.S. occupation authorities to avoid some of the serious mistakes that stoked the insurgency and made Iraq almost ungovernable for several years.

Under the Clean Bill of Health scenario, by assumption, the threat posed by Iraq would have been much reduced from prewar estimates of its capabilities. The main danger in this case would be that a relaxation of international pressure would have enabled Saddam Hussein eventually to acquire an arsenal of WMD and the means to produce them. Presumably, however, even after inspections had established with a high degree of confidence that Iraq lacked any WMD, the international community would have still wanted to put in place monitoring and surveillance systems that would have made it difficult for Saddam Hussein to reconstitute his WMD programs and stockpiles. Thus, although Saddam Hussein and his successors might have stayed in power for many more years, their ability to threaten the United States and its regional allies and other security interests would have remained highly circumscribed.

Instead, the biggest challenge comes with evaluating the Return to Containment scenario. Further inspections would presumably have given reason to conclude that the threat posed by Iraq was something less than what was believed by many during the run up to the invasion. In addition, although inspections would not have generated an international consensus on how to proceed, it seems quite plausible that there would have been broad support for their continuation. Also, enduring doubts about the adequacy of Iraqi compliance might have helped to parry the previous pressure to eliminate the UN sanctions.

Despite such possible improvements in the situation, some observers would have inevitably remained pessimistic about the prospects for containing Iraq. First, there would still have been a chance, perhaps even the likelihood, that Saddam Hussein would eventually have been able to acquire nuclear weapons. The sanctions, which constituted the most critical element of containment, had become increasingly ineffective, and it might have been difficult to prevent the holes from growing, let alone to close them up. As Kenneth Pollack concluded in late 2002, "There is no meaningful support for a tough containment policy toward Iraq."[71]

If and when Saddam Hussein acquired a nuclear arsenal, he might have become increasingly aggressive and difficult to deter. As Pollack argued, "Saddam Hussein is one of the most reckless, aggressive, violence-prone, risk-tolerant, and damage-tolerant leaders of modern history." These traits, Pollack continued, "do not seem to make him impossible to deter, but they do appear to make him difficult to deter in most circumstances and impossible to deter in some."[72] The problem, however, was not that Saddam Hussein would initiate a nuclear war. Rather, "the much greater threat is that he will believe that his possession of nuclear weapons will allow him to carry out lesser acts of aggression because the United States, Israel, and anyone else would themselves be deterred from responding effectively."[73] Pollack concluded, "If we allow him to acquire nuclear weapons, we are likely to find ourselves in a new crisis with him in which we will not be able to predict what he will do, and his personality and his history can only lead us to expect the worst."[74]

As others have written, however, there are also good reasons to believe that containment could have been successful. "Despite its flaws," Steven Miller argued in late 2002, containment had been "effective in limiting Saddam's power and containing his ambitions."[75] Even if Iraq possessed some WMD and had the potential to acquire nuclear weapons, its military capabilities were and would have remained much more limited than if efforts to constrain them had been abandoned. Even if imperfect, continued inspections could have been useful for limning the magnitude of the threat.

Nevertheless, even some of those who favored a continuation of containment believed that it "may not be enough to prevent Iraq from acquiring nuclear weapons someday." But they also believed that even a nuclear-armed Iraq under Saddam Hussein could be deterred from acts of aggression. Although he had started two wars against his neighbors, they argued, he had attacked both times "because Iraq was vulnerable and because he believed his targets were weak and isolated."[76] Likewise, although he had used WMD (in this case chemical weapons) against Iran and Kurds in Iraq, his victims had lacked the ability to respond in kind. Thus, Iraq would be unable to use or even threaten to use nuclear weapons so long as the United States was willing to retaliate.

The proponents of continued containment also addressed the possibility, invoked by members of the Bush administration, that Saddam Hussein might clandestinely transfer nuclear weapons to a terrorist group hostile to the United States. They argued that the likelihood of such a nuclear handoff was extremely small, for at least four reasons. First, there was no evidence of any genuine connection between Saddam Hussein and such groups, especially al Qaeda; to the contrary, a history of enmity existed between them. Second, if Saddam Hussein did give nuclear weapons to a terrorist group, he would lose control over how they would be used. Third, if he nevertheless went ahead, he could not be sure that the transfer would go undetected, especially given the U.S. imperatives to monitor the situation carefully. And even if a transfer went undetected, Saddam Hussein could not assume that the United States would not retaliate against him anyway if a terrorist nuclear attack were to occur.[77]

Finally, there was the possibility, however small, that Saddam Hussein's regime would be replaced by one that was less threatening to the United States. A coup, assassination, or other violent form of overthrow seemed unlikely. But Saddam Hussein was nearly sixty-six years old when the war began, so it would not have been surprising if he had died within a decade or two, and there was no way to know how smoothly any planned transfer of power would go. The economists Davis, Murphy, and Topel assumed a 3 percent annual probability of positive regime change in their calculations of the cost of containment.

In sum, there were and still are good arguments for both the pessimistic and optimistic views on containment. One might note, however, that on the eve of the war, the prospects for successful containment may have been better than they had been in several years. As Steven Miller observed, "Having created momentum toward war, the Bush administration [was] in a strong position to extract cooperation both from those states who are essential to the containment of Iraq and from Iraq itself."[78]

Prosecution of the War and Occupation: Plausible Alternatives

A second set of counterfactuals concerns how the Bush administration conducted the war and occupation, once the decision to attack was taken. The administration made thousands of decisions big and small about how the war should be fought, and many appear to have been bad. Consequently, many supporters of the initial invasion have subsequently backtracked with the explanation that they had no idea the administration would be so incompetent in managing the day-to-day operations of the conflict. That is, if they had known how ineffectual U.S. political and military leadership would be, they would not have supported such a risky venture. In terms of a counterfactual approach, this is the equivalent of "death by a thousand cuts." It is not so much the fateful initial decision to invade as the many subsequent choices that determined the outcome. In this section, we consider the most consequential political and military decisions associated with the management of the war once the basic decision had been made and ask whether plausible alternative choices could have significantly altered the overall costs and benefits of the war for American national security.

Better Military Management There is a substantial and growing body of evidence that the Bush administration did not heed the advice of military professionals prior to undertaking the Iraq invasion and in managing its aftermath. Numerous military officers, including General Tommy Franks, the commander in chief of the U.S. Central Command at the time of the invasion, and Lieutenant General Ricardo Sanchez, the V Corps commander of coalition forces in Iraq, have detailed military mistakes, miscalculations, and organizational failures.[79] Although many of these can be attributed to the decisions of military professionals, some appear to lie with civilian leaders in the Pentagon, the National Security Council, and perhaps, the Office of the Vice President.

But what would more successful planning, execution, and implementation of military operations have meant for U.S. national security? To examine this question we focus on two critical military decisions: (1) the decision to limit the size of the invasion force; and (2) the initial decision to limit U.S. participation in postwar reconstruction and stabilization. Early accounts of the war lauded the "small footprint" of the original invasion force. The trouble was that once the Iraq regular army had been defeated, the small numbers of coalition troops were unable to provide security for the Iraqi people or guard the vast ammunition dumps and sensitive government facilities left behind by the disintegrating Iraqi regular army and internal security forces. Thus, as many former Iraqi officers and soldiers joined insurgent groups and provided military expertise to extremists of all sorts, the emerging resistance was able to amass large quantities of weapons and otherwise exploit the opportunities provided by the thin military presence.[80] These developments greatly complicated the missions of coalition forces. For U.S. national security more broadly, this mistake and its military consequences raised questions about U.S. competence and, eventually as the insurgency proved difficult to overcome, contributed to a general sense that the U.S. military was not the formidable adversary it had seemed after the Persian Gulf War.

In a similar fashion, confusion reigned about the role of coalition forces in providing security (and eventually military support for postwar stabilization and reconstruction) in the immediate aftermath of the invasion. Anecdotal accounts suggest that some military leaders assumed that once Saddam's army had been defeated, the military part of the operation would somehow be over.[81] U.S. and other coalition forces would withdraw and the process of rebuilding Iraq, including its government structures, economy, and security capabilities, would fall to the Iraqi's themselves and, to some extent, the Office for Reconstruction and Humanitarian Assistance (OHRA) headed by retired Army Lieutenant General Jay Garner (and later the Coalition Provision Authority [CPA] led by Ambassador Paul Bremer). Whomever historians deem responsible, the problem for the United States, which resonates to this day, is that the interim government of Iraq and its successors had to struggle mightily with the question of providing basic security for the Iraqi state and its populace. American forces had not planned or even trained adequately for so-called Phase IV operations—general postconflict activities or what some have deemed the transition from war to peace and all the complexities involved.[82]

Events in the last two years suggest that the Bush administration belatedly learned lessons about fighting in Iraq, and certainly the military itself has learned how better to fight counterinsurgency operations and conduct stabilization operations. General Petraeus was apparently given a much freer hand in running Iraqi operations than his predecessors. By most accounts the "surge" helped reduced violence in central Iraq and at least opened the door for negotiations and a potential political settlement. But, however successful these adaptations and new leaders have been, the past cannot be undone. The ability of the United States to achieve one of its central war aims—the overthrow of Saddam's regime and its replacement with an effective democratic Iraqi regime that would be a beacon for progress in the entire Middle East—was undermined, at least in part, by poor military management of the problems of postconflict operations. Had the Department of Defense placed more emphasis on postconflict planning and devoted more training and resources to what at least in retrospect seems like a foreseeable problem, the costs borne by the United States and its armed forces would have been substantially lower across all dimensions. Although we can never know with certainty, Iraq might have progressed much faster toward becoming an effective nation-state once again.

Better Political Management In recent years, key civilian leaders in the CPA, such as Bremer, and in the Department of Defense, such as former undersecretary of defense Douglas Feith, have published retrospective accounts of their roles in the Bush administration that highlight real or perceived political mistakes associated with the management of the Iraq War.[83] While some might be tempted to discount such accounts as the self-serving efforts of disgruntled losers in Washington policy wars seeking to clear themselves of responsibility for policy failures, they nevertheless help to identify critical junctures on which the success of the war and occupation turned.

One of the most critical decisions was that to disband the Iraqi army. Although the facts are in dispute, most accounts suggest that one of the first major decisions (Order Number 2) made by Ambassador Bremer was to disband the Iraqi army, at least in part to begin the de-Ba'thification process and, it is thought, to protect against the possibility of a resurgent Iraqi army powerful enough to pose an internal and external threat. Whether Bremer was acting on the instruction of someone highly placed within the Bush administration or made the decision on his own remains unclear. What is clear, however, is that this decision deprived the rump Iraqi government and the coalition of a key source of social control at a time when American and coalition forces on the ground were either too few in numbers or ill-prepared to provide security. Moreover, the decision helped unleash thousands of armed militarily trained young men on Iraqi society without visible means of support for themselves or their families. By some accounts, these former soldiers subsequently formed the backbone of various tribal militias and the Iraqi insurgency.

From a military perspective, this political decision affected the course of the war and eventually wider U.S. national security in several ways. First and foremost, it placed a large burden on coalition forces in Iraq. As tribal militias, terrorists of various sorts, and others gradually coalesced from disorganized sources of looting and other relatively minor operational inconveniences into a full-fledged insurgency or perhaps even parties in a civil war, coalition forces, most notably American combat troops, were eventually forced to play a larger role in providing security than planners had ever envisioned.[84] It also added greatly to the war's expense in terms of both personnel and materiel. As battle deaths mounted, largely due to improvised explosive devices (IEDs) and occasional firefights with anti-American forces, public opinion both in the United States and abroad solidified against the war.

In sum, better political and military management of the invasion and occupation could arguably have reduced many of the costs associated with the war. Most obviously, it could have reduced the human and economic costs and hastened the establishment of a stable, if not necessarily democratic, post-Saddam regime in Iraq. Although a larger initial deployment would have been accompanied by more strain on the military and greater strategic risk in the short run, the United States would probably have been able to reduce its forces more quickly and thus to devote more resources to other national security challenges, such as the war on terror and containing Iran's nuclear ambitions. Whether and how much a different approach would have blunted some of the damage done by the war to U.S. democracy promotion efforts and the image of the United States abroad is more difficult to say, and the overall costs of the war would still have been high.

At the same time, however, we must acknowledge the political and perhaps ideological constraints that limited the Bush administration's flexibility. How the war and occupation were conducted was closely bound up with the decision to go to war itself. Thus we cannot plausibly tinker too much with such choices as the size of the invasion force or the amount of planning for postconflict activities without calling into question the very premise—a war launched in March 2003 in the face of considerable international opposition—on which they are based. For example, the war was justified in no small part on the assumption that only a relatively small force would be required and that the force could be quickly withdrawn. If the Bush administration had acknowledged that several hundred thousands of troops might be necessary, as even some proponents of the war maintained, and that they might have to remain in Iraq for a prolonged period, would it still have been able to persuade Congress and the American people that war was the best option?[85]

Thus how much better the Bush administration could in fact have managed the war, once the basic decision had been made, remains questionable.

In this section, we have identified what we believe to be the most plausible counterfactual scenarios to the path actually pursued by the Bush administration. Under these alternative scenarios, we have argued:

1. the demands on U.S. national security resources would have been less than was in fact the case;
2. other security threats and challenges facing the United States—from proliferation to terrorism to regional conflicts, for example—would be no greater, and probably less serious, than they are today; and
3. the challenges posed to the United States by Iraq now and in the future would have been no greater, and probably smaller, than they are likely to be under the present circumstances.

We conclude this discussion, however, with an acknowledgment of the limits of the confidence we can ascribe to these findings. Not only is counterfactual analysis necessarily speculative, but this particular analysis must necessarily be brief and somewhat superficial. How one regards these comparisons, moreover, depends on which alternatives one finds most plausible. In presenting these scenarios, we have rendered no judgment as to their relative probabilities. Nevertheless, we believe that these conclusions are at least suggestive and arguably make a useful contribution, when combined with the insights and analyses of our chapter authors, to the construction of a comprehensive portrait of the Iraq War's implications. Whether we analyze specific issues or perform counterfactual thought experiments, we find that the war has undermined key aspects of U.S. national security in ways that will have long-term repercussions.

LESSONS FOR U.S. NATIONAL SECURITY POLICY

What lessons can be drawn from our analysis for future U.S. national security policy? When we began this project in earnest in the fall of 2007, we expected that our findings would have important implications for U.S. policy toward Iraq. As this book goes to press, however, we are not so sure. In the first place, the question of what to do next in Iraq is very different from the question of whether it was wise to invade Iraq in the first place. Thus conclusions about the costs and benefits of the war as a whole may be largely irrelevant to considerations about future steps. Indeed, as suggested by the results of the "surge," it may sometimes be advisable to augment one's investment in a losing cause in order to increase the chances of success rather than simply to cut one's losses, although the ultimate results of the surge remain to be determined. If Bob Woodward's recent account is accurate, President Bush essentially chose to escalate by committing more American resources to the fight in Iraq when many others, including military leaders on the ground such as General George Casey, loyal members of his own party, and outside critics, sought to withdraw or at least initiate a serious redeployment of U.S. soldiers away from the counterinsurgency operations.[86]

Since we began this project, moreover, the principal issue has been largely transformed from that of whether the United States should reduce its forces in Iraq to how quickly it should do so. It may be easy to forget that in the fall of 2007, a major debate was raging over U.S. policy in Iraq. Indeed, it was arguably the single most important issue in the presidential campaign at the time and continued to be well into the following year. Thanks to the temporary increase in U.S. force levels, changes in U.S. tactics, and other important developments within Iraq itself, however, the security situation on the ground had improved dramatically by mid-2008.

Attacks on Iraqi civilians and U.S. forces had dropped sharply, as had the numbers of casualties. In July 2008, fewer Americans were killed than in any month since the war began.[87] As a result of these positive developments, the Bush administration and Iraqi government were able to negotiate a status-of-forces agreement that foresaw the withdrawal of all U.S. forces from Iraq by the end of 2011.[88] Such a timeline was not so different from the plan proposed by Barack Obama during the presidential campaign, which called for the removal of all U.S. combat brigades by the summer of 2010.[89] In other words, the range of plausible alternative policies had narrowed markedly.

Not only are the findings of this book of limited utility for informing future U.S. policy toward Iraq, but some might argue that there are few if any useful lessons to be learned for U.S. national security policy more generally. The circumstances leading up to the Bush administration's decision to go to war—Iraq's record of aggression and status as an international pariah, the shock of 9/11 and the imperative to prosecute the war on terror—are so unique in nature that we are extremely unlikely to encounter anything like them any time soon. Moreover, some of the problems caused by the Iraq War may be solved simply by having a new face in the White House. Many international polls show that anti-American attitudes have as much or more to do with

President Bush than with the United States as a whole. Thus the change in administration alone could go a long way toward repairing the international standing of the United States, undoing any remaining damage in alliance relations, and defusing some of the anti-American attitudes that have fueled international terrorism.

It is also possible to make too much of the Iraq War in terms of its effects on large-scale trends such as the relative decline (or not) of the United States versus other nations or the prospects for peace in the Middle East. Perhaps several decades from now, when scholars write histories of U.S. security policy in the early twenty-first century, other developments in the United States, the greater Middle East, and perhaps elsewhere will seem much more significant than Iraq. After all, in some important respects, the Iraq War is a relatively minor affair in comparison to the great wars of the twentieth century—from World War One to Vietnam—much less the American Civil War.[90]

Nevertheless, we believe that one can draw important lessons of relevance to future U.S. national security policy. These follow from our overall diagnosis of the errors made by the Bush administration. We argue that the administration made two sets of interrelated and mutually reinforcing mistakes. First, it chose to fight a war that was not in fact necessary. Second, it chose to fight the war with very limited international support, insufficient planning, and inadequate military and other resources. These mistakes are interrelated because the limited international support reflected a lack of consensus on the necessity of the war, while the insufficiency of preparation and resources followed from the administration's miscalculations about the requirements of success and thus the wisdom of going to war in the first place.

We do not deny that the war could theoretically have been prosecuted more successfully and at less cost, although the overall outcome would not have necessarily been more favorable than in the alternative scenarios explored above. But we are not convinced that the administration had much greater discretion with regard to how it went about fighting the war, given its determination to invade Iraq no later than March 2003. After all, the administration made several major efforts to generate international support for a war on its terms, including a dramatic presentation by Secretary of State Colin Powell in the UN Security Council about Iraq's WMD programs and ties to international terrorism that turned out to be riddled with inaccuracies. Likewise, given the doubts that existed about the need for military action, Congress and the American public would have offered much less support for, if not outright resistance to, the war if the Bush administration had asked for a much greater commitment of military and financial resources.

This analysis suggests several general ways in which the costs of future U.S. national security policies can be reduced and their benefits maximized:

1. make sure there is a problem that requires action;
2. when the United States does decide that action is necessary, try to maximize international support;
3. use military force only when alternatives are unavailable or clearly inferior;
4. especially when force is used, make sure that adequate resources are employed; and
5. most importantly, carefully weigh the expected costs and benefits of any proposed course of action against those of the alternatives.

One of the most striking features of the Iraq War experience was the discovery that Iraq's military capabilities and ties to international terrorism were far less than those cited by the Bush administration as a justification for war.[91] This embarrassing discrepancy has been variously attributed to two factors: the failure of the intelligence agencies to produce accurate estimates and the Bush administration's selective use of the available intelligence to achieve a predetermined result. Each has been the subject of an extensive report by the Senate Select Committee on Intelligence.[92]

With regard to addressing these failings, we acknowledge that others are better informed about the technical processes of gathering and analyzing intelligence for national security and thus in a better position to suggest how those processes can be improved. Thus what concerns us more here is ensuring that future administrations take a more critical approach to threat assessment—so that it is neither overly complacent nor overly alarmist—and, in the worst case, preventing the gross misuse of intelligence for partisan purposes or to advance an ideological agenda. Unfortunately, however, we see no easy solutions.

One possibility would be to develop robust internal mechanisms and structures for generating alternative assessments, while avoiding the ideological failings of the "Team B" analysis conducted during the Ford administration. It was such a failing that helped get the Bush administration into the Iraq quagmire in the first place. In effect, some factions within the administration, including the Office of the Vice President, were dissatisfied with the tempered, even cautious, analyses of the intelligence community with regard to Iraqi weapons of mass destruction and the relationship between Saddam Hussein's regime and al Qaeda. In subtle and not-so-subtle ways, they pressured various intelligence agencies with on-site visits by high-ranking administration officials, by asking for direct access to raw intelligence, by using foreign governments as conduits for injecting into the system controversial information (for example, on Nigerian yellowcake and meetings between Iraqi operatives and al Qaeda) that had been disregarded or questioned by American analysts, and by sponsoring sources from the Iraqi exile community (for example, "Curve Ball") that had little if any credibility. The Bush administration, in short, created an informal, highly secret "Team B" to challenge career civil servants, including experts on Iraq, terrorism, and WMD.

Many of these questionable activities were the result of a particular confluence of the specific individuals charged with making decisions and an especially permissive bureaucratic and oversight environment engendered by 9/11. Indeed, several Bush advisors, including Deputy Secretary of Defense Paul Wolfowitz, had been intimately involved with the original Team B effort. But if the United States is to develop mechanisms for generating relatively unbiased alternative assessments and getting them into the hands of decision makers, care will have to be taken to ensure sufficient checks and balances as well as procedural transparency.

Another possibility is to provide greater access to classified intelligence findings to members of Congress and their staffs so that the legislative branch can serve as a greater check on potential executive misbehavior. Yet more intelligence for Congress alone will not suffice; effective congressional oversight of national security, including how wars are fought, is a much more complex process.[93] Individual senators and representatives must be willing and able to act effectively, through committees and the various highways and byways of legislative action, to hold the executive branch accountable. And representatives of the executive branch must be willing to provide accurate information in a timely manner when requested, a tradition sorely tested by the last eight years. If not, Congress must use the power of the purse and its power to subpoena and sanction, with the support of the federal court systems and, indeed, if necessary, of the Supreme Court.

In any case, the experience of the Iraq War suggests the importance of taking the time needed to gauge accurately the nature and magnitude of the presumed threat. Even seemingly urgent challenges posed by rogue regimes like Saddam Hussein's Iraq—whether from conventional means or weap-

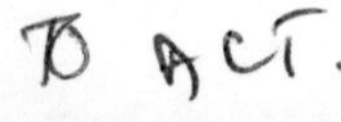

ons of mass destruction—must be evaluated carefully. Certainly, the United States should not rush to eliminate an uncertain threat that is less than imminent. In the case of the Iraq War, little was gained and much was lost by not waiting at least a few more months before launching the invasion. Clearly, the Bush administration could have prosecuted the war more successfully if it had taken more time to prepare, and costs that it would have incurred by postponing the attack would probably have been more than made up for in terms of greater international support. By proceeding more deliberately, the administration might even have discovered, however reluctantly, that war was not necessary after all because Iraq lacked any meaningful stockpiles of WMD or the programs to build them. In many cases, a more careful approach to threat assessment may mean having to live with uncertainty and accepting some risk. But as the Iraq War has shown, the overall costs of eliminating any single threat can easily exceed the benefits.

A second lesson concerns the critical importance of obtaining international legitimacy and, where necessary, material support for potentially controversial and costly U.S national security policies. This imperative need not always mean obtaining authorization from the UN Security Council for military action, although the United States would be wise to seek such authorization except when the threat it faces is "instant, overwhelming, leaving no choice of means, and no moment for deliberation."[94] At a minimum, however, it does entail listening carefully to the views and concerns of America's allies, even those that may disagree, and only in rare cases proceeding without their support, especially when undertaking something as momentous as preventive war. After all, their views may turn out to be more accurate at least some of the time. More generally, international opinion provides a potentially useful confirmation—or disconfirmation—of the wisdom of any action and thus should not be summarily dismissed.

Two further lessons from the experience of the Iraq War concern the use of force in particular. Obviously, some goals of national security policy can be accomplished only through military action. But there are also many goals that cannot be achieved through the use of force, or that can be accomplished just as effectively and at less cost by nonmilitary means. As the Iraq War amply illustrates, when force is used, the potential for unexpected and unintended consequences rises substantially. Certainly, the war has confirmed the deep doubts many people have long harbored about the utility of preventive war, even under the most favorable circumstances. Thus, the United States must not respond to future threats and challenges with only a portion of its national security tool kit or use only coercive means, but rather should draw on the full range of policy instruments available. To do otherwise is to endanger further the nation in a challenging period of international history. Yet, changing this tendency may require a much more significant rethinking of U.S. national security than is suggested by the simple notion that the United States must employ force more carefully; after all, one reason that presidents reach for the military instrument is that the military is by far the most robust tool available. The nation funds the military and intelligence communities to a far greater extent than it does soft-power means, such as traditional diplomacy, foreign assistance programs, or public diplomacy, to name just a few alternative methods of accomplishing national objectives.

A related lesson is that when force is used, the United States would be wise to err where possible on the conservative side with regard to preparation and force requirements. One can point to few, if any, episodes of history in which the United States employed forces that were excessively large or too well prepared. To be sure, U.S. policymakers should not adhere slavishly to any particular formula governing the use of force, although the Weinberger and Powell doctrines do provide useful guidance. But when it comes to determining the military requirements of an operation, future political leaders would do well to listen carefully to the generals and admirals, as those with the greatest familiarity with the technical issues involved. Although U.S. military leaders have a record of caution when it comes to advising on military operations, their views should be taken seriously rather than summarily dismissed, as occurred when then army chief of staff Eric Shinseki warned that "something on the order of several hundred thousand soldiers" would probably be required for postwar Iraq.[95] At least the Bush administration appears to have learned this lesson eventually, when it nearly pushed the army to the breaking point to provide General Petraeus with the five additional combat brigades he believed were needed to conduct an effective campaign of counterinsurgency and stabilization. If a substantial mismatch exists between what forces military leaders say are necessary and what are actually available, it may be necessary to rethink the use of force.[96]

Finally, and perhaps most importantly, the Iraq War underscores the constant need to consider carefully the costs and benefits of alternative policy options. Even a nation as wealthy and willing as the United States faces limits to its resources, especially in a international environment where large security challenges remain on the horizon—from China to nontraditional threats like global pathogens and virulent brands of terrorism. Even more to the point, strategies and policies in response to threats that are based on military preemption and preventive war rather than careful diplomacy demand special scrutiny in view of what happened in Iraq.

This last lesson would seem to be especially relevant to the determination of future U.S. policy in Iraq. Even within the greatly narrowed range of possibilities, critical choices remain to be made about how quickly to withdraw American forces from the country, with important implications for other dimensions of U.S. national security, such as the United States's ability to prosecute the war in Afghanistan, the health of the U.S. military, and U.S. readiness to engage in other conflicts that might erupt.

During its last two years, the Bush administration finally hit upon a successful strategy in Iraq and devoted the resources needed to implement it. But as the administration came to an end, the United States was still planning to maintain nearly 140,000 troops in Iraq, leaving very few for other contingencies. This was some four times the number of U.S. troops planned for Afghanistan, where the level of violence was increasing and had already surpassed that in Iraq. Now the United States risked making the opposite mistake of 2003 by not moving military resources from one theater to another. It may be useful that the person most responsible for the successful implementation of the surge, General Petraeus, will be in charge of U.S. military policy in both Iraq and Afghanistan as well as the rest of the Middle East and Central Asia. But the evaluation of the trade-offs should not stop there. It will be important to consider the broader implications of U.S. military policy in the region for the U.S. armed forces, the federal budget, the war on terror, relations with allies and other major powers, and other values. As the Iraq War has clearly shown, U.S. national security is ill served by a single-minded focus on just one of the many challenges that the country faces.

Thus as the Obama administration reviews and reformulates U.S. national security policy, it must constantly strive to balance the costs and risks in Iraq against those that it might incur elsewhere. What is likely to happen in Iraq if the United States quickly reduces its force levels there? How much greater are the chances of a positive outcome if we delay troop withdrawals as long as possible? And how profitably can U.S. military and other resources that might otherwise be devoted to Iraq be employed in other theaters and for other purposes? Clearly, considerable uncertainty attaches to any answers that might be offered to these questions, and even experts will advance conflicting theories about what is likely to happen in Iraq and elsewhere under various circumstances. No one knows—or can know—for sure. What is important is that alternative predictions be subjected to careful scrutiny and that U.S. national security policy not proceed on the basis of unchallenged assumptions.

NOTES

Chapter 1

1. "Opening Statement of Chairman Ike Skelton (D-MO), Joint Hearing on Status of the War and Political Developments in Iraq," September 10, 2007, http://armedservices.house.gov/apps/list/speech/armedsvc_dem/skeltonos091007.shtml (accessed May 13, 2008).

2. "How Will War in Iraq Be Judged in the Future?" *London Financial Times*, October 6, 2003.

3. On the initial emergence and early evolution of the Iraqi insurgency, see Ahmed S. Hashim, *Insurgency and Counter-Insurgency in Iraq* (London: Hurst & Co., 2006).

4. It is unlikely many Bush supporters consider the Iraq War a success in terms of American domestic politics. Arguably, the president's political party lost its hold over both houses of Congress in 2006 because of the war. Moreover, much of President Bush's extreme unpopularity with the electorate—in late 2008, his favorability ratings stood at historically unprecedented lows—derives from dissatisfaction with the war. For an early account of this phenomenon, see John Mueller, "The Iraq Syndrome," *Foreign Affairs* 84, no. 6 (November/December 2005).

5. "Remarks by Vice President Cheney, General David Petraeus and Ambassador Ryan Crocker in Press Availability," U.S. Embassy, Baghdad, Iraq, March 17, 2008, http://www.whitehouse.gov/news/releases/2008/03/print/20080317-6.html (accessed May 5, 2008). See also "Mission Still Not Accomplished," *New York Times*, March 20, 2008.

6. Jay Bookman, "Mission Still Not Accomplished," *Atlanta Journal-Constitution*, March 23, 2008, p. B6.

7. Joseph E. Stiglitz and Linda J. Bilmes, *The Three Trillion Dollar War: The True Cost of the Iraq Conflict* (New York: W. W. Norton, 2008).

8. Sherry Ricchiardi, "Whatever Happened to Iraq? How the Media Lost Intere in a Long-Running War with No End in Sight," *American Journalism Review* 30, no. (June/July 2008), http://ajr.org (accessed June 15, 2008).

9. Brian Stelter, "Reporters Say Networks Put Wars on Back Burner," *New Yo Times*, June 23, 2008, p. C4.

10. For example, in a poll of more than three thousand people conducted four t five weeks before the war began, only 32 percent of the respondents answered, "The U should invade Iraq even if we have to go it alone." See PIPA-Knowledge Networks Poll, "Americans on Iraq & UN Inspections II," http://www.worldpublicopinion.org/pipa/pdf/feb03/IraqUNInsp2%20Feb03%20quaire.pdf (accessed June 2, 2008).

11. The continuing uncertainty over the long-term political outcome in Iraq is not necessarily due to the inherent difficulty of the task of rebuilding Iraq alone. Rather, there is now a broad consensus that the Bush administration mismanaged the invasion and occupation of Iraq, perhaps at least until the implementation of the so-called surge of U.S. military forces in 2007, some four years after the war began.

12. As of October 31, 2008, the Universal Catalog of the University System of Georgia listed more than 1,750 books under the subject heading "Iraq War."

13. For example, Thomas E. Ricks, *Fiasco: The American Military Adventure in Iraq* (New York: Penguin, 2006); Michael R. Gordon and Bernard E. Trainor, *Cobra II: The Inside Story of the Invasion and Occupation of Iraq* (New York: Pantheon, 2006); George Packer, *The Assassins' Gate: America in Iraq* (New York: Farrar, Straus and Giroux, 2005); Peter W. Galbraith, *The End of Iraq: How American Incompetence Created a War Without End* (New York: Simon & Schuster, 2006); Eric Herring and Glen Rangwala, *Iraq in Fragments: The Occupation and Its Legacy* (Ithaca, NY: Cornell University Press, 2006); Charles H. Ferguson, *No End in Sight: Iraq's Descent into Chaos* (New York: Public Affairs, 2008); and Ali A. Allawi, *The Occupation of Iraq: Winning the War, Losing the Peace* (New Haven, CT: Yale University Press, 2008).

14. Stiglitz and Bilmes, *Three Trillion Dollar War.* See also Amy Belasco, *The Cost of Iraq, Afghanistan, and Other Global War on Terror Operations Since 9/11*, CRS Report for Congress, April 11, 2008.

15. Rick Fawn and Raymond A. Hinnebusch, eds., *The Iraq War: Causes And Consequences* (Boulder, CO: Lynne Rienner, 2006).

16. Steven E. Miller, "Mired in Mesopotamia: The Iraq War and American Interests," in *No More States? Globalization, National Self-Determination, and Terrorism*, ed. Richard N. Rosecrance and Arthur A. Stein (Lanham, MD: Rowman & Littlefield, 2006), pp. 183–206.

17. Peter W. Galbraith, *Unintended Consequences: How War in Iraq Strengthened America's Enemies* (New York: Simon & Schuster, 2008).

18. Peter Baker, "Democracy in Iraq Not a Priority in U.S. Budget," *Washington Post*, April 5, 2006, p. A01.

19. "President Bush Announces Major Combat Operations in Iraq Have Ended," Remarks by the President from the *USS Abraham Lincoln*, At Sea Off the Coast of San Diego, California, May 1, 2003, http://www.whitehouse.gov/news/releases/2003/05/20030501-15.html (accessed May 5, 2008).

20. "President Bush Discusses Freedom in Iraq and Middle East," Remarks by the President at the 20th Anniversary of the National Endowment for Democracy, United States Chamber of Commerce, Washington, DC, November 6, 2003, http://www.whitehouse.gov/news/releases/2003/11/20031106-2.html (accessed May 5, 2008).

21. For example, Fawn and Hinnebusch, *Iraq War*; and Richard A. Falk, *The Costs of War: International Law, the UN, and World Order after Iraq* (New York: Routledge, 2007).

Chapter 2

The author would like to thank Sara Bjerg Moller and Alex Noyes of the Council on Foreign Relations for their assistance in preparing this chapter.

1. Daniel Benjamin and Steven Simon, *The Next Attack* (New York: Times Books, 2005), p. 33.

2. Ibid.

3. Ayman al-Zawahiri, "Selected Questions and Answers from Dr. Ayman al-Zawahiri—Part 1," NEFA Foundation, April 17, 2008, http://www.nefafoundation.org/miscellaneous/FeaturedDocs/nefazawahiri0508.pdf (accessed February 20, 2009).

4. Ayman al-Zawahiri, "Shaykh Ayman al-Zawahiri: On the Fifth Anniversary of the Invasion and Torture of Iraq," NEFA Foundation, April 21, 2008, http://www.nefafoundation.org/miscellaneous/FeaturedDocs/nefazawahiri0408-2.pdf (accessed February 20, 2009).

5. Abu Bakr Naji, "The Management of Savagery," trans. William McCants, West Point Combatting Terrorism Center, May 2006, http://www.wcfia.harvard.edu/olin/images/Management%20of%20Savagery%20-%2005-23-2006.pdf (accessed February 20, 2009).

6. "Excerpts from the 'Bin Laden' Audio Tape," *Guardian*, January 19, 2006, http://www.guardian.co.uk/world/2006/jan/19/alqaida.terrorisml (accessed February 20, 2009).

7. "Transcript of Usama Bin Laden Audio Recording Produced by the As-Sahab Media Foundation: The Way to Frustrate the Conspiracies," NEFA Foundation, December 29, 2007.

8. Ayman al-Zawahiri, "Shaykh Ayman al-Zawahiri," NEFA Foundation, April 17, 2008.

9. Reuters, "Bin Laden Urges Muslims to Join Iraq Fight—Web," October 24, 2007, http://in.reuters.com/article/worldNews/idINIndia-30126220071023 (accessed February 20, 2009).

10. "Trends in Global Terrorism: Implications for the United States," Declassified Key Judgments of the National Intelligence Estimate, April 2006, http://www.dni.gov/press_releases/Declassified_NIE_Key_Judgments.pdf (accessed February 20, 2009).

11. Pew Global Attitudes Project, "America's Image Slips, But Allies Share U.S. Concerns Over Iran, Hamas," June 13, 2006, http://pewglobal.org/reports/display.php?ReportID=252 (accessed February 20, 2009).

12. Peter Bergen and Alec Reynolds, "Blowback Revisited," *Foreign Affairs* 84, no. 6 (November/December 2005).

13. Peter Bergen and Paul Cruickshank, "The Iraq Effect: The War in Iraq and Its Impact on the War on Terrorism," *Mother Jones*, March/April 2007.

14. Don Van Natta Jr. and David Johnston, "Threats and Responses: Terror Network; A Terror Lieutenant with a Deadly Past," *New York Times*, February 10, 2003.

15. George Tenet, *At the Center of the Storm* (New York: Harper Collins, 2007), p. 277.

16. "Irhabi" is the Arabic term for terrorist.

17. Evan Kohlmann, "The Real Online Terrorist Threat," *Foreign Affairs* 85, no. 5 (September/October 2006); Rita Katz and Michael Kern, "Terrorist 007, Exposed," *Washington Post*, March 26, 2006.

18. BBC News, "Journey of a Belgian Female 'Bomber,'" December 2, 2005, http://news.bbc.co.uk/2/hi/europe/4491334.stm (accessed February 20, 2009).

19. Associated Press, "Zarqawi's Terror Network Rivals Bin Laden's, U.S. Intelligence Says," October 24, 2005.

20. Raymond Bonner, Jane Perlez, and Eric Schmitt, "British Inquiry of Failed Plots Points to Iraq's Qaeda Group," *New York Times*, December 14, 2007.

21. Cf. Quintan Wiktorowicz, *Radical Islam Rising: Muslim Extremism in the West* (Lanham, MD: Rowman & Littlefield, 2005).

22. Workshop on Muslim/Non-Muslim Relations in Europe, London, October 29–30, 2007. This workshop, held at the International Institute for Strategic Studies, was jointly sponsored by the Council on Foreign Relations, the Brookings Institution's Center on the United States and Europe, and the Center on Law and Security at New York University.

23. Elaine Sciolino, "Fears of Iraq Becoming a Terrorist Incubator Seem Overblown, French Say," *New York Times*, April 8, 2008.

24. The total thus far falls well below the numbers of British volunteers to the Afghan jihad in the 1990s, which UK officials place at about three thousand.

25. Richard Oppel, "Foreign Fighters in Iraq Are Tied to Allies of US," *New York Times*, November 22, 207.

26. Joseph Felter and Brian Fishman, "Al Qaida's Foreign Fighters in Iraq: A First Look at the Sinjar Papers," Combating Terrorism Center at West Point, December

2007, p. 8, http://www.ctc.usma.edu/harmony/pdf/CTCForeignFighter.19.Dec07.pdf (accessed February 20, 2009).

27. Graphs of these figures can be viewed at ibid.

28. Christopher Boucek, "Extremist Reeducation and Rehabilitation in Saudi Arabia," *Terrorism Monitor* 5, no. 16 (August 16, 2007); Christopher Boucek, "Jailing Jihadis: Saudi Arabia's Special Terrorist Prisons," *Terrorism Monitor* 6, no. 2 (January 24, 2008).

29. Joshua Kurlantzick, "A Radical Solution: Using Former Terrorists to Turn Around Militants in the Making Is Showing Remarkable Success," *Los Angeles Times*, January 6, 2008.

30. Ibid.

31. Cf. Fawaz Gerges, *The Far Enemy: Why the Jihad Went Global* (New York: Cambridge University Press, 2005), pp. 251–76; and Benjamin and Simon, *The Next Attack*, pp. 17–50.

32. Peter Bergen, "The Taliban, Regrouped and Rearmed," *Washington Post*, September 10, 2006.

33. The two deadliest months of 2005 were August and October, with seventy-seven deaths each. The previous record, set in April and November 2004, was one hundred twenty-six. See "Military Casualty Information," http://siadapp.dmdc.osd.mil/personnel/CASUALTY/castop.htm (accessed February 20, 2009).

34. Glenn Kessler and Michael Abramowitz, "Bush Brings Afghanistan, Pakistan to the Table," *Washington Post*, September 27, 2006.

35. Benjamin and Simon, *The Next Attack*, p. 35.

36. Azzam was the cofounder, with bin Laden, of the Office for Services in Peshawar during the anti-Soviet jihad.

37. Mary Anne Weaver, "The Short, Violent Life of Abu Musab al-Zarqawi," *Atlantic*, June 8, 2006, http://www.theatlantic.com/doc/200607/Zarqawi/3 (accessed February 20, 2009).

38. Tenet, *Center of the Storm*, p. 277.

39. An estimated two hundred fighters are reported to have traveled to Iraq from Afghanistan during this period. Ibid., p. 350.

40. Gretchen Peters and Aleem Agha, "Weary Taliban Coming in from the Cold," *Christian Science Monitor*, December 14, 2004.

41. Sami Yousafzai and Ron Moreau, "Taliban Gets Help, Inspiration from Iraq," *Newsweek*, September 26, 2005.

42. In March 2006, the Asia Times Online reported that five hundred fighters who had trained in Iraq had returned to the Afghan-Pakistan region. Anna Badkhen, "Foreign Jihadists Seen as Key to Spike in Afghan Attacks," *San Francisco Chronicle*, September 25, 2006.

43. Yousafzai and Moreau, "Taliban Gets Help."

44. In the fall of 2003, there were a reported one hundred IED attacks a month. By the following February, IED attacks in Iraq had reached nearly one hundred per week. Rick Atkinson, "The IED Problem Is Getting Out of Control. We've Got to Stop the Bleeding," *Washington Post*, September 30, 2007.

45. Rick Atkinson, "The Single Most Effective Weapon Against Our Deployed Forces," *Washington Post*, September 30, 2007.

46. Afghanistan Conflict Monitor, http://www.afghanconflictmonitor.org/incidents.html#docs4 (accessed February 20, 2009).

47. *JIEDDO FY 2007 Annual Report*,https://www.jieddo.dod.mil/ANNUALREPORTS/20080130_FULL_Annual%20Report%20UNCLS%208.5%20x%2011_v6.pdf (accessed February 20, 2009).

48. Sean Rayment, "Troops Face Huge Rise in Taliban Bombs," *Sunday Telegraph*, July 13, 2008.

49. Clay Wilson, "Improvised Explosive Devices (IEDs) in Iraq and Afghanistan: Effects and Countermeasures," Congressional Research Service, Washington, DC, August 28, 2007.

50. Nathan Hodge, "JIEDDO Chief Highlights Rising IED Threat in Afghanistan," *Jane's Defence Weekly*, February 20, 2008.

51. Joanna Wright, "Increasing Afghan IED Threat Gives Forces Cause for Concern," *Jane's Intelligence Review*, August 1, 2006.

52. A British unit walked into a "daisy chain" ambush in Helmand Province in midsummer 2008. Sean Rayment, "Afghanistan: The 'Forgotten' War Is Back in the Spotlight," *Sunday Telegraph*, July 21, 2008.

53. "Suicide Bombings in Afghanistan," *Jane's Islamic Affairs Analyst*, September 1, 2007.

54. Ibid.

55. Ibid.

56. Mohammed Hafez, *Suicide Bombers in Iraq* (Washington, DC: United States Institute of Peace Press, 2007), p. 89.

57. UN Assistance Mission in Afghanistan, "Suicide Attacks in Afghanistan (2001–2007)," September 2007, http://hsrp.typepad.com/afghanistan/UNAMA_suicideattacks200107.pdf (accessed February 20, 2009).

58. There were no suicide attacks reported in Afghanistan in 2002. The following year there were two attacks, and in 2004 there were three. UN, "Suicide Attacks in Afghanistan."

59. Brian Glyn Williams and Cathy Young, "Cheney Attack Reveals Taliban Suicide Bombing Patterns," *Terrorism Monitor*, March 1, 2007.

60. Tom Vanden Brook, "IEDs Go Beyond Iraq, Afghanistan: Bombing Tactic Used in Russia, India, Elsewhere," *USA Today*, April 4, 2008.

61. Souad Mekhennet et al., "Ragtag Insurgency Gains a Lifeline from Al Qaeda," *New York Times*, July 1, 2008.

62. "An Interview with Abdelmalek Droukdal," *New York Times*, July 1, 2008.

63. *Landmine Monitor 2007 Report*, http://www.icbl.org/lm/2007/algeria.html (accessed February 20, 2009).

64. "Counter-terrorism Successes Force Algerian Militias to Evolve," *Jane's Intelligence Review*, June 1, 2006, http://www.washingtoninstitute.org/opedsPDFs/ 44c9141 fa913a.pdf (accessed February 20, 2009).

65. State Department, *Country Reports on Terrorism*, chap. 2, April 2007, http://www.state.gov/s/ct/rls/crt/2006/82733.htm (accessed February 20, 2009).

66. Reuters, "Islamist Group Says it Carried Out Algeria Attack," December 11, 2006.

67. Andrew Black, "Recasting Jihad in the Maghreb," *Terrorism Monitor* 5, no. 20 (October 25, 2007).

68. Warren Hoge, "Algeria Angered by UN Plans for Bombing Inquiry," *New York Times*, January 19, 2008.

69. Reuters, "Al-Qaeda Claims Responsibility for Algiers Bombing," April 11, 2007.

70. Black, "Recasting Jihad in the Maghreb."

71. "Counter-terrorism Successes Force Algerian Militants to Evolve," *Jane's Intelligence Review*, June 1, 2006.

72. Joseph Felter and Brian Fishman, "Al-Qaeda's Foreign Fighters in Iraq: A First Look at the Sinjar Record," Combating Terrorism Center at West Point, December 19, 2007.

73. See Daniel Kimmage and Kathleen Ridolfo, "Iraqi Insurgent Media: The War of Images and Ideas," *RFE/RL* Special Report, June 2007, for an astounding portrait of the insurgent media industry in Iraq.

74. Moss and Mekhennet, "An Internet Jihad Aims at U.S. Viewers.".

75. Yousafzai and Moreau, "Taliban Gets Help."

76. Moss and Mekhenent, "An Internet Jihad Aims at U.S. Viewers."

77. Anna Badkhen, "Foreign Jihadists Seen as Key to Spike in Afghan Attacks," *San Francisco Chronicle*, September 25, 2006.

78. Tom Pyszczynski et al., "Mortality Salience, Martyrdom, and Military Might: The Great Satan Versus the Axis of Evil," *Personality and Social Psychology Bulletin* 32, no. 4 (April 2006): 525–37.

79. Rudolph Peters, "Dutch Extremist Islamism: Van Gogh's Murder and His Ideas," in *Jihadi Terrorism and the Radicalization Challenge in Europe*, ed. Rik Coolsaet (Burlington, VT: Ashgate Publishing Company, 2008), pp. 115–27.

80. BBC News, "Bomber Video 'Points to al-Qaeda,'" http://news.bbc.co.uk/2/hi/uk_news/4208250.stm (accessed February 20, 2009).

81. BBC News, "London Bomber Video Aired on TV," September 2, 2005, http://news.bbc.co.uk/2/hi/uk_news/4206708.stm (accessed February 20, 2009); BBC News, "Video of 7 July Bomber Released," July 6, 2006, http://news.bbc.co.uk/2/hi/uk_news/5154714.stm (accessed February 20, 2009).

82. Tony Thompson, "Terror Suspect Gives First Account of London Attack," *Observer,* July 31, 2005.

83, Ghaith Abdul-Ahad, "Jordan Turns its Back on Zarqawi," *Guardian*, November 18, 2005.

84. Arthur Bright, "Has Al Qaeda Demoted Zarqawi?" *Christian Science Monitor,* April 5, 2006, http://www.csmonitor.com/2006/0405/dailyUpdate.html?s=mesdu (accessed February 20, 2009).

85. Letter from al-Zawahiri to al-Zarqawi, Office of the Director of National Intelligence, October 11, 2005, http://www.fas.org/irp/news/2005/10/letter_in_english.pdf (accessed February 20, 2009).

86. Ibid.

87. Pew Global Attitudes Project, "Global Opinion Trends Survey," July 24, 2007, p. 7, http://news.bbc.co.uk/2/shared/bsp/hi/pdfs/24_07_07pewglobal.pdf (accessed February 20, 2009).

88. Ibid., p. 57.

89. Pew Global Attitudes Project, "Global Unease with World Powers," June 27, 2007, p. 68, http://pewglobal.org/reports/pdf/256.pdf (accessed February 20, 2009).

90. Bruce Hoffman, "Reports of Al-Qaeda's Death May Be Greatly Exaggerated" (unpublished paper), 2008.

91. Lawrence Wright, "The Rebellion Within: An Al Qaeda Mastermind Questions Terrorism," *New Yorker,* June 2, 2008, pp. 46–47.

92. Peter Bergen and Paul Cruickshank, "The Unraveling," *New Republic,* June 11, 2008.

93. Hoffman, "Reports of Al-Qaeda's Death."

94. Omar Ashour, "Lions Tamed? An Inquiry into the Causes of De-Radicalization of Armed Islamist Movements: The Case of the Egyptian Islamic Group," *Middle East Journal* 61, no. 4 (autumn 2007): 596–625.

95. See, for example, Caroline Wadhams and Lawrence Korb, "The Forgotten Front," Center for American Progress, November 6, 2007, http://www.americanprogress.org/issues/2007/11/afghanistan_report.html (accessed February 20, 2009).

96. Ibid.

97. Barton Gellman, "Afghanistan, Iraq: Two Wars Collide," *Washington Post,* October 22, 2004.

98. Benjamin and Simon, *The Next Attack*, p. 176.

99. Ibid., p. 176.

100. The incident in question occurred in 2006. Mark Mazzetti and David Rohde, "Amid U.S. Policy Disputes, Qaeda Grows in Pakistan," *New York Times*, June 30, 2008.

101. Testimony to Congress, January 25, 2008. See also Thom Shanker and Steven Lee Myers, "Afghan Mission Is Reviewed as Concerns Rise," *New York Times*, December 16, 2007.

102. Gates is alleged to have told Democratic members of the U.S. House of Representatives that Afghanistan was "underresourced" both in terms of equipment and personnel, due to the war in Iraq. When asked about the comments, Pentagon spokesman Geoff Morrell acknowledged that the U.S. focus on Iraq was hurting the effort in Afghanistan: "We have a finite number of resources. . . . We have chosen to use the vast majority of those resources to fight the war in Iraq." Hans Nichols, "Gates Tells Lawmakers Iraq War Is Hurting Afghanistan Mission," *Bloomberg*, October 1, 2007.

103. Lt. Gen. John Sattler, *Testimony Before the Senate Armed Services Committee*, February 14, 2008.

104. Mark Mazzetti, "Military Death Toll Rises in Afghanistan," *New York Times*, July 2, 2008.

105. "Trends in Global Terrorism: Implications for the United States," Declassified Key Judgments of the National Intelligence Estimate, April 2006.

106. Robert Burns, "Petraeus: Al-Qaeda Fighters May Be Migrating," *USA Today*, July 19, 2008.

107. Associated Press, "Ambassador: Al-Qaeda Leaving Iraq for Afghanistan," *New York Times*, July 23, 2008.

108. Ibid.

109. Figures taken from transcript of AP's interview with General Petraeus on July 19, 2008, MNF-I Press Desk.

110. Amit R. Paley, "Al-Qaeda in Iraq Leader May Be in Afghanistan," *Washington Post*, July 31, 2008. Whether the move was a temporary one or part of a larger strategic shift within the group is unclear. Yet former insurgents told U.S. officials that Masri, an Egyptian who uses the nom de guerre Abu Hamza al-Muhajer, is unpopular among Iraqi insurgents and has been criticized for attacking the Awakening Movement instead of trying to win back their support. Although his supporters say Masri has visited Afghanistan twice before and is doing so this time in order to "review the situation of al-Qaeda in Iraq with Bin Laden" and will return, others point to a recent communiqué to al Qaeda in Iraq leaders signed by a new figure, Abdul Khalil al-Souri, as proof that Masri's leadership role in the group has diminished. Little is known about Souri, who is a member of "the first line," a group of thirty-three fighters who accompanied Abu Musab al-Zarqawi to Iraq in 2003.

111. Ibid.

112. Author interviews with UK and Dutch intelligence officials.

113. Bruce Hoffman and Seth Jones, "Cell phones in the Hindu Kush," *National Interest Online*, June 24, 2008.

114. Hoffman, "Reports of Al-Qaeda's Death."

115. Bruce Hoffman, "The 'Cult of the Insurgent': Its Tactical and Strategic Implications," *Australian Journal of International Affairs* 61, no. 3 (September 2007): 312–29.

Chapter 3

1. President John F. Kennedy, "Address Before the General Assembly of the United Nations," September 25, 1961, http://www.jfklibrary.org/Historical%2BResources/Archives/Reference%2BDesk/Speeches/JFK/003POF03UnitedNations09251961.htm (accessed February 20, 2009).

2. Associated Press, "No Nations Should Have Nukes, Most in USA Say," *USA Today*, March 31, 2005, http://www.usatoday.com/news/nation/2005-03-31-nuclear-fears_x.htm (accessed February 20, 2009).

3. John Bolton, "A Legacy of Betrayal," *Washington Times*, May 12, 1999, http://www.aei.org/publications/filter.all,pubID.17258/pub_detail.asp (accessed February 20, 2009).

4. Gary Schmitt, "Memorandum to Opinion Leaders," Project for the New American Century, December 13, 2001, http://www.newamericancentury.org/defense -20011213.htm (accessed February 20, 2009).

5. Letter to President Bill Clinton, January 26, 1998, available at the Web site of the Project for the New American Century, http://www.newamericancentury.org/iraq clintonletter.htm (accessed February 20, 2009).

6. Ibid.

7. Elliott Abrams, special assistant to the president and senior director on the National Security Council for Near East and North African Affairs (2002–2005) and deputy national security advisor (2005–2009); John Bolton, undersecretary of state for arms control and international security (2001–2005) and U.S. ambassador to the UN (2005); Richard Perle, defense policy board chairman (2001–2003); Donald Rumsfeld, secretary of defense (2001–2006); Paul Wolfowitz, deputy secretary of defense (2001–2005) and State Department International Security Advisory Board chairman (2008–2009).

8. John S. Wolf, "Remarks to the 12th Annual International Arms Control Conference," April 19, 2002, http://www.state.gov/t/isn/rls/rm/9635.htm (accessed February 20, 2009).

9. President George W. Bush, "President Announces New Measures to Counter the Threat of WMD," National Defense University, February 11, 2004, http://www.state.gov/t/isn/rls/rm/29290.htm (accessed February 20, 2009).

10. Paul Wolfowitz, "Campaign Against Terror," *Frontline*, PBS, April 22, 2002.

11. President George W. Bush, "President Bush Delivers Graduation Speech at

West Point," June 1, 2002, http://usa.usembassy.de/gemeinsam/bush060102.htm (accessed February 20, 2009).

12. President George W. Bush, "State of the Union," January 28, 2003, http://frwebgate.access.gpo.gov/cgi-bin/getdoc.cgi?dbname=2003_presidential_documents&docid=pd03fe03_txt-6.pdf (accessed February 20, 2009).

13. National Security Council, *The National Security Strategy of the United States of America* (Washington, DC: White House, 2002), http://www.globalsecurity.org/military/library/policy/national/nss-020920.pdf (accessed February 20, 2009); National Security Council, *National Strategy to Combat Weapons of Mass Destruction* (Washington, DC: White House, 2002), p. 1, http://www.defenselink.mil/pdf/NMS-CWMD2006.pdf (accessed February 20, 2009).

14. Ibid.

15. Thomas Donnelly, "The Top Ten Questions for the Post-9/11 World," American Enterprise Institute *National Security Outlook*, July 23, 2004, http://www.aei.org/publications/pubID.20965/pub_detail.asp (accessed February 20, 2009).

16. President Bill Clinton, November 18, 1998.

17. National Security Council, *National Strategy to Combat Weapons of Mass Destruction*, http://www.defenselink.mil/pdf/NMS-CWMD2006.pdf (accessed February 20, 2009).

18. President George W. Bush, "State of the Union Address," January 29, 2002, http://frwebgate.access.gpo.gov/cgi-bin/getdoc.cgi?dbname=2002_presidential_documents&docid=pd04fe02_txt-11.pdf (accessed February 20, 2009).

19. Ibid.

20. Spencer Ackerman and John B. Judis, "The Selling of the Iraq War: The First Casualty," *New Republic*, June 30, 2003.

21. President George W. Bush, "State of the Union Address," January 28, 2003, http://frwebgate.access.gpo.gov/cgi-bin/getdoc.cgi?dbname=2003_presidential_documents&docid=pd03fe03_txt-6.pdf (accessed February 20, 2009).

22. President George W. Bush, "President Says Saddam Hussein Must Leave Iraq Within 48 Hours," Address to the Nation, March 17, 2003, http://www.defenselink.mil/news/newsarticle.aspx?id=29285 (accessed February 20, 2009).

23. Ibid.

24. U.S. Senate, *Report on the U.S. Intelligence Community's Power Intelligence Assessment on Iraq Committee on Intelligence* (Washington, DC, July 2004), p. 388, quote from *Iraqi Military Capabilities Through 2003* (NIE 99–04/II, April 1999), http://www.intelligence.senate.gov/phaseiiaccuracy.pdf (accessed February 20, 2009).

25. Ibid., p. 390, from *Key Warning Concerns for 2003* (ICA 2003–2005, January 2003).

26. Hans Blix, "Briefing of the Security Council," February 14, 2003, http://www.un.org/Depts/unmovic/blix14Febasdel.htm (accessed February 20, 2009).

27. See Stephen Pullinger, "Lord Butler's Report on UK Intelligence," *Disarmament Diplomacy*, no. 78 (July/August 2004), http://www.acronym.org.uk/dd/dd78/78sp.htm (accessed February 20, 2009).

28. See remarks of Hans Blix and Mohammed ElBaradei at the Carnegie International Non-Proliferation Conference, June 2004, http://www.ProliferationNews.org.

29. James Risen, "The Struggle for Iraq: Intelligence; Ex-Inspector Says C.I.A. Missed Disarray in Iraqi Arms Program," *New York Times*, January 26, 2004, http://query.nytimes.com/gst/fullpage.html?res=9A02E6D71738F935A15752C0A9629C8B63 (accessed February 20, 2009).

30. See Joseph Cirincione, Jessica T. Mathews, and George Perkovich, "WMD in Iraq: Evidence and implications," Carnegie Endowment for International Peace, January 2004, pp. 54–56, http://www.carnegieendowment.org/files/Iraq3FullText.pdf (accessed February 20, 2009).

31. Richard Cheney, "Remarks to Veterans of Foreign Wars 103rd National Convention," Nashville, Tennessee, August 26, 2002, http://www.defenselink.mil/news/newsarticle.aspx?id=4352 (accessed February 20, 2009).

32. Donald Rumsfeld, "Interview with the National Journalist Roundtable," August 7, 2002, http://www.globalsecurity.org/military/library/news/2002/08/mil-020805-dod01b.htm (accessed February 20, 2009).

33. Trevor Findlay, "The Lessons of UNSCOM and UNMOVIC," in *Verification Yearbook 2004* (VERTIC, 2003), p. 76, http://www.vertic.org/assets/YB04/Findlay%208.pdf (accessed February 20, 2009).

34. For a more complete view of the French position, see Joseph Cirincione, "The French Were Right," Carnegie Analysis, February 24, 2004, http://www.carnegieendowment.org/npp/publications/index.cfm?fa=view&id=15020 (accessed February 20, 2009).

35. "The Truth About the War," *New York Times*, June 6, 2008, http://www.nytimes.com/2008/06/06/opinion/06fri1.html?scp=1&sq=The%20Truth%20About%20the%20War,%94%20&st=cse (accessed February 20, 2009).

36. Jay Rockefeller, "Senate Intelligence Committee Unveils Final Phase II Reports on Prewar Iraq Intelligence," Press Release, June 5, 2008, http://intelligence.senate.gov/press/record.cfm?id=298775 (accessed February 20, 2009).

37. PBS, "The War Behind Closed Doors," *Frontline*, January 25, 2003, http://www.pbs.org/wgbh/pages/frontline/shows/iraq/ (accessed February 20, 2009).

38. Joshua Muravchik, "Democracy's Quiet Victory," *New York Times*, August 19, 2002, http://query.nytimes.com/gst/fullpage.html?res=9A00EFDE123DF93AA2575BC0A9649C8B63 (accessed February 20, 2009).

39. Ibid.

40. Stan Crock, "Bush Dusts Off Bill's Pyongyang Playbook," *Business Week*, September 20, 2005, http://www.businessweek.com/bwdaily/dnflash/sep2005/nf20050920_2248_db016.htm (accessed February 20, 2009).

41. Leslie Gelb, "In the End, Every President Talks to the Bad Guys," *Washington Post*, April 27, 2008, p. B03, http://www.washingtonpost.com/wp-dyn/content/article/2008/04/24/AR2008042401459.html (accessed February 20, 2009).

42. Gareth Porter, "Burnt Offering," *American Prospect*, May 21, 2006, http://www.prospect.org/cs/articles?articleId=11539 (accessed February 20, 2009).

43. Ibid.

44. Glenn Frankel and Keith B. Richburg, "Europeans Seek Arms Accord in Tehran," *Washington Post*, October 21, 2003, p. A1.

45. William Kristol, "And Now Iran," *Weekly Standard* 011, no. 8 (January 23, 2006), http://www.weeklystandard.com/Content/Public/Articles/000/000/006/585tdlqf.asp (accessed February 20, 2009).

46. Charles Krauthammer, "The Iran Charade, Part II," *Washington Post*, January 18, 2006, p. A17, http://www.washingtonpost.com/wp-dyn/content/article/2006/01/17/AR2006011700893.html (accessed February 20, 2009).

47. Jeffery Lewis, "Iran & the Bomb 1: How Close Is Iran?" *Arms Control Wonk*, January 19, 2006, http://www.armscontrolwonk.com/945/iran-focus-part-1-how-close-is-iran-to-the-bomb (accessed February 20, 2009).

48. National Intelligence Council, "Iran: Nuclear Intentions and Capabilities," National Intelligence Estimate, November 2007, http://www.dni.gov/press_releases/20071203_release.pdf (accessed February 20, 2009).

49. Ibid.

50. Blaine Harden, "N. Korea Misses Deadline, but U.S. Response Is Restrained," *Washington Post*, January 1, 2008, p. A07, http://www.washingtonpost.com/wp-dyn/content/article/2007/12/31/AR2007123102233.html (accessed February 20, 2009).

51. John Bolton, "The North Korea Climbdown," *Wall Street Journal*, March 5, 2007, http://www.opinionjournal.com/extra/?id=110009746 (accessed February 20, 2009).

52. Glenn Kessler, "Conservatives Assail North Korea Accord," *Washington Post*, February 15, 2007, p. A01, http://www.washingtonpost.com/wp-dyn/content/article/2007/02/14/AR2007021401695.html (accessed February 20, 2009).

53. Paul Kerr, "Libya Vows to Dismantle WMD Program," *Arms Control Today* 34, no. 1 (January/February 2004), http://www.armscontrol.org/act/2004_01-02/Libya (accessed February 20, 2009).

54. Flynt L. Leverett, "Why Libya Gave Up on the Bomb," *New York Times*, January 23, 2004, http://query.nytimes.com/gst/fullpage.html?res=9E02E6DC1139F930A15752C0A9629C8B63&sec=&spon= (accessed February 20, 2009).

55. For a chronology of the network, see Michael Laufer, "A. Q. Khan Nuclear Chronology," *Carnegie Proliferation Brief* 7, no. 8 (September 7, 2005), http://www.carnegieendowment.org/publications/index.cfm?fa=view&id=17420&prog=zgp&proj=znpp (accessed February 20, 2009).

56. At their February 2005 meeting in Bratislava, Slovakia, Presidents Bush and

Putin emphasized the importance of protecting nuclear material. In July 2005, the two countries resolved a liability dispute that had been holding up a program to eliminate sixty-eight tons of weapons-grade plutonium.

57. Condoleezza Rice, "Remarks on the Second Anniversary of the Proliferation Security Initiative," May 31, 2005, http://www.nuclearfiles.org/menu/key-issues/nuclear-weapons/issues/proliferation/psi/2005-05-31_rice-2nd-anniversary-remarks.htm (accessed February 20, 2009).

58. Robert Joseph, "Remarks at the Carnegie International Non-Proliferation Conference," November 7, 2005, http://www.carnegieendowment.org/static/npp/2005conference/presentations/Robert_Joseph_transcript.pdf (accessed February 20, 2009).

59. Zbigniew Brzezinski, "George Bush's Suicidal Statecraft," *International Herald Tribune*, October 13, 2005, http://www.iht.com/articles/2005/10/13/opinion/edzbig.php (accessed February 20, 2009).

60. Zbigniew Brzezinski, "Iraq: Next Steps for U.S. Policy," Keynote Address, Center for American Progress, March 16, 2007, http://www.americanprogress.org/atf/cf/%7BE9245FE4-9A2B-43C7-A521-5D6FF2E06E03%7D/BREZENSKI%20KEYNOTE%2016MARCH06.PDF (accessed February 20, 2009).

61. In 2002, the number of "significant" international terrorist incidents was 136; in 2003 it was 175; in 2004, it was 651. See U.S. Department of State, *Patterns of Global Terrorism 2002*; and *Patterns of Global Terrorism 2003*. See also National Counterterrorism Center, "A Chronology of Significant International Terrorism for 2004."

62. Porter J. Goss, "DCI's Global Intelligence Challenges Briefing," Testimony before the Senate Select Committee on Intelligence, February 16, 2005, http://www.fas.org/irp/congress/2005_hr/031705goss.pdf (accessed February 20, 2009). See also Vice Admiral Lowell E. Jacoby, "Current and Projected National Security Threats to the United States," Testimony before the Senate Select Committee on Intelligence, 109th Cong., 1st sess., February 16, 2005, http://www.intelligence.senate.gov/threats.pdf (accessed February 20, 2009).

63. Matthew Bunn and Anthony Wier, *Securing the Bomb 2005: The New Global Imperatives* (Cambridge, MA, and Washington, DC: Project on Managing the Atom, Harvard University, and Nuclear Threat Initiative, May 2005), pp. 30–32, http://www.nti.org/e_research/cnwm/overview/cnwm_home.asp (accessed February 20, 2009). See also U.S. Department of Energy, "NNSA Expands Nuclear Security Cooperation with Russia," NNSA Fact Sheet, October 2005, http://nnsa.energy.gov/news/988.htm (accessed February 20, 2009).

64. Associated Press, "Officials Fear New Terrorist Attacks," February 17, 2005.

65. Nicholas Burns, "We Should Talk to Our Enemies," *Newsweek*, October 25, 2008.

66. Chuck Hagel and Peter Kaminsky, *America: Our Next Chapter, Tough Questions, Straight Answers* (New York: Harper Collins Press, 2008), p. 93.

67. Former secretaries of state Colin Powell, Madeleine Albright, Warren Christopher, James Baker, and Henry Kissinger said they favored talking to Iran as part of a strategy to stop Tehran's development of a nuclear weapons program during a forum hosted by the George Washington University on September 15, 2008. Former national security advisors Brent Scowcroft and Zbigniew Brezinski also praised engagement at a July 2008 event at the Center for Strategic and International Studies.

68. Ian Cobain and Ian Traynor, "Intelligence Report Claims Nuclear Market Thriving," *Guardian*, January 4, 2006.

69. Brazil, Iran, and South Korea have all announced their intentions to enrich their own uranium.

70. Presidents Bush and Putin signed the Strategic Offensive Reductions Treaty (SORT) in June 2002. Now, for the first time since the negotiated threat-reduction process began with SALT in the early 1970s, there are no plans for additional agreements. Under SORT, both sides are required to reduce their deployed strategic nuclear weapons to between seventeen hundred and twenty-two hundred by the end of 2012. Under the proposed START III agreement, negotiated by Presidents Clinton and Yeltsin in 1997, each side would have drawn down to similar numbers of deployed strategic nuclear weapons by 2007, five years earlier than envisioned under SORT. START III would also have provided a framework for discussions on reductions in tactical nuclear weapons and dismantlement of warheads. See Joseph Cirincione, Jon B. Wolfsthal, and Miriam Rajkumar, *Deadly Arsenals: Tracking Weapons of Mass Destruction* (Washington, DC: Carnegie Endowment for International Peace, 2002), pp. 204–5, 209–11.

71. In April 2008, former Pentagon director of operational test and evaluation Philip Coyle told the House Committee on Oversight and Government Reform, Subcommittee on National Security and Foreign Affairs, "The [anti-missile being deployed in Europe] still has no demonstrated effectiveness to defend the U.S., let alone Europe, against enemy attack under realistic operational conditions." Dr. Lisbeth Gronlund, a senior scientist with the Union of Concerned Scientists, commented at the same hearing, "The United States is no closer today to being able to effectively defend against long-range ballistic missiles than it was 25 years ago."

72. Richard N. Haass, "Regime Change and Its Limits," *Foreign Affairs* 84, no.4 (July/August 2005): 70, http://www.foreignaffairs.org/20050701faessay84405/richard-n-haass/regime-change-and-its-limits.html (accessed February 20, 2009).

73. John M. Spratt, "Stopping a Dangerous Drift in U.S. Arms Control Policy," *Arms Control Today* 33, no. 2 (March 2003), http://www.armscontrol.org/act/2003_03/spratt_mar03 (accessed February 20, 2009).

74. John Wolf, "Addressing Today's Nuclear Nonproliferation Challenges: Iran, North Korea, and the U.S.-India Nuclear Deal," Arms Control Association Press Briefing, September 16, 2005, http://www.armscontrol.org/events/20050916_Nuclear Nonproliferation (accessed February 20, 2009).

75. Ibid.

76. Mohamed ElBaradei, "Reflection on Nuclear Challenges Today," Lecture to the International Institute for Strategic Studies, London, December 6, 2005, http://www.iaea.org/NewsCenter/Statements/2005/ebsp2005n019.html (accessed February 20, 2009).

77. Francis Fukuyama, "The Neoconservative Moment," *National Interest*, June 1, 2004, http://www.nationalinterest.org/General.aspx?id=92&id2=11358 (accessed February 20, 2009).

Chapter 4

1. http://muse.tau.ac.il/maslool/boidem/118chou.html (accessed July 9, 2008).

2. The International Crisis Group reports that approximately 20 percent of the Iraqi population either left the country as refugees or became internally displaced as a result of the war. ICG, "Failed Responsibility: Iraqi Refugees in Syria, Jordan and Lebanon," *Middle East Report* no. 77, July 10, 2008, http://www.crisisgroup.org/home/index.cfm?id=5563&l=1 (accessed July 19, 2008).

3. President Bush announced the "Bush Doctrine" in the graduation speech at the United States Military Academy at West Point on June 1, 2002: "When the spread of chemical and biological and nuclear weapons, along with ballistic missile technology—when that occurs, even weak states and small groups could attain a catastrophic power to strike great nations. Our enemies have declared this very intention, and have been caught seeking these terrible weapons. . . . We must take the battle to the enemy, disrupt his plans, and confront the worst threats before they emerge. In the world we have entered, the only path to safety is the path of action. And this nation will act." http://www.whitehouse.gov/news/releases/2002/06/20020601-3.html (accessed July 15, 2008).

4. See, for one example, President Bush's speech to the National Defense University on March 8, 2005: "Our strategy to keep the peace in the longer term is to help change the conditions that give rise to extremism and terror, especially in the broader Middle East. Parts of that region have been caught for generations in the cycle of tyranny and despair and radicalism. When a dictatorship controls the political life of a country, responsible opposition cannot develop and dissent is driven underground and toward the extreme. And to draw attention away from their social and economic failures, dictators place blame on other countries and other races and stir the hatred that leads to violence. This status quo of despotism and anger cannot be ignored or appeased, kept in a box or bought off." http://www.whitehouse.gov/news/releases/2005/03/20050308-3.html (accessed July 15, 2008).

5. The clearest statement of this new thinking was delivered by Secretary of State Rice in a speech at the American University in Cairo on June 20, 2005: "For sixty years, my country, the United States, pursued stability at the expense of democracy in this region here in the Middle East—and we achieved neither. Now, we are taking a differ-

ent course. We are supporting the democratic aspirations of all people." http://www.state.gov/secretary/rm/2005/48328.htm (accessed July 16, 2008).

6. F. Gregory Gause III, "Can Democracy Stop Terrorism?" *Foreign Affairs* 84, no. 5 (September/October 2005).

7. The debate over the causes of the Iraq War is hardly settled. My assertion that the American decision to go to war in Iraq was a major change from past policy in the region and that it was grounded in the larger framework of seeking to change the domestic politics of the region as a whole is contested by those who see the invasion as motivated by a long-standing interest of the United States in controlling regional oil supplies and/or protecting Israeli interests. On the oil motivation for the war, see Michael Klare, *Blood and Oil* (New York: Metropolitan Books, Henry Holt, 2004); and Paul Roberts, *The End of Oil: On the Edge of a Perilous New World* (Boston: Houghton Mifflin, 2004). Roberts says the war in Iraq, "whether openly acknowledged or not, was clearly meant to restore Middle Eastern stability and maintain Western access to a steady supply of oil" (p. 10). On the Israeli rationale, see John J. Mearsheimer and Stephen M. Walt, *The Israel Lobby and U.S. Foreign Policy* (New York: Farrar, Straus and Giroux, 2007), chap. 8. For examples of the argument that the Iraq War was simply a culmination of previous American policy patterns in the Persian Gulf, not a departure, see Marc J. O'Reilly, *Unexceptional: America's Empire in the Persian Gulf, 1941–2007* (Lanham, MD: Lexington Books, 2008); John S. Duffield, *Over a Barrel: The Costs of U.S. Foreign Oil Dependence* (Stanford, CA: Stanford University Press, 2008).

8. Nuclear Threat Initiative, "Country Profile: Libya," http://www.nti.org/e_research/profiles/Libya/index.html (accessed July 15, 2008); James Martin Center for Nonproliferation Studies, Monterrey Institute for International Studies, "Weapons of Mass Destruction in the Middle East: Libya," http://cns.miis.edu/research/wmdme/libya.htm (accessed July 15, 2008).

9. Joel Brinkley, "U.S. Will Restore Diplomatic Links with the Libyans," *New York Times*, May 16, 2006.

10. Gary Hart, "My Secret Talks with Libya, and Why They Went Nowhere," *Washington Post*, January 18, 2004; Martin Indyk, "Was Kadafi Scared Straight? The Record Says No," *Los Angeles Times*, March 28, 2004.

11. The definitive statement of the absence of WMD is the "Comprehensive Report of the Special Advisor to the DCI on Iraq's WMD," September 30, 2004, http://www.cia.gov/library/reports/general-reports-1/iraq_wmd_2004/index.html (accessed July 15, 2008). On the intelligence failures, see Commission on the Intelligence Capabilities of the United States regarding Weapons of Mass Destruction, "Report to the President of the United States," March 31, 2005, http://www.wmd.gov/report (accessed July 15, 2008); and U.S. Senate, Select Committee on Intelligence, *Report on the U.S. Intelligence Community's Prewar Intelligence Assessments on Iraq*, 108th Cong., 2d sess., July 7, 2004.

12. Ali Ansari, *Confronting Iran: The Failure of American Foreign Policy and the Next Great Conflict in the Middle East* (New York: Basic Books, 2006), pp. 197–201.

13. Office of the Director of National Intelligence, National Intelligence Estimate, "Iran: Nuclear Intentions and Capabilities," November 2007, http://www.dni.gov/press_releases/20071203_release.pdf (accessed July 15, 2008).

14. Ansari, *Confronting Iran*, pp. 202–6, 221–25.

15. The Iranian overture in 2003 was revealed by Flynt Leverett, "Dealing with Teheran: Assessing U.S. Diplomatic Options Toward Iran," A Century Foundation Report, 2006, http://tcf.org/publications/internationalaffairs/leverett_diplomatic.pdf (accessed July 17, 2008). Leverett served on the National Security Council as senior director for Middle East affairs from March 2002 to March 2003, having previously held Middle East positions on the Policy Planning staff at the State Department and at the CIA. He subsequently became a vocal critic of Bush administration policy.

16. David Albright and Corey Hinderstein, "The Clock Is Ticking, But How Fast?" Institute for Science and International Security Issue Brief, March 27, 2006, p. 2, http://www.isis-online.org/publications/iran/clockticking.pdf (accessed July 17, 2008): "In early January 2006, Iran removed 52 seals applied by the International Atomic Energy Agency (IAEA) that verified the suspension of Iran's P-1 centrifuge uranium enrichment program. The seals were located at the Natanz, Pars Trash, and Farayand Technique sites, Iran's main centrifuge facilities. On February 11, Iran started to enrich uranium in a small number of centrifuges at Natanz, bringing to a halt Iran's suspension of uranium enrichment that had lasted since October 2003." Ansari, *Confronting Iran*, contends that the decision to renew enrichment was made before Ahmadinejad became president, p. 231. However, it is hard to separate the new president's more aggressive rhetoric from the decision to renew the enrichment program.

17. Steven Lee Myers, "U.S. Envoy to Join Meeting with Iranian," *New York Times*, July 16, 2008.

18. Paul Richter and Greg Miller, "CIA to Describe North Korea-Syria Nuclear Ties," *Los Angeles Times*, April 23, 2008; Robin Wright, "N. Koreans Taped at Syrian Reactor," *Washington Post*, April 24, 2008; Joby Warrick, "Experience with Syria Exemplifies Challenge that Detection Presents," *Washington Post*, May 12, 2008.

19. William J. Broad and David E. Sanger, "Eye on Iran, Rivals Pursuing Nuclear Power," *New York Times*, April 15, 2007.

20. Roula Khalaf, "Gulf Arabs Weigh Joint Nuclear Programme," *Financial Times*, December 11, 2006.

21. Molly Moore, "Sarkozy Pushes Nuclear Energy in the Mideast," *Washington Post*, January 20, 2008; "Saudi Arabia, US Sign Nuke Energy Pact," *Saudi Gazette*, May 17, 2008; "US, Bahrain Sign Deal on Nuclear Energy Cooperation," Agence France Presse, March 24, 2008.

22. For an overview of nuclear programs (outside of Iran's) in the Middle East, see

International Institute for Strategic Studies, *Nuclear Programmes in the Middle East: In the Shadow of Iran* (London: IISS, 2008).

23. Mark Mazzetti, "Intelligence Chief Says Al Qaeda Improves Ability to Strike in U.S.," *New York Times*, February 6, 2008.

24. Steven Simon, "The Price of the Surge," *Foreign Affairs* 87, no. 3 (May/June 2008); International Crisis Group, "Iraq after the Surge I: The New Sunni Landscape," *Middle East Report* no. 74, April 30, 2008, http://www.crisisgroup.org/home/index.cfm?id=5415&l=1 (accessed July 18, 2008).

25. On AQAP, see Roel Meijer, "The 'Cycle of Contention' and the Limits of Terrorism in Saudi Arabia," in *Saudi Arabia in the Balance: Political Economy, Society and Foreign Affairs*, ed. Paul Aarts and Gerd Nonneman (London: Hurst and Company, 2005), pp. 271–314; Thomas Hegghammer, "Political Violence in Saudi Arabia: The Rise and Fall of al-Qaida on the Arabian Peninsula," FFI—Norwegian Defense Research Establishment, March 2, 2007, http://www.mil.no/multimedia/archive/00091/Political_Violence_i_91403a.pdf (accessed July 18, 2008).

26. David Ignatius, "Beirut's Berlin Wall," *Washington Post*, February 23, 2005.

27. On the results of the January 2005 election, see *al-Hayat* (London), March 17, 2005, p. 5 (story on the opening meeting of the parliament). On the December 2005 election, see Ellen Knickmeyer, "Iraqi Election Results Show Sunni Gains," *Washington Post*, January 21, 2006. Unfortunately, the Independent Electoral Commission of Iraq, which posted detailed official results of each election, has taken down its Web site. For a chart of the results of the two elections, based on the IECI results, see http://www.uvm.edu/fgause/168read.htm#Iraqi%20elections (accessed July 19, 2008).

28. I discuss these election results in an on-line posting, F. Gregory Gause III, "Beware of What You Wish For," *Foreign Affairs* (February 8, 2006), http://www.foreignaffairs.org/20060208faupdate85177/f-gregory-gause-iii/beware-of-what-you-wish-for.html (accessed July 19, 2008).

29. Deputy Secretary of Defense Paul Wolfowitz told a congressional committee in March 2003 that "the oil revenues of that country could bring between $50 and $100 billion over the course of the next two or three years. . . . We're dealing with a country that can really finance its own reconstruction, and relatively soon." Dana Milbank and Robin Wright, "Off the Mark on Cost of War, Reception by Iraqis," *Washington Post*, March 19, 2004. Wolfowitz's estimate assumed a substantial increase in Iraqi production, as Iraqi oil revenues in 2002 could not have been more than $20 billion, based on average daily Iraqi production of around 2 MBD and oil prices averaging between $20 and $25 per barrel that year.

30. U.S. Department of Energy, Energy Information Administration, *Monthly Energy Review*, June 2008, Table 11.1a, http://www.eia.doe.gov/emeu/mer/pdf/pages/sec11_2.pdf (accessed July 18, 2008).

31. British Petroleum, "Statistical Review of World Energy 2008," Oil Prices

section, http://www.bp.com/sectiongenericarticle.do?categoryId=9023773&contentId=7044469 (accessed July 18, 2008).

32. Rajiv Chandrasekaran, "Economic Overhaul for Iraq, Only Oil Excluded from Foreign Ownership," *Washington Post*, September 22, 2003.

33. Andrew E. Kramer, "Deals with Iraq Are Set to Bring Oil Giants Back," *New York Times*, June 19, 2008.

34. Peter S. Goodman, "For Iraq's Oil Contracts, A Question of Motive," *New York Times*, June 29, 2008.

35. Andrew E. Kramer and Campbell Robertson, "Iraq Cancels Six No-Bid Oil Contracts," *New York Times*, September 11, 2008.

36. Amit Paley, "Iraq and China Sign $3 Billion Oil Contract," *Washington Post*, August 29, 2008.

37. Ben Lando, "Return of International Oil Companies to Iraq Begins," United Press International, October 14, 2008, http://www.upi.com/Energy_Resources/2008/10/13/Return_of_international_oil_companies_to_Iraq_begins/UPI-78571223938986/ (accessed February 20, 2009).

38. Mary Beth Sheridan, "Iraq Opens Bidding on Oil Field Contracts," *Washington Post*, October 14, 2008.

39. Karen DeYoung, "U.S., Iraq Scale Down Negotiations Over Forces," *Washington Post*, July 13, 2008.

40. In his speech to the Veterans of Foreign Wars on August 26, 2002, Vice President Cheney listed among the benefits to be realized by removing Saddam Hussein from office: "And our ability to advance the Israeli-Palestinian peace process would be advanced, just as it was following the liberation of Kuwait in 1991." http://www.whitehouse.gov/news/releases/2002/08/20020826.html (accessed July 19, 2008).

41. Ethan Bronner, "Israel Holds Peace Talks with Syria," *New York Times*, May 22, 2008.

42. For a review of the peace process in this period, see International Crisis Group, "The Israeli-Palestinian Conflict: Annapolis and After," *Middle East Briefing* no. 22, November 20, 2007, http://www.crisisgroup.org/home/index.cfm?id=5174&l=1 (accessed July 19, 2008).

43. Reuters, "U.S., Iraq Agree Pact Giving U.S. Troops Until 2011," October 15, 2006; Karen DeYoung, "Lacking an Accord on Troops, U.S. and Iraq Seek a Plan B," *Washington Post*, October 14, 2008.

44. After the war, Deputy Secretary of State Wolfowitz told a reporter that an "almost unnoticed but huge" benefit of the war was that it allowed the United States to remove its troops from Saudi Arabia, where there presence was a destabilizing element and a spur to al Qaeda's hostility. Wolfowitz went on to say that "just lifting that burden from the Saudis is itself going to open the door" to a more peaceful Middle East. Sam Tanenhaus, "Bush's Brain Trust," *Vanity Fair*, July 2003.

45. On Iran's influence in Iraq, see International Crisis Group, "Iran in Iraq: How Much Influence?" *Middle East Report* no. 38, March 21, 2005, http://www.crisisgroup.org/home/index.cfm?id=3328&l=1 (accessed July 19, 2008). On the rise of Iranian power in Iraq and more generally in the region, see Vali Nasr, *The Shia Revival* (New York: W. W. Norton, 2006), chap. 8; Ray Takeyh, *Hidden Iran: Paradox and Power in the Islamic Republic* (New York: Times Books/Henry Holt, 2006), chaps. 3, 7; and an article coauthored by these two scholars, Vali Nasr and Ray Takeyh, "The Costs of Containing Iran," *Foreign Affairs* 87, no. 1 (January/February 2008).

46. On the details of Lebanese politics in this period, see a number of recent reports by the International Crisis Group, "Hizballah and the Lebanese Crisis," *Middle East Report* no. 69, October 10, 2007; "Lebanon: Hizballah's Weapons Turned Inward," *Middle East Briefing* no. 23, May 15, 2008; "The New Lebanese Equation: The Christians' Central Role," *Middle East Report* no. 78, July 15, 2008. All can be accessed at: http://www.crisisgroup.org/home/index.cfm?id=2743&l=1 (accessed July 19, 2008).

47. See, for example, the article by the distinguished Israeli historian Benny Morris in which he not only predicted an Israeli attack on Iran before the end of 2008 but also raised the possibility that the Israelis might use their own nuclear weapons in such an attack. Benny Morris, "Using Bombs to Stave Off War," *New York Times*, July 18, 2008.

48. Mojtaba Zolnour, representative of Iran's Supreme Leader Ali Khamene'i to the Revolutionary Guards, said that Iran would target "the heart of Israel" and thirty-two American bases in the Persian Gulf if it were subject to attacks. BBC News, "Iran to target Israel, US bases," http://news.bbc.co.uk/2/hi/middle_east/7399403.stm (accessed July 19, 2008).

Chapter 5

1. Richard K. Betts, *Military Readiness: Concepts, Choices, Consequences* (Washington, DC: Brookings, 1995), pp. 115–43.

2. Quoted in Deborah Clay-Mendez, Richard L. Fernandez, and Amy Belasco, *Trends in Selected Indicators of Military Readiness, 1980 Through 1993* (Washington, DC: Congressional Budget Office, 1994), p. 1, citing the definition from the Joint Chiefs of Staff, *The Dictionary of Military and Associated Terms*, JCS Publication 1 (Washington, DC: Department of Defense, 1986).

3. Betts, *Military Readiness*, pp. 43–62.

4. Ibid., pp. 87–114.

5. Thomas E. Ricks, *Fiasco: The American Military Adventure in Iraq* (New York: Penguin, 2006), pp. 149–202; Susan L. Marquis, *Unconventional Warfare: Rebuilding U.S. Special Operations Forces* (Washington, DC: Brookings Institution, 1997), pp. 1–5; Frederick W. Kagan, *Finding the Target: The Transformation of American Military Policy* (New York: Encounter Books, 2006), pp. 92–100; and Ivo H. Daalder and Michael E.

O'Hanlon, *Winning Ugly: NATO's War to Save Kosovo* (Washington, DC: Brookings, 2000), pp. 125–26.

6. Julian E. Barnes, "Military Recruiters Are Seeing Better Days," *Los Angeles Times*, October 11, 2008.

7. Heidi Golding and Adebayo Adedeji, *Recruiting, Retention, and Future Levels of Military Personnel* (Washington, DC: Congressional Budget Office, 2006), p. 6; and John Allen Williams, "Anticipated and Unanticipated Consequences of the Creation of the All-Volunteer Forces," in McCormick Tribune Conference Series, *The U.S. Citizen-Soldier at War: A Retrospective Look and the Road Ahead* (Chicago: McCormick Tribune Foundation, 2008), pp. 37–38.

8. Anita Dancs, "Military Recruiting 2007: Army Misses Benchmarks by Greater Margin," National Priorities Project, January 22, 2008, http://www.nationalpriorities.org/militaryrecruiting2007 (accessed April 2, 2008).

9. Barnes, "Military Recruiters."

10. Lt. Col. Bryan Hilferty, "Information Paper: West Point Graduate Retention After 5–Year Active Duty Service Obligation," West Point, New York, December 5, 2007.

11. U.S. Army Fact Sheet, "U.S. Army Officer Retention Fact Sheet as of May 25, 2007," U.S. Army, Washington, DC, May 25, 2007, http://www.armyg1.army.mil/docs/public%20affairs/officer%20retention%20fact%20sheet%2025may07.pdf (accessed March 25, 2008).

12. Stephen J. Lofgren, "Retention During the Vietnam War and Today," U.S. Army Center of Military History Information Paper, U.S. Army, Washington, DC, February 1, 2008.

13. Michele A. Flournoy, "Strengthening the Readiness of the U.S. Military," Testimony before the House Armed Services Committee, February 14, 2008, p. 3.

14. "U.S. Army Officer Retention Fact Sheet as of May 25, 2007," http://www.armyg1.army.mil/docs/public%20affairs/Officer%20Retention%20Fact%20Sheet%2025May07.pdf (accessed April 2, 2008).

15. Heidi Golding and Adebayo Adedeji, *The All-Volunteer Military: Issues and Performance* (Washington, DC: Congressional Budget Office, July 2007), pp. 14–17.

16. Ann Scott Tyson, "Military Waivers for Ex-Convicts Increase," *Washington Post*, April 22, 2008, p. A1.

17. Barnes, "Military Recruiters."

18. Leslie Kaufman, "After War, Love Can Be a Battlefield," *New York Times*, April 6, 2008, p. ST1; and Pauline Jelinek, "Military Divorce Rate Holding Steady," *WTOPnews.com*, March 1, 2008, http://www.wtopnews.com (accessed April 1, 2008).

19. Pauline Jelinek, "Army Suicides Highest in 26 Years," *Washington Post*, August 15, 2007, http://www.washingtonpost.com/wp-dyn/content/article/2007/08/15/AR2007081502027_pf.htm (accessed April 1, 2008); and "Suicide Statistics," http://www.suicide.org/suicide-statistics.htm/#death-rates (accessed April 15, 2008).

20. Thom Shanker, "Army Is Worried by Rising Stress of Return Tours," *New York Times*, April 6, 2008, p. A1.

21. Laurinda Zeman, *Making Peace While Staying Ready for War: The Challenges of U.S. Military Participation in Peace Operations* (Washington, DC: Congressional Budget Office, 1999), p. xiii.

22. U.S. Department of Defense, *Quarterly Readiness Report to the Congress, April–June 2000* (Washington, DC: Department of Defense, August 2000).

23. Carla Tighe Murray, *Evaluating Military Compensation* (Washington, DC: Congressional Budget Office, 2007), pp. 1–20.

24. Steven M. Kosiak, *Military Compensation: Requirements, Trends and Options* (Washington, DC: Center for Strategic and Budgetary Assessments, 2005), pp. 20–21; Cindy Williams, "Introduction," in *Filling the Ranks: Transforming the U.S. Military Personnel System*, ed. Cindy Williams (Cambridge, MA: MIT Press, 2004), pp. 1–28, at pp. 16–20; and Paul F. Hogan, "Overview of the Current Personnel and Compensation System," in *Filling the Ranks*, pp. 29–54, at pp. 49–51.

25. In 1990, the Air Force budgeted for 19.5 hours per air crew per month of flying, and the Navy for 24. In 2008–2009, the respective figures were down to roughly 14 and 18 a month. The decline was gradual; about half occurred during the Clinton years, the other half during the George W. Bush years. See Tamar A. Mehuron and Heather Lewis, "Defense Budget at a Glance," *Air Force Magazine* 91, no. 4 (April 2008): 61.

26. Frances M. Lussier, *Replacing and Repairing Equipment Used in Iraq and Afghanistan: The Army's Reset Program* (Washington, DC: Congressional Budget Office, 2007), pp. 1–15.

27. Frederick W. Kagan, *Finding the Target: The Transformation of American Military Policy* (New York: Encounter Books, 2006), pp. 36–73; Richard K. Betts, *Military Readiness: Concepts, Choices, Consequences* (Washington, DC: Brookings, 1995), pp. 202–4; and Andrew F. Krepinevich Jr., *The Army and Vietnam* (Baltimore, MD: Johns Hopkins University Press, 1986), pp. 27–127, 258–75.

28. See, for example, U.S. Army and U.S. Marine Corps, *Counterinsurgency Field Manual* (Chicago: University of Chicago Press, 2007); John A. Nagl, *Learning to Eat Soup with a Knife: Counterinsurgency Lessons from Malaya and Vietnam* (Chicago: University of Chicago Press, 2005); and Thomas E. Ricks, *Fiasco: The American Military Adventure in Iraq* (New York: Penguin Press, 2006), pp. 221, 419–28.

29. See General David H. Petraeus, "Report to Congress on the Situation in Iraq," April 8–9, 2008, http://www.defenselink.mil (accessed April 11, 2008); and Statement by Stephen Biddle before the Senate Committee on Foreign Relations, April 2, 2008, http://www.cfr.org (accessed May 1, 2008).

30. Andrew F. Krepinevich and Dakota L. Wood, *Of IEDs and MRAPs: Force Protection in Complex Irregular Operations* (Washington, DC: Center for Strategic and

Budgetary Assessments, 2007), pp. ix, 8–10, 59–65. Krepinevich and Wood also note, however, the potential downsides of MRAPs—including cost, high fuel consumption, and potential for further removing counterinsurgent troops from the populations they are trying to protect.

31. See Stephen Biddle, *Military Power: Explaining Victory and Defeat in Modern Battle* (Princeton, NJ: Princeton University Press, 2004), pp. 196–205; and Michael O'Hanlon, *Technological Change and the Future of Warfare* (Washington, DC: Brookings, 2000), pp. 81–93.

Chapter 6

I am grateful to Michael Busch for his invaluable research assistance for this article.

1. Fareed Zakaria, *The Post-American World* (New York: W. W. Norton, 2008), p. 224.

2. Data drawn from Amy Belasco, "The Cost of Iraq, Afghanistan, and Other Global War on Terror Operations Since 9/11," CRS Report for Congress (updated April 11, 2008), http://www.fas.org/sgp/crs/natsec/RL33110.pdf (accessed February 20, 2009).

3. Center for International Cooperation, *Annual Review of Global Peace Operations 2008* (Boulder, CO: Lynne Rienner, 2008).

4. Joseph Stiglitz and Linda Bilmes, *The Three Trillion Dollar War: The True Cost of the Iraq Conflict* (New York: W. W. Norton, 2008).

5. Senlis Council, "Stumbling into Chaos: Afghanistan on the Brink," November 2007, http://www.foreignpolicyjournal.com/research/afghanistan/2007/senlis_afghan istan_on_the_brink.pdf (accessed February 20, 2009).

6. James P. Rubin, "Building a New Atlantic Alliance," *Foreign Affairs* 87, no. 4 (July/August 2008): 99–110, at p. 102.

7. See Thomas G. Weiss and Barbara Crossette, "The United Nations: The Post-Summit Outlook," in *Great Decisions 2006*, ed. Karen M. Rohan (New York: Foreign Policy Association, 2006), pp. 9–20.

8. Edward Luck, *Mixed Messages: American Politics and International Organization 1919–1999* (Washington, DC: Brookings Institution Press, 1999).

9. For a discussion, see Stephen Schlesinger, "The Bush administration's Stealth UN Policy," *World Policy Journal* 25, no. 2 (summer 2008): 1–9.

10. Edward Luck, "Bush, Iraq, and the UN," in *Wars on Terrorism and Iraq*, ed. Thomas G. Weiss, Margaret E. Crahan, and John Goering (New York and London: Routledge, 2004), pp. 135–54.

11. Pew Global Attitudes Project, *Rising Environmental Concern in 47-Nation Survey: Global Unease with Major World Powers* (Washington, DC: Pew Research Center, 2007), pp. 13–28.

12. "Gates Says Anger Over Iraq Hurts Iraq Efforts," *New York Times*, February 9, 2008.

13. Quoted in "The View From Berlin: America's Failure in Afghanistan," *Spiegel International*, February 11, 2008.

14. Robert Kagan, "The September 12 Paradigm," *Foreign Affairs* 87, no. 5 (September/October 2008): 25–39.

15. For a discussion on the particular challenges of dealing with the Iraq and Afghanistan wars in light of damaged U.S. foreign policy and reputation in the Middle East and Central Asia, see Richard Holbrooke, "The Next President," *Foreign Affairs* 87, no. 5 (September/October 2008): 2–24; and Stephen Biddle, Michael E. O'Hanlon, and Kenneth M. Pollack, "How to Leave a Stable Iraq," *Foreign Affairs* 87, no. 5 (September/October 2008): 40–58.

16. Michael J. Glennon, "Why the Security Council Failed," *Foreign Affairs* 82, no. 3 (May/June 2003): 16–35.

17. Richard Perle, "Thank God for the Death of the UN," *Guardian*, March 21, 2003.

18. See Sean Murphy, "Assessing the Legality of Invading Iraq," *Georgetown Law Journal* 92, no. 4 (2004): 173–258.

19. Jean-David Levitte as quoted by Adam Gopnik, "The Human Bomb," *New Yorker*, August 27, 2007.

20. United Nations, Report of the High-level Panel on Threats, Challenges and Change, *A More Secure World: Our Shared Responsibility* (New York: UN, 2004).

21. Kofi A. Annan, "In Larger Freedom: Towards Development, Security and Human Rights for All," UN document A/59/2005, March 21, 2005.

22. Quoted in "To Paris, US Looks Like a Hyper Power," *International Herald Tribune*, February 5, 1999.

23. United Nations, "2005 World Summit Outcome," UN document A/60/L.1, September 15, 2005.

24. "The Lost U.N. Summit Meeting," *New York Times*, September 14, 2005.

25. See Robert Jenkins, *Peacebuilding: From Concept to Commission* (London: Routledge, 2009).

26. See International Commission on Intervention and State Sovereignty, *The Responsibility to Protect* (Ottawa: International Development Research Centre, 2001). For an overview, see Thomas G. Weiss, *Humanitarian Intervention: Ideas in Action* (Cambridge: Polity, 2007).

27. "U.N. Adopts Modest Goals on Reforms and Poverty," *New York Times*, September 14, 2005. Paragraphs 57–64 of the *Draft Outcome Document*, August 5, 2005, had been devoted to this topic.

28. For a discussion of this and related issues, see Jane Boulden, Ramesh Thakur, and Thomas G. Weiss, eds., *The United Nations and Nuclear Orders* (Tokyo: UN University Press, 2009).

29. See M. J. Peterson, "Using the General Assembly," in *Terrorism and the UN:*

Before and After September 11, ed. Jane Boulden and Thomas G. Weiss (Bloomington: Indiana University Press, 2004), pp. 173–97.

30. UN, *A More Secure World*, par. 161.

31. Annan, *In Larger Freedom*, par. 91.

32. UN, "2005 World Summit Outcome," par. 81.

33. See Roger Norman and Sarah Zaidi, *Human Rights Issues at the UN: The Political History of Universal Justice* (Bloomington: Indiana University Press, 2008); and Julie Mertus, *UN Human Rights Machinery*, 2d ed. (London: Routledge, 2009).

34. UN, "2005 World Summit Outcome," par. 160.

35. Yvonne Terlinghen, "The Human Rights Council: A New Era in UN Human Rights Work?" *Ethics & International Affairs* 21, no. 2 (summer 2007): 167–78.

36. Human Rights Watch, "UN: Rights Council Ends First Year With Much To Do," Geneva, June 19, 2007, http://hrw.org/english/docs/2007/06/18/global16208.htm (accessed February 20, 2009).

37. John Bolton, *Surrender Is Not an Option: Defending America at the United Nations and Abroad* (New York: Simon & Schuster, 2007), p. 234.

38. Paul A. Volcker, Richard J. Goldstone, and Mark Pieth, *The Management of the Oil-for-Food Programme*, vol. 1, Independent Inquiry Committee into the United Nations Oil for Food Programme, September 7, 2005, http://www.iic-offp.org/Mgmt_Report.htm (accessed February 20, 2009).

39. UN, "2005 World Summit Outcome," pars. 161–67, quote from par. 163. This is a central theme in Thomas G. Weiss, *What Is Wrong with the United Nations and How to Fix It* (Cambridge: Polity Press, 2009).

40. Volcker et al., *Management*, p. 5.

41. Rhea Myerscough, "Military Spending: CDI Analysts Take a Close Look at Defense Budgets," *Defense Monitor* 35, no. 2 (March/April 2006), http://www.cdi.org/PDFS/DMMarApr06.pdf (accessed February 20, 2009).

42. Zakaria, *Post-American World*.

43. Joseph E. Nye Jr., *Soft Power: The Means to Success in World Politics* (New York: Public Affairs, 2004); Matthew Fraser, *Weapons of Mass Distraction: Soft Power and American Empire* (New York: St. Martin's Press, 2005).

44. "Statement of H. E. George W. Bush, President of the United States of America," 2005 World Summit, High Level Plenary Meeting, September 14, 2005, http://www.un.org/webcast/summit2005/statements/usa050914.pdf (accessed February 20, 2009).

45. Intergovernmental Panel on Climate Change, *Climate Change 2007: Mitigation of Climate Change* (New York: Cambridge University Press, 2007).

46. Richard Goldstone and Adam Smith, *International Judicial Pursuit* (London: Routledge, 2008).

47. "Speech Given by the Prime Minister in Sedgefield, Justifying Military Action in Iraq and Warning of the Continued Threat of Global Terrorism," *Guardian*,

March 5, 2004, http://www.guardian.co.uk/politics/2004/mar/05/iraq.iraq (accessed February 20, 2009).

48. J. Martin Rochester, *Between Peril and Promise: The Politics of International Law* (Washington, DC: CQ Press, 2006), p. 95.

49. Madeleine K. Albright and William S. Cohen, cochairs, *Preventing Genocide: A Blueprint for U.S. Policymakers* (Washington, DC: American Academy of Diplomacy, United States Holocaust Memorial Museum, and the U.S. Institute of Peace, 2008).

50. Quoted in *The Economist*, December 13, 2008, p. 43.

51. Barack Obama, "Renewing American Leadership," *Foreign Affairs* 86, no. 4 (July-August, 2007): 2–16, at p. 3.

52. See Ian Johnstone, ed., "Developmental and Cultural Nationalisms," special issue, *Third World Quarterly* 29, no. 3 (2008).

53. Kofi A. Annan, "A Glass at Least Half Full," *Wall Street Journal*, September 19, 2005.

54. Joseph E. Nye Jr., *The Paradox of American Power: Why the World's Only Super power Can't Go it Alone* (Oxford and New York: Oxford University Press, 2002).

55. Zakaria, *Post-American World*, p. 248.

56. Ivo H. Daalder and Robert Kagan, "America and the Use of Force: Sources of Legitimacy," in *Bridging the Foreign Policy Divide: Liberals and Conservatives Find Common Ground on 10 Key Global Challenges*, ed. Derek Chollet, Tod Lindberg, and David Shorr (New York: Routledge, 2008), pp. 7–20, at p. 18.

57. Condoleezza Rice, "Rethinking the National Interest," *Foreign Affairs* 87, no. 4 (July/August 2008): 2–26.

58. Ahmed Rashid, *Descent into Chaos* (New York: Viking, 2008), p. liv.

59. "Announcement of National Security Team," December 1, 2008, available at http://change.gov/newsroom/entry/the_national_security_team/ (accessed February 1, 2009).

60. Mark P. Lagon and David Shorr, "How to Keep From Overselling or Underestimating the United Nations," in *Bridging the Foreign Policy Divide: Liberals and Conservatives Find Common Ground on 10 Key Global Challenges*, ed. Derek Chollet, Tod Lindberg, and David Shorr (New York: Routledge, 2008), pp. 21–33, at p. 29.

61. Stephen G. Brooks and William C. Wohlforth, "International Relations Theory and the Case of Unilateralism," *Perspectives on Politics* 3, no. 3 (September 2005): 509–24, at p. 509.

62. See Jane Boulden and Thomas G. Weiss, "Tactical Multilateralism: Coaxing America Back to the UN," *Survival* 46, no. 3 (2004): 103–14.

63. Theodore C. Sorensen, "JFK's Strategy of Peace," *World Policy Journal* 20, no. 3 (fall 2003): 2–6, at p. 4.

64. G. John Ikenberry, "Is American Multilateralism in Decline?" *Perspectives on Politics* 1, no. 3 (September 2003): 533–50, at p. 545.

65. Anne-Marie Slaughter et al., *Strategic Leadership: Framework for a 21st Century National Security Strategy* (Washington, DC: Center for a New American Security, 2008), p. 5.

66. Dan Plesch, "How the United Nations Beat Hitler and Prepared the Peace," *Global Society* 22, no. 1 (January 2008): 137–58, at p. 137.

67. Brian Urquhart, "The New American Century," *New York Review of Books* 52, no. 13 (August 11, 2005): 42.

Chapter 7

1. All of CCGA's studies are available at http://www.thechicagocouncil.org/pos_overview.php. Pew's studies can be found at http://people-press.org/?s=prc; a question search feature permits quick retrieval by question text. GMF's studies can be found at http://www.transatlantictrends.org. PIPA's studies and its work, together with GlobeScan, for the BBC World Service are all available at two searchable sites, http://worldpublicopinion.org or http://www.pipa.org. Polls by Gallup, CBS News, Newsweek, the 2000 Election Issues Survey, were all accessed for this study through the IPOLL online database maintained by the Roper Center, University of Connecticut.

2. Will Lester, "Poll Finds Americans More Likely to Want United States' Focus on Issues at Home," Associated Press, November 17, 2005.

3. Andrew Kohut, "Speak Softly and Carry a Smaller Stick," *New York Times*, March 24, 2006, p. A19.

4. Andrew Kohut, "What Foreign Policy Agenda?" *New York Times*, March 13, 2008.

5. Susan Page and David Jackson, "More Say U.S. Focus Should Be Home," USA Today, April 14, 2006, p. 1A.

6. Peter Beinart, "The Isolation Pendulum: Expect a Cyclical U.S. Retreat from World Affairs After the Iraq War," *Washington Post*, January 22, 2006, p. B7.

7. David Brooks, "It's not Isolationism, But It's not Attractive," *New York Times*, March 6, 2006, p. 15.

8. The reader should remember that at the time of writing, *there was, as yet, no "public after Iraq."* All that existed was a public that continued to carry the burden of the war in Iraq. Once the war eventually comes to a close and a period of reflection follows, the public's views may evolve further.

9. For responses to this question from 1945 to 1988, see Benjamin I. Page and Robert Y. Shapiro, *The Rational Public: Fifty years of Trends in Americans' Policy Preferences* (Chicago: Chicago University Press, 1992), pp. 174–77. For the 1990s, see Steven Kull and I. M. Destler, *Misreading the Public: The Myth of a New Isolationism* (Washington, DC: Brookings Institution Press, 1999), p. 43.

10. German Marshall Fund's "Transatlantic Trends" Web site: http://www.transatlantictrends.org/trends/doc/TTToplineData2005.pdf (accessed February 20, 2009).

11. Responses to this question are collected in a table in a PIPA Web site: http://

www.americans-world.org/digest/overview/us_role/foot_note1.cfm#2 (accessed February 20, 2009).

12. German Marshall Fund conducted a "Post-Election Study 2004" in the United States, Germany and France. See http://washdchub.gmfus.org/Web/GMFWebFinal.nsf/A83E5672A0DAACE985256F9F007045C7/$File/Post%20Election%20Study%202004_%20Final%20Topline%20Data.pdf (accessed February 20, 2009).

13. In 2006 there was a further drop to 33 percent calling China a critical threat. In this case there is the consideration of CCGA's shift from telephone polling with random digit dial (RDD) samples to Knowledge Networks, with its panel recruited through telephone RDD and its questionnaire administrated on-line. Due to this shift in mode we cannot regard the drop to 33 percent as part of a perfect trendline.

14. CNN, "Top Bush Officials Push Case Against Saddam," September 8, 2002, http://archives.cnn.com/2002/ALLPOLITICS/09/08/iraq.debate/ (accessed February 20, 2009).

15. The drop in support from 2002 (65 percent) to 2004 (54 percent) could be challenged on the grounds that CCGA shifted from telephone polling to Knowledge Networks in 2004, which uses the random digit dial method to recruit its panel and then conducts surveys on the Internet, providing on-line access to panel members who lack it. The further drop in 2006 to 45 percent is not open to that criticism.

16. Time/Cable News Network, February and May 2003; GMF, June 2003; Pew, February 2004; GMF, June and December 2004; Gallup, February 2005; Pew, March 2005; GMF, May 2005.

17. Pew, October 2005 and May 2006; GMF, June 2006; Pew, July 2006.

18. A long account can be found in Kull and Destler, *Myth of a New Isolationism*, pp. 113–33. A recent update on the topic is on-line at the "Americans and the World" section of PIPA's Web site: http://www.americans-world.org/ (accessed February 20, 2009).

19. "More See America's Loss of Global Respect as Major Problem," June 16, 2008, http://people-press.org/report/429/america-loss-of-respect (accessed February 20, 2009).

20. Pew asked this question again immediately after the 2008 Republican convention (September 9–14) and found the numbers who said the loss of respect for the United States is a major problem had dropped to earlier levels. The future will tell whether the May 2008 finding is an aberration, or the September 2008 finding is a momentary interruption in a trend.

21. Space prohibits fully supporting this assertion here, but see the following studies by PIPA, all of which included public responses to budget exercises: "Seven in Ten Americans Favor Congressional Candidates Who Will Pursue a Major Change in Foreign Policy," October 19, 2006, http://www.worldpublicopinion.org/pipa/articles/brunitedstatescanadara/262.php?lb=brusc&pnt=262&nid=&id (accessed February 20, 2009); "U.S. Budget: The Public's Priorities," March 7, 2005, http://

www.worldpublicopinion.org/pipa/articles/brunitedstatescanadara/85.php?lb=brusc&pnt=85&nid=&id (accessed February 20, 2009); "Americans on Federal Budget Priorities," October 3, 2000 (available on request); and Kull and Destler, *Myth of a New Isolationism*, pp. 180–92.

Chapter 8

1. Jill Zuckman, "Senate Grills Petraeus on Iraq Strategy," *Chicago Tribune*, September 12, 2007, http://www.chicagotribune.com/news/nationworld/chi-petraeus_12sep12,1,5340957.story (accessed September 20, 2007).

2. For a detailed treatment of several major unintended consequences including, for example, the impact of the war on Turkey, see Peter W. Galbraith, *Unintended Consequences: How War in Iraq Strengthened America's Enemies* (New York: Simon and Shuster, 2008).

3. Such claims are detailed in U.S. Senate Select Committee on Intelligence, *Whether Public Statements Regarding Iraq by U.S. Government Officials Were Substantiated By Intelligence*, 110th Cong., 2d sess., June 5, 2008, http://intelligence.senate.gov/080605/phase2a.pdf (accessed February 20, 2009).

4. "President George Bush Discusses Iraq in National Press Conference," March 6, 2003, http://merln.ndu.edu/MERLN/PFIraq/archive/wh/PresBush6Mar03.pdf (accessed February 20, 2009).

5. The first three items are part of what Gause deems the Bush administration's new approach to regional security in the Middle East; the next two are traditional regional security objectives dating back to World War Two.

6. Philip Dine, "Democracy Movement in Iraq Would Face Series of Hurdles," *Tribune*, March 3, 2003, and "President Discusses the Future of Iraq," February 26, 2003, http://www.whitehouse.gov/news/releases/2003/02/20030226-11.html (accessed August 28, 2008).

7. Peter Baker, "Mideast Strides Lift Bush, But Challenges Remain," *Washington Post*, March 8, 2005, p. A01.

8. Steven E. Miller, "Mired in Mesopotamia? The Iraq War and American Interests," in *No More States? Globalization, National Self-Determination, and Terrorism*, ed. Richard N. Rosecrance and Arthur N. Stein (Lanham, MD: Rowman & Littlefield, 2006), pp. 183–206, at p. 183.

9. Bryan Bender, "Analysis Says War Could Cost $1 Trillion: Budget Office Sees Effect on Taxpayers for Decade," *Boston Globe*, August 1, 2007.

10. Elizabeth Bumiller, "White House Cuts Estimate of Cost of War with Iraq," *New York Times*, December 31, 2002.

11. Brent Scowcroft, "Don't Attack Saddam," *Wall Street Journal*, August 15, 2002; Dan Reiter, "Deterrence Has Worked in Past; Use it With Iraq," *Atlanta Journal-Constitution*, September 6, 2002, p. A17; Jack F. Matlock Jr., "Deterring the Undeter-

rable," *New York Times*, October 20, 2002; John Mearsheimer and Stephen Walt, "An Unnecessary War," *Foreign Policy*, no. 134 (January/February 2003): 50–59; Avishai Margalit, "The Wrong War," *New York Review of Books* 50, no. 4 (March 13, 2003).

12. William B. Nordhaus, "The Economic Consequences of a War with Iraq," in *War with Iraq: Costs, Consequences, and Alternatives*, ed. Carl Kaysen et al. (Cambridge, MA: American Academy of Arts and Sciences, 2002), pp. 51–85.

13. Scowcroft, "Don't Attack Saddam."

14. James A. Baker III, "The Right Way to Change a Regime," *New York Times*, August 25, 2002.

15. Steven E. Miller, "Gambling on War: Force, Order and the Implications of Attacking Iraq," in *War with Iraq*, pp. 7–50, at p. 25.

16. As former U.S. secretary of state Madeleine K. Albright has argued, the Iraq War "generated a negative reaction that has weakened support for cross border interventions even for worthy purposes. Governments, especially in the developing world, are now determined to preserve the principle of sovereignty, even when the human costs of doing so are high." See "The End of Intervention," *New York Times*, June 11, 2008, p. A29.

17. Peter Dombrowski and Rodger Payne, "The Emerging Consensus for Preventive War," *Survival* 48, no. 2 (summer 2006): 115–36.

18. U.S. Senate Select Committee on Intelligence, "Postwar Findings About Iraq's WMD Programs and Links to Terrorism and How They Compare with Prewar Assessments," 109th Cong., 2d sess., September 8, 2006, http://intelligence.senate.gov/phaseiiaccuracy.pdf (accessed February 20, 2009).

19. Ivo H. Daalder and James M. Lindsay, *America Unbound: The Bush Revolution in Foreign Policy* (Hoboken, NJ: Wiley, 2005), p. 159.

20. "Vice President Speaks at VFW 103rd National Convention," August 26, 2002, http://georgewbush-whitehouse.archives.gov/news/releases/2002/08/20020826.html (accessed February 20, 2009).

21. Dexter Filkins, "Exiting Iraq, Petreaus Says Gains Are Fragile," *New York Times*, August 21, 2008, p. A6.

22. Jim Michaels, "Odierno Takes Reins in Iraq," *USA Today*, September 17, 2008, http://www.usatoday.com/news/world/iraq/2008-09-16-iraq-news_N.htm (accessed September 30, 2008).

23. On the continued possibility of civil war, see Stephen Biddle, Michael E. O'Hanlon, and Kenneth M. Pollack, "How to Leave a Stable Iraq," *Foreign Affairs* 87, no. 2 (October 2008): 40–58, at p. 50.

24. Peter W. Galbraith, "Is This a Victory," *New York Review of Books* 55, no. 16 (October 23, 2008): 76.

25. Miller, "Mired in Mesopotamia?" p. 199.

26. Thomas Carothers and Marina Ottaway, eds., *Uncharted Journey: Promoting*

Democracy in the Middle East (Washington, DC: Carnegie Endowment, 2005), pp. 4, 9, 252; and Thomas Carothers, *U.S. Democracy Promotion During and After Bush* (Washington, DC: Carnegie Endowment, 2007), p. 4.

27. Carothers, *U.S. Democracy Promotion*, pp. 1, 9, 11.

28. Ted Galen Carpenter and Malou Innocent, "The Iraq War and Iranian Power," *Survival* 49, no. 4 (winter 2007–2008): 67–82.

29. F. Stephen Larrabee, *Turkey as a US Security Partner* (Santa Monica, CA: Rand Corporation, 2008).

30. John J. Mearsheimer and Stephen M. Walt, *The Israel Lobby and U.S. Foreign Policy* (New York: Farrar, Straus and Giroux, 2008), pp. 229–62.

31. John S. Duffield, "Oil and the Iraq War: How the United States Could Have Expected to Benefit, and Might Still," *Middle East Review of International Affairs* 9, no. 2 (June 2005): 109–41, at pp. 118–19.

32. Duffield, "Oil and the Iraq War," pp. 129–30; Energy Information Administration, *Annual Energy Review* 2007, Report No. DOE/EIA-0384(2007), June 2008, http://www.eia.doe.gov/aer/pdf/aer.pdf309 (accessed September 30, 2008).

33. Joseph E. Stiglitz and Linda J. Bilmes, *The Three Trillion Dollar War: The True Cost of the Iraq Conflict* (New York: W. W. Norton, 2008), p. 116.

34. Stiglitz and Bilmes, *Three Trillion Dollar War*, pp. 220, 117.

35. Communication with Edward Morse, November 11, 2007.

36. Sabrina Tavernise and Andrew E. Kramer, "Iraq to Open Oil Fields for 35 Foreign Companies," *New York Times*, July 1, 2008, p. A10.

37. Andrew Gray, "Iran May Be Biggest Threat to Iraq—U.S. General," Reuters, March 4, 2008.

38. "U.S. Casualties in Iraq," http://www.globalsecurity.org/military/ops/iraq_casualties.htm (accessed September 19, 2008); and "Iraqi Coalition Casualty Count," http://icasualties.org/oif/ (accessed September 19, 2008).

39. Pauline Jelinik, "Study: 300,000 US Troops from Iraq, Afghanistan Have Mental Problems, 320,000 Brain Injuries," Associated Press, April 17, 2008, http://www.armytimes.com/news/2008/04/ap_mental_041708/ (accessed September 19, 2008).

40. Stiglitz and Bilmes, *Three Trillion Dollar War.*

41. "Eyeing the Wages of War," *Economist*, March 13, 2008; and Tunku Varadarajan, "A War Appraisal too Vast to Swallow," *Financial Times*, March 3, 2008.

42. Lawrence J. Korb, Brian Katulis, Sean Duggan, and Peter Juul, "How Does This End? Strategic Failures Overshadow Tactical Gains in Iraq," Center for American Progress, April 2, 2008, p. 14, http://www.americanprogress.org/issues/2008/04/pdf/iraq_end.pdf (accessed February 20, 2009).

43. Lawrence Korb, "The State of America's Ground Forces: Testimony Before the House Committee on Armed Services," April 16, 2008, http://www.americanprogress.org/issues/2008/04/military_readiness.html (accessed May 8, 2008); Michèle A.

Flournoy, "Life After the Surge: Prospects for Iraq and for the U.S. Military," Prepared Statement for the Senate Foreign Relations Committee, April 2, 2008, http://www.cnas.org/files/documents/publications/CNASTestimony_FlournoySFRC_April%202,%202008.pdf (accessed May 8, 2008). See also Ann Scott Tyson, "Military Is Ill-Prepared for Other Conflicts," *Washington Post*, March 19, 2007, p. A1.

44. John A. Nagl et al., *The U.S. Army/Marine Corps Counterinsurgency Field Manual* (Chicago: University of Chicago Press, 2007).

45. Miller, "Mired in Mesopotamia?" pp. 193–95.

46. Richard Bernstein, "Foreign Views of U.S. Darken Since Sept. 11," *New York Times*, September 11, 2003.

47. Program on International Policy Attitudes, "Muslim Public Opinion on US Policy, Attacks on Civilians and al Qaeda," April 24, 2007, http://www.worldpublicopinion.org/pipa/pdf/apr07/START_Apr07_rpt.pdf (accessed September 23, 2008).

48. House Committee on Foreign Affairs, Subcommittee on International Organizations, Human Rights, and Oversight, "Testimony of Dr. Steven Kull," May 17, 2007, http://foreignaffairs.house.gov/110/kul051708.htm (accessed September 23, 2008).

49. Pew Global Attitudes Project, "Global Economic Gloom—China and India Notable Exceptions: Some Positive Signs for U.S. Image," June 12, 2008, http://pewglobal.org/reports/pdf/260.pdf (accessed February 20, 2009).

50. German Marshall Fund of the United States, *Transatlantic Trends 2008*, p. 6, http://www.transatlantictrends.org/trends/doc/2008_English_Key.pdf (accessed September 23, 2008).

51. "Global Economic Gloom," and Meg Bortin, "Global Survey Finds Shift in Attitudes Toward U.S.," *New York Times*, June 13, 2008, p. A11.

52. *Transatlantic Trends 2008*, p. 6.

53. Norman J. Ornstein and Thomas E. Mann, "When Congress Checks Out," *Foreign Affairs* 85, no.6 (November/December 2006). For a contrary view, see William G. Howell and Jon C. Pevehouse, "When Congress Stops Wars," *Foreign Affairs* 86, no. 5 (September/October 2007). Some of the difference in interpretation about the extent to which Congress has exercised oversight over the conduct of the war stems from the different approaches taken by the Republican-controlled Congress President Bush enjoyed until 2006 and the less malleable Democratic-controlled Congress of the remainder of his second term.

54. See, for example, the far-ranging Center for Strategic and International Studies (CSIS) project, *Beyond Goldwater Nichols: Government and Defense Reform for a New Strategic Era*, led by CSIS experts Clark Murdock, Christine Wormuth, Kathleen Hicks, Anne A. Witkowsky, and Samuel Brannen. Details including numerous project reports are available at http://www.csis.org/isp.bgn (accessed February 20, 2009).

55. Paul R. Pillar, "Intelligent Design? The Unending Saga of Intelligence Reform," *Foreign Affairs* 87, no. 2 (March/April 2008).

56. Thomas E. Ricks, *Fiasco: The American Military Adventure in Iraq* (New York: Penguin, 2006), esp. pp. 193–95.

57. Iraq Study Group conclusion quoted in Richard A. Best, *Intelligence Issues for Congress* (Washington, DC: Library of Congress, updated May 30, 2008), p. CRS 14.

58. Amy Zegart, "An Empirical Analysis of Failed Intelligence Reforms Before September 11," *Political Science Quarterly* 121, no. 1 (spring 2006). For a skeptical overview of academic perspectives on intelligence and its reforms, see Pillar, "Intelligent Design?"

59. One prominent example from a professional historian is the set of essays edited by Niall Ferguson, *Virtual History: Alternatives and Counterfactuals* (New York: Basic Books, 2000). Another by well-respected political scientists is Philip E. Tetlock and Aaron Belkin, eds., *Counterfactual Thought Experiments in World Politics* (Princeton, NJ: Princeton University Press, 1996).

60. Philip E. Tetlock and Aaron Belkin, "Counterfactual Thought Experiments in World Politics: Logical, Methodological, and Psychological Perspectives," in *Counterfactual Thought Experiments*, pp. 1–38, at pp. 23–25.

61. David Ignatius, "War of Choice, and One Who Chose It," *Washington Post*, November 2, 2003, p. B01. See also Richard N. Haass, "Wars of Choice," *Washington Post*, November 23, 2003, p. B07.

62. On the implications of the delay and its impact on the course of the invasion and ongoing conflict, see, for example, Williamson Murray and Robert H. Scales Jr., *The Iraq War: A Military History* (Cambridge, MA: Harvard University Press, 2003), pp. 62, 63, 186.

63. Hans Blix, *Disarming Iraq* (New York: Pantheon, 2004), p. 11.

64. See, among others, the findings of the United Nations Monitoring, Verification, and Inspection Commission (UNMOVIC), including its report on nonnuclear WMD, *Compendium of Iraq's Proscribed Weapons Programmes in the Chemical, Biological and Missile Areas* (June 2007), http://www.un.org/Depts/unmovic/new/pages/document_list.asp (accessed February 20, 2009), and the Iraq Survey Group's report "Comprehensive Report of the Special Advisor to the DCI on Iraq's WMD," commonly known as the Duelfer Report, https://www.cia.gov/library/reports/general-reports-1/iraq_wmd_2004/index.html (accessed February 20, 2009).

65. The additional financial costs of and strain on the troops deployed during the buildup would have ensured that these forces would have had a relatively short stay in the region.

66. Daalder and Lindsay, *America Unbound*, p. 160. See also Blix, *Disarming Iraq*.

67. Lyla M. Hernandez, Jane S. Durch, Dan G. Blazer II, and Isabel V. Hoverman, eds., "Gulf War Veterans: Measuring Health," Committee on Measuring the Health of Gulf War Veterans, Institute of Medicine (Washington, DC: National Academies Press, 1999).

68. Steven J. Davis, Kevin M. Murphy, and Robert H. Topel, "War in Iraq Versus Containment: Weighing the Costs" (University of Chicago, 2003), http://www.uchicago.edu/fac/steven.davis/research/ (accessed February 20, 2009); and Steven J. Davis, Kevin M. Murphy, and Robert H. Topel, "War in Iraq Versus Containment," NBER Working Paper No. 12092, March 2006, http://www.nber.org/papers/w12092 (accessed February 20, 2009).

69. John S. Duffield, *Over a Barrel: The Costs of U.S. Foreign Oil Dependence* (Stanford, CA: Stanford University Press, 2008), pp. 167–68, 177–78.

70. Karen DeYoung and Sudarsan Raghavan, "U.S., Iraqi Negotiators Agree on 2011 Withdrawal," *Washington Post*, August 22, 2008, p. 1.

71. Kenneth A. Pollack, *The Threatening Storm: The Case for Invading Iraq* (New York: Random House, 2002), p. 225.

72. Ibid., pp. 271–72.

73. Ibid., p. 272.

74. Ibid., p. 280.

75. Steven E. Miller, "Gambling on War: Force, Order and the Implications of Attacking Iraq," in *War with Iraq*, pp. 7–50, at p. 45.

76. Mearsheimer and Walt, "Unnecessary War," p. 52.

77. Mearsheimer and Walt, "Unnecessary War."

78. Miller, "Gambling on War," p. 49.

79. Tommy R. Franks, *American Soldier* (New York: HarperCollins, 2005); and Ricardo S. Sanchez and Donald T. Phillips, *Wiser in Battle: A Soldier's Story* (New York: HarperCollins, 2008).

80. For insights into the effects of Bremer's decree on the security situation in Iraq and, more generally, an account of the Iraq insurgency and counterinsurgency, see Ahmed S. Hashim, *Insurgency and Counterinsurgency in Iraq* (London: Hurst and Company, 2006), esp. pp. 92–99.

81. "[General Tommy] Franks had told his commanders in early August 2002 that the State Department would take the lead in planning for the leap into the unknown that would follow the ouster of Saddam Hussein." Michael R. Gordon and Bernard E. Trainor, *Cobra II: The Inside Story of the Invasion and Occupation of Iraq* (New York: Pantheon, 2006), p. 8. For the consequence of this line of thought, see also chap. 8, pp. 138–63. Another excellent account is Ricks, *Fiasco*, esp. pp. 179–300.

82. Conrad C. Crane, "Phase IV Operations: Where Wars are Really Won," *Military Review* 85, no. 3 (May/June 2005).

83. L. Paul Bremer with Malcolm McConnell, *My Year in Iraq: The Struggle to Build a Future of Hope* (New York: Simon & Schuster, 2006); and Douglas J. Feith, *War and Decision: Inside the Pentagon at the Dawn of the War on Terrorism* (New York: Harper, 2008).

84. James D. Fearon, "Iraq's Civil War," *Foreign Affairs* 86, no. 2 (March/April 2007).

85. Pollack, *Threatening Storm*, p. 398.

86. Bob Woodward, *The War Within: A Secret White House History, 2006–2008* (New York: Simon & Schuster, 2008).

87. Dexter Filkins, "Exiting Iraq, Petraeus Says Gains Are Fragile," *New York Times*, August 21, 2008.

88. Thom Shanker and Steven Lee Myers, "Draft of Iraq Deal Sets U.S. Pullout by End of 2011, With Some Flexibility," *New York Times*, October 18, 2008.

89. "War in Iraq," http://www.barackobama.com/issues/Iraq (accessed October 27, 2008).

90. Obviously, by this we do not mean to minimize the very human costs of those who have lost family members or directly suffered due to the war effort; these sacrifices can and should be honored and not forgotten.

91. James Bamford, *A Pretext for War: 9/11, Iraq, and the Abuse of America's Intelligence Agencies* (New York: Doubleday, 2004); and Ron Suskind, *The One Percent Doctrine: Deep Inside America's Pursuit of Its Enemies Since 9/11* (New York: Simon & Schuster, 2007).

92. See Senate Select Committee on Intelligence, *Report of the Select Committee on Intelligence on the U.S. Intelligence Community's Prewar Intelligence Assessments on Iraq*, 108th Cong., 2d sess., July 9, 2004, http://www.gpoaccess.gov/serialset/creports/iraq.html (accessed February 20, 2009); and Senate Select Committee on Intelligence, *Report of the Select Committee on Intelligence on Postwar Findings about Iraq's WMD Programs and Links to Terrorism and How They Compare with Prewar Assessments*, 109th Cong., 2d sess, September 8, 2006, http://intelligence.senate.gov/phaseiiaccuracy.pdf (accessed February 20, 2009).

93. Norman J. Ornstein and Thomas E. Mann, "When Congress Checks Out," *Foreign Affairs* 87, no. 6 (November/December 2006).

94. This is the traditional formulation of the conditions required to justify preemptive military action in self-defense under customary international law, as articulated by U.S. Secretary of State Daniel Webster in 1842. See Anthony C. Arend, "International Law and the Preemptive Use of Military Force," *The Washington Quarterly* 26, no. 2 (spring 2003), pp. 89–103.

95. Richard K. Betts, *Soldiers, Statesmen, and Cold War Crises* (Cambridge, MA: Harvard University Press, 1977). Shinseki is quoted in PBS, "Rumsfeld's War: Transcript," November 10, 2004, http://www.pbs.org/wgbh/pages/frontline/shows/pentagon/etc/script.html (accessed April 3, 2009).

96. Of course, as Elliot Cohen has convincingly argued, sometimes political intervention, even against received military judgment, may be exactly what is necessary to protect the national interest or win a nation's war. See Elliot A. Cohen, *Supreme Command: Soldiers, Statesmen, and Leadership in Wartime* (New York: Free Press, 2004).

INDEX

OIL - HONDURAN. OIL TANKER DOCKS IN NK.
NK SHOCKS UP ROBBERS